LOOSE SALLIES
ESSAYS

Daniel J. Kornstein

authorHOUSE®

AuthorHouse™ LLC
1663 Liberty Drive
Bloomington, IN 47403
www.authorhouse.com
Phone: 1-800-839-8640

Published by AuthorHouse   01/20/2014

ISBN: 978-1-4918-4481-6 (sc)
ISBN: 978-1-4918-4480-9 (hc)
ISBN: 978-1-4918-4479-3 (e)

Library of Congress Control Number: 2013923123

To the Memory of My Father

ROBERT J. KORNSTEIN

1916-1975

A Member of the "Greatest
Generation" Who in 1944-45
Fought at the Battles of
Saipan and Okinawa

Essay—A loose sally of the mind;

an irregular undigested piece; not a

regular and orderly composition.

Dr. Johnson's *Dictionary*

CONTENTS

Preface xi

1. In the Court of Sex Appeals 1

PART ONE
THOUGHTS ON DRAFTING THE CONSTITUTION

2. The Annapolis Convention 8
3. A Historic Alliance 14
4. Shays' Rebellion 18
5. The Big-State Virginia Plan 22
6. The Small-State New Jersey Plan 26
7. Hamilton's Long Speech 30
8. The Great Compromise 35
9. The Not-So-Great Compromise: Slavery 38
10. The Original Debate Over Original Intent 44
11. Those Machiavellian Framers 53
12. The Convention and Partial Verdicts 57
13. A Written Constitution 61
14. The Library Exhibit on the Constitution 66
15. Changing Public Perceptions 70

PART TWO
CIVIL LIBERTIES

16. "Areopagitica" Remembered 79
17. Eloquence, Reason and Necessity: Gitlow v. New York
    in a New Age of Terrorism 82
18. The Great Dissent 103
19. Anthony Lewis and the First Amendment 110
20. The Free Speech Paradox 120

21. Religious Liberty 135
22. Defining Privacy—A Task Still Undone 142

PART THREE
PERSONALITIES

23. Hugo Black, Felix Frankfurter and Civil Liberties 149
24. Eric Neisser and the Spirit of Civil Liberties 155
25. Hitchens vs. Holmes 159
26. Bill Buckley the Witness 163
27. Simon Rifkind—A Sachem of the Law 167
28. Arthur Liman, Lawyer of Virtue 172
29. Ben Franklin and Claude-Anne Lopez 176

PART FOUR
OBITER DICTA

30. The Success of the Word: The Literary Critic as
    Constitutional Theorist 183
31. Adam and Eve Hire a Lawyer 200
32. Politics and Litigation 203
33. English Revolution Redux 207
34. Bill Clinton and the Draft 211
35. Abolish Private Schools? 219
36. The Bertrand Russell Case Revisited, Or Do We Ever Learn? 224
37. In the Opinion of the Court 229
38. The Latest Legal Fiction 233
39. Jump in, Judge Cardozo 236
40. Riot as Alternative Dispute Resolution 239
41. Liberalism Undressed 242
42. Vichy Law and the Holocaust 246
43. New York—London: A Tale of Two Cities' Anti-Semitism 250
44. Steve Jobs and Ayn Rand 257

Acknowledgments 261

PREFACE

The title of this book—*Loose Sallies*—might be ambiguous and misleading, so let me clear up any confusion right away. It is not a book about fast women named Sally. It is a collection of essays, a series of reflections, mostly about topics of general interest. I apologize to any readers with a prurient interest who are disappointed, but I do not know any loose women named Sally. The "loose sallies" of my title are the essays between these covers. The title comes instead from an entry in Samuel Johnson's celebrated eighteenth-century *Dictionary*.

Dr. Johnson famously defined "essay" with humor and sarcasm, but also with accuracy. According to Johnson, who himself was a master of the essay form, an essay is a "loose sally of the mind; an irregular undigested piece; not a regular and orderly composition." We can smile at this classic definition by the esteemed author of *The Rambler* essays, but we can also examine it. A "sally" is, in modern usage, an "outburst" or "a venture or excursion off the beaten track." That is a good way to think of an essay, and I have tried to view it that way. At least some of the essays here qualify as excursions off the beaten track. Whether the essays here are "irregular undigested pieces" and "not regular and orderly compositions" will be for you to decide.

I am a full-time, practicing lawyer who also likes to write. If you like to write, the law is a good profession for you, for a lawyer is at heart a writer. A lawyer's main weapon is wielding the written word; words are the only tools lawyers have. "[O]urs is a profession of writers," says Bryan Garner, a leading expert on legal writing. "Our success or failure depends in large part on how adept we are at getting ideas across in writing, and doing it convincingly."

Much, maybe the overwhelming part, of a lawyer's professional life is spent writing. Every day, in addition to piles of correspondence, memos and e-mails, I have to write court papers such as pleadings, motions and briefs. I really enjoy drafting those legal documents, especially briefs; it gives me a chance to clarify my thinking and arrange my thoughts in the form of an argument. I also like the idea of using language to try to persuade a reader to my point of view.

But lawyers' writing often has problems. It has long been an object of ridicule. Usually marred by "legalese," it is frequently confusing, unclear, stilted, long-winded, with a secret vocabulary known only to members of the guild. In *Gulliver's Travels*, Jonathan Swift described a society of lawyers who spoke in "a peculiar cant and jargon of their own, that no other mortal can understand." And E.B. White, co-author of the classic *Elements of Style*, said, "I honestly worry about lawyers. They never write plain English themselves." Of course even legal writing need not be so bad, but that is its reputation.

I try hard to avoid these pitfalls. What good is writing if you cannot be understood or appreciated? One way to step around these land mines of legal writing is to write other than for professional reasons. Quite apart from trying to persuade judges to decide in my clients' favor, I like to write about the law and related subjects. It is fun, not work. I read a book or a new court decision, and it gets me thinking. I see a connection I did not see before, and I want to explore it. I want to see where it leads. I want to communicate that excitement, that discovery. I need to do that on paper. It is how I think.

The result has been occasional essays, some of which are in this volume. I have found the essay to be a useful genre, convenient and congenial. An essay is a free play of the mind, a form of discovery. "What one discovers," explains essayist Joseph Epstein, is "where one stands on complex issues, problems, questions, subjects. In writing the essay, one tests one's feelings, instincts, thoughts in the crucible of composition." I really like that phrase "the crucible of composition," for the act of writing does severely concentrate the mind on the intense effort and difficult attempt to produce or develop something new and good.

An essay can be as short or as long as the topic requires, but is neither exhaustive nor definitive. It calls for focus on one theme. It allows communication from mind to mind, from the writer to the reader. It reveals aspects of the writer's personality and interests, mood and temperament. In some ways it is intimate, informal and reflective, as if you are sitting at home in your living room or dining room and having a pleasant, sometimes provocative, sometimes stimulating, but always, one hopes, insightful and enlightening conversation.

Friends and colleagues often ask me how I find the time to write. "What with the demands of a busy law practice, when do you write?" they ask. "Are you one of those people who sleep only two hours a night?" They do not understand. This kind of writing is a joy, a diversion. It is self-expression. "The secret of writing a good essay," according to J.B. Priestley, "is to let yourself go." Ideas knock and my brain has to let them in and give them voice. You find the time for that pleasure, just as you find time for going to the gym and for being with those you love. Am I compelled to write? Perhaps, but I like to think of it more as an urgent, pleasant desire to write.

The physical act of writing, while hard work, gives me genuine pleasure. I do not use a computer to write. I write longhand with a pen or pencil on yellow paper. I usually write only one paragraph to a page, which gives me an aesthetic sense of how each paragraph is built and then how the whole composition is constructed. I say the words out loud, to hear if they sound right. There is something special and sensual about actually writing, feeling the ideas travel from their birthplace among the neurons and across the synapses of your brain, down the nerves and muscles of your neck, shoulder and arm to your hand and fingers through the tip of your writing instrument (preferably a fountain pen), and then watching them spill out and take shape on the page in words. Writing like that makes me feel good. (Sublimation wears many faces.)

Writing is also part of my double life. I have a life other than the lawyer's life I lead on the surface. The two sides—law and writing—reinforce and complement each other. The somewhat clandestine, secret nature of the writing is, at least in part, the very wellspring of my inspiration. Without writing, my life would be impoverished. It is fun, like playing hooky, to snatch time from my profession in order to scribble away. "The lawyer's world," writes Hillary Mantel in *Bringing Up the Bodies*, a novel about Thomas Cromwell, King Henry VIII's lawyer, "is entire unto itself, the human pared away." Not so. The "human" is very much a part of the lawyer's world, as I try to show in these pieces.

The essays included here, while often about some general aspect of American history or law, have no narrow, single theme other than the unity of a single mind. They are divided into four categories. The first are some thoughts on drafting the U.S. Constitution. The second deals with our Constitution's most cherished gift: civil liberties. In the third section, I write about some personalities I have found to be special. The fourth and final section is a miscellaneous collection of different topics.

I wrote these essays and reviews over a number of years. A few have never been published before, and those that have previously seen the light of day have since been updated and revised, some substantially. A good essay should defy its date of birth; it should live. The first selection stands alone as a bit of entertaining fluff, an appetizer designed to whet your interest, make you smile and, with luck, continue reading. I have tried to let myself go and launch some loose sallies of my mind.

1

IN THE COURT OF SEX APPEALS

The first year of law school can be something of a grind, which can make first-year law students look for distractions, for ways to break the monotony of reading and briefing too many cases and preparing for class. In my first month of law school, September 1968, I was browsing around the law school library and came upon an intriguing new case from New York's highest state court, the Court of Appeals. The case was called *Millington v. Southeastern Elevator* and had only been decided two months earlier, in July 1968. It was a case about sexual double standards, a topic that caught my interest that late summer day when I was twenty years old.

The issue in *Millington* was whether a wife could sue for what the law ever so quaintly calls the loss of her husband's "consortium." The legal concept of consortium includes, as the New York court stated, "not only loss of support or service, it also embraces such elements as love, companionship, affections, society, sexual relations, solace and more." But there was a catch.

Up until then, the law in New York was that a wife could recover nothing for the loss of her husband's ability to have sex caused by an injury. A husband, in contrast, did have a good cause of action if a defendant negligently injured his wife so that she could no longer have sexual relations. This discrepancy created a double standard if there ever was one. It brought to mind the famous comment by Mr. Bumble in Dickens's *Oliver Twist*: "If the law supposes that, the law is a ass, a idiot."

Millington tried to even up the double standard. In a four-to-three decision written by Judge Kenneth Keating (a former U.S. Senator), New York's highest court ridiculed an earlier case that had denied a wife's action for loss of consortium as "based on outworn theory." The *Millington* opinion quoted from and rejected an old case that had

1

regarded a wife "in law in some respects as her husband's chattel" so that a husband, unlike a wife, could get damages as he would "for the loss or injury of one of his domestic animals."

Overruling precedent, and finding for the wife in *Millington*, the court stated, "The loss of companionship, emotional support, love, felicity and sexual relations are real injuries." The court went on: "That both spouses suffer when the marriage relationship is adversely affected by physical injury to either is a fact evidenced, if not by logic, by human experience since the institution of marriage became a basic part of our mores . . . . Today, at least, it is unquestioned that the desire to have children and the pleasure of sexual intercourse are mutually shared."

Millington inspired me, in between classes that first month of law school, to try my hand at a low form of verse or doggerel (poetry would be much too fine a word for it) celebrating the *Millington* decision. Perhaps one of the greatest attributes of the common law is its ability to adapt to changed attitudes and moral conditions. It is with this high ideal in mind that I offered the following ditty in the law school newspaper:

> In the Empire State, not too very long ago
> Husbands recovered for lack of consortium, though
> If the husband himself was badly injured so
> > His sex life was ended
> > Nuptial joys suspended
> The courts gave the unhappy little wife no dough.
>
> So when Millington while in an elevator
> Fell and was paralyzed from the waist down later
> His wife decided money only would sate her.
> > Her marriage now in ruin,
> > Celibacy too soon,
> She sued for consortium, hoping soft judges paid her.
>
> Now New York's highly respected Court of Appeals
> Rarely takes judicial notice of bedroom squeals.
> But the precedents smacked of double standard deals:
> > It was thought only men

Had any sexual yen
And women though maybe alive were only half real.

So in 1968 that great and noble court dared
To talk of delicate subjects forthrightly bared,
And in words aimed at remediless wives declared,
    Of libido study,
    Clear, not at all muddy;
Joys "of sexual intercourse are mutually shared."

The moral is very simple, far from complex,
Just Victorian prudes should it really perplex:
That old maxim "De minimis non curat lex,"*
(Though liked and too much true,
Left wives no way to sue,)
No longer applies to womens' suits for loss of sex!

---

*   Latin for "the law does not concern itself with trifles."

PART ONE

THOUGHTS ON DRAFTING
THE CONSTITUTION

The story of how the Constitution came into being has been told, and retold, often and well. We Americans appear to have an endless appetite for stories about the founding of our country and the framing of our basic charter of government. This craving for information about our nation's beginnings is understandable. We all like origin stories, and, like the Book of Genesis, the U.S. Constitution has in a sense become a sacred, talismanic text for its people.

The Constitution unites us in more senses than one. Americans are not joined together as a people by birth or religion, blood or by soil. We are bound together by ideas and values that move us beyond our backgrounds, lift us above our interests and teach us what it means to be citizens. Those ideas and values find expression in, among other places, the Constitution. The Constitution is our certificate of incorporation and our mission statement. When we Americans talk about "democracy," we are essentially talking about the Constitution.

To many, the Constitution is a large part of what makes America different from all other countries. It contributes much to the concept of American exceptionalism. The very idea of a written constitution is one of America's greatest gifts to history and political science and the art of government. Examining the path to the Constitution's final form throws light on the differences between our country and others. In taking another look at the framing of the Constitution, we look at our own origins. And we may be surprised—even disappointed—at some of what we find.

Yet, for all that has been written, there is still more to be said about how the Constitution was conceived. Something can always be learned, some new perspective, some new insight, about the genesis of our form of government, often in terms that resonate today. Today's controversial issues can give new meaning, a new interpretation, to what the Framers did in 1787, and vice versa. The issues that occupied the Constitutional Convention of 1787 offer brightly lit windows onto our own age. Merely to study the Constitutional Convention of 1787 and meditate on its implications will help us with our issues. Compromise, flexibility, debate, federalism, sectionalism—they are with us still.

In different periods of American history, the Constitution has meant different things. The drafting of the Constitution has become almost a wishing well for historians, lawyers and judges to search for what they hope to find. We "discover" in the text of the Constitution whatever we expect to locate there, according to fashion. We are never done with the Constitutional Convention. In many ways, our current debates about constitutional issues—federalism, separation of powers, and civil liberties, for example—reflect the Framers' arguments, more than two centuries ago. "The compromises, misjudgments, and failures of the men in Philadelphia," wrote Jeffrey Toobin in a December 2013 issue of *The New Yorker* magazine, "haunt us still today. But the Founders also left just enough room between the lines to allow for a continuing reinvention of their work."

As a result, the desire to learn about the birth of the Constitution is always there. In 1987, on the two-hundredth anniversary of the signing of the Constitution, there was a year-long national celebration. That Bicentennial of the Constitution brought forth a flood of interesting books, articles and exhibits about the drafting of that organic document. I too got caught up in the enthusiasm and submitted a series of essays on the Bicentennial to the daily *New York Law Journal*. In revised form, they comprise the core of this section of the volume and, drawing on what happened at the Convention and just before, deal with some important current issues of constitutional attitudes and interpretations.

It is one man's perspective, idiosyncratic and personal, on some important aspects, some high points, of the drafting of the Constitution. It is in a sense an attempt to capture the mystery of who and what we are, and then to contemplate that mystery. I can only hope that the taste for reading about the mystery of the Constitutional Convention is still insatiable.

2

THE ANNAPOLIS CONVENTION

The Constitution, that hallowed document, did not spring full-blown and all at once from the heads of the Framers in Philadelphia on September 17, 1787. On the contrary, it was the product of much planning, thought, debate and struggle. The Constitution resulted, in short, from a process.

To be sure, there are those who can trace any event to much earlier historical antecedents and causes. Our Constitution could thus be said to have originated in seventeenth-century England with Parliament's struggle against the Stuart kings, or in the ideas of the Enlightenment, or in the writings of philosophers Locke and Montesquieu. And yet, if the time frame is to be kept within reasonable bounds, the timeline has to be drawn somewhere closer to the final event itself. The trick, as with proximate cause in the law of torts, is to find the time and place that is the turning point, the catalyst, for accelerating the historical process to its ultimate conclusion.

For the Constitution, that time is September 11-14, 1786—ten years after the Delcaration of Independence and three years after the peace treaty that ended the Revolutionary War—and the place is Annapolis, Maryland, on the shore of Chesapeake Bay. On those days more than two hundred twenty-five years ago, twelve delegates from five states met in Maryland's capital. The specific notable and history-altering result of their meeting, known ever after as the Annapolis Convention, was a call for a constitutional convention in May 1787. In view of this crucial summons, it is appropriate to regard the Annapolis Convention as the real, concrete start of the framing of the Constitution.

The Annapolis Convention grew out of the weaknesses of the Articles of Confederation. During the Revolution, the Articles had created a loose federation of sovereign states without a strong national government. Congress under the Articles had little power generally, and almost none to coerce the states to do anything. Sensing these defects, some farsighted leaders had for years been saying that a more powerful central government was needed. Under the Articles, trade barriers between the states threw up road blocks to commerce. One of those commercial disputes was the immediate cause of the Annapolis Convention.

Maryland and Virginia were quarreling over navigation of the Potomac River. In spring 1785, their legislatures sent delegates to Mount Vernon to discuss the dispute as well as east-west communication generally. At Mount Vernon, the delegates saw an opportunity to get other states to cooperate. They enlarged the committee and scheduled it to meet in Annapolis in September 1786 to discuss regulating trade among the states.

What started as a trade conference ended up seeking adjustment of the entire federal system. Only five states—New York, New Jersey, Pennsylvania, Delaware, and Virginia—attended the Annapolis Convention. Among the twelve representatives were such luminaries as Alexander Hamilton, James Madison, and Edmund Randolph. Of these, Hamilton deserves much of the credit for the lasting importance of the Annapolis Convention.

Hamilton drafted the convention's report. As a commercial convention, the meeting at Annapolis failed. It accomplished nothing in that regard. But under Hamilton's guidance, the Annapolis Convention snatched victory from seeming defeat.

Hamilton's report, dated September 14, 1786 and addressed to the legislatures of the five states that had sent representatives, made the Annapolis Convention memorable. It is a subtle masterpiece, a basic document in American history, that started the wheels turning that led directly to the Philadelphia Convention.

Hamilton began his report by reviewing the scope of the delegates' powers. Since only five states sent delegates—and they were sent for the limited purpose of discussing "the Trade and Commerce of the United States"—Hamilton announced the failure of the Annapolis Convention, at least in terms of its original goal. The delegates, said Hamilton, "did not conceive it advisable to proceed on the business of their mission, under the circumstances of so partial and defective representation."

Having recorded the Convention's failure in one sense, Hamilton turned that failure into something else, something positive—the proverbial lemon into lemonade. "Deeply impressed, however, with the magnitude and importance of the object confided to them on this occasion," wrote Hamilton with an eye toward what should happen next, "your Commissioners cannot forebear to indulge an expression of their earnest and unanimous wish, that speedy measures may be taken, to effect a general meeting of the States, in a future Convention, for the same, and such other purposes, as the situation of public affairs, may be found to require."

Hamilton knew that by making such a suggestion he and the other delegates were going beyond the limited scope of their assigned task. So he sought to modify any bad reaction by using a subtle style: "If in expressing this wish, or in intimating any other sentiment, your Commissioners should seem to exceed the strict bounds of their appointment, they entertain a full confidence, that a conduct, dictated by an anxiety for the welfare, of the United States, will not fail to receive an indulgent construction." This statement by Hamilton was a harbinger of what was to come, and would be echoed at the Constitutional Convention itself.

Then Hamilton's larger plans became more explicit. The "idea of extending the powers" of the delegates "to other objects than those of Commerce" should "be incorporated into that of a future Convention." For a partial explanation, the report offered: "the power of regulating trade is of such comprehensive extent, and will enter so far into the general system of the federal government, that to give it efficacy, and to obviate questions and doubts concerning its precise nature and limits may require a correspondent adjustment of other parts of the federal system." The Annapolis report thus hinted that not only trade and commerce but the entire federal system might need realignment.

According to the report, all the states had acknowledged "important defects in the system of the federal government." Hamilton referred to "the embarrassments which characterize the present state of our national affairs." Such defects and embarrassments merit, said the report, "a deliberate and candid discussion." They are "of a nature so serious, as, in the view of your Commissioners, to render the situation of the United States delicate and critical, calling for an exertion of the united virtue and wisdom of all the members of the Confederacy."

Finally came the historic call. The delegates "suggest their unanimous conviction, that it may essentially tend to advance the interests of the union, if the States . . . would themselves concur, and use their endeavors to procure the concurrence of the other States, in the appointment of Commissioners to meet at Philadelphia on the second Monday in May next, to take into consideration the situation of the United States, to devise such further provisions as shall appear to them necessary to render the constitution of the Federal Government adequate to the exigencies of the Union; and to report such an Act for that purpose to the United States in Congress assembled, as when agreed to, by them, and afterwards confirmed by the Legislatures of every State, will effectually provide for the same." The key phrase is "render the constitution of the Federal Government adequate to the exigencies of the union."

The Annapolis report went to the five states that sent delegates, as well as to the other states and the Continental Congress. It was a report calling for a constitutional convention that boldly asserted that grave conditions required a powerful government. Hamilton had turned a call for a general commercial convention into a call for a genuine constitutional convention.

This is the story of the Annapolis Convention as told in history books. But books are not the only way to appreciate history, nor necessarily the most meaningful. It is one thing to read about a historical event, it is quite another to be there, to touch a relic, to stand on the same spot, in the same room. Like Proust's madeleine, the physical presence stimulates memories and emotional responses, but unlike Proust's "remembrances of things past," our memories of bygone historical events are given us not by our own earlier, first-hand experience, but by reading, culture, and oral tradition, a collective conscious. When thus properly triggered by a symbol—be it a building, a monument or even a setting—the cultivated mind enhances the sense of history and our reaction to it. If you visit a battlefield, say Gettysburg, the Alamo or the Normandy beaches, you inevitably somehow *feel* the clash of armies and vividly imagine what it was like. In a sense—an important, evocative sense—the mind's eye sees the event.

This Proustian aspect of history applies as well to the Annapolis Convention. In July 1986, as the countdown to the Constitutional

11

Bicentennial began, I argued a case in a court in Annapolis, a city laid out today much as it was in colonial times. After the oral argument, I explored the city a little. From the docks on the edge of Chesapeake Bay, I walked on that bright sunny day past fashionable stores and wonderful crab restaurants and up Francis Street, toward the Maryland State House at the top of a hill. Even from the bottom of the hill, I could see the impressive wooden dome and cupola of the State House.

Built in 1772-79, the Maryland State House was the site of the Annapolis Convention. In front of the main entrance, amid blooming yellow marigolds and black-eyed susans, was a large statue of Roger Taney, a Marylander who became attorney general and chief justice of the United States. It seemed fitting and symmetrical that one chief justice (Warren Burger) should preside over the Bicentennial of our Constitution and another should guard the site from which came the call for the Constitutional Convention itself.

The presence of Taney's statue is also symbolic for other, less pleasant but equally historic reasons of constitutional magnitude. In 1857, Taney, as chief justice, wrote the awful *Dred Scott* decision for the Supreme Court. In that infamous ruling, the eighty-year-old Taney declared, on behalf of himself and six of his fellow justices, that blacks were property and could not, under the Constitution, be citizens of the United States or of any state, and that Congress had no power to exclude slavery from new territories. As a result, the Court voided the Missouri Compromise, by which Congress in 1820 had banned the extension of slavery into American territory north of latitude 36°30'.

Taney's controversial judicial decision—perhaps the worst and most tragic in American history—highlighted a number of basic constitutional issues not yet fully appreciated at the Annapolis Convention in 1786. First was the fundamental problem of slavery and how it should be treated in the Constitution. Second was the issue of judicial review. *Dred Scott* was the first time the Supreme Court invalidated an important federal law. Thus Taney's statue at the site where the idea of a constitution was first conceived stimulates mixed reactions.

The Annapolis Convention itself was held in the Old Senate Chamber, now open to public view on the first floor. That Chamber, not a particularly large room as far as legislative chambers go, is preserved to look as it did then. The walls are light green, the ceiling white, and legislators' desks are neatly arranged. A large fireplace and chandelier complete the furnishings.

The Old Senate Chamber was the scene of several historic events. In addition to the Annapolis Convention, General Washington there resigned his commission as commander-in-chief of the Continental Army and the Continental Congress there ratified the Treaty of Paris ending the Revolutionary War.

But for me, on that warm afternoon in July 1986, the most pressing feeling had to do with the Annapolis Convention. Here, over two hundred twenty-five years ago, twelve prescient Americans met for one purpose and wound up calling another meeting for another, larger purpose, a purpose that is unfolding still.

3

A HISTORIC ALLIANCE

The Annapolis Convention had another unintended consequence. It forged an important, if temporary, friendship. At the end of the classic film "Casablanca," Humphrey Bogart says to Claude Rains, "Louie, this could be the start of a beautiful friendship." We can pause a moment to imagine a similar scene not at the end but near the beginning of the process that led to the U.S. Constitution. The real-life, unlikely friends in our imaginary scene are James Madison and Alexander Hamilton.

Madison and Hamilton, one from plantation Virginia and the other form commercial New York, formed a working relationship that was a major factor in the genesis of the Constitution. Each played an important individual role. Madison is called the "Father of the Constitution," and Hamilton more than anyone else was instrumental in assembling the Constitutional Convention. However important their individual achievements, though, their great work on the Constitution resulted from their joint efforts as a team.

Madison and Hamilton knew each other from the Continental Congress. As members of the same congressional committee, they supported stronger federal funding measures in 1782 and 1783. Together, they defended in Congress our crucial alliance with France. With their national outlook, they opposed "partial conventions" of states trying to settle their own commercial and boundary disputes.

At one of those "partial conventions," Madison and Hamilton first joined forces to produce what ultimately became our basic charter of government. They both went to the Annapolis Convention in September 1786 and quickly realized that it could do nothing to solve the immediate commercial problems facing it. Instead, they were able to maneuver the meeting to go beyond its purpose and call for a national convention to form a new constitution. A historic alliance was beginning.

After the Annapolis Convention, Madison and Hamilton traveled together to Philadelphia. Doubtless, they took pride and pleasure in what they had done in Annapolis. They had come to general agreement on the goal of a stronger central government. At some point during the trip from Annapolis to Philadelphia, perhaps the twenty-nine-year-old Hamilton, in a moment of high sprits and good fellowship and with an awareness of the important work that lay ahead, put his arm around thirty-five-year-old Madison and said, "Mr. Madison, this could be the start of a beautiful friendship."

Whatever they said to each other, these two young men shared the vision, energy, intellect, and ability to conceive the need for a new constitution. They both knew that to meet that need would require hard practical work over time. What makes their joint efforts and especially close ties even more interesting are the different paths they traveled to arrive at the same point in their thinking.

Madison acquired his nationalist views of government by study and reflection. Born to wealth, he had the luxury to read and think while others had to spend their time earning a living. The shy and withdrawn Madison was, moreover, predisposed to a life of contemplation. A notorious hypochondriac, he complained of frail health for all of his eighty-five years, and avoided traveling when he could, and spent countless hours poring over books about past governments.

By the time he entered public life in 1776 as a young member of the Virginia Convention, Madison had already formed certain fundamental views. He was from the start an outspoken champion of religious freedom. Although he loathed slavery, he took inconsistent and timid public stands on that controversial issue. During the Revolutionary War, he served in the state legislature and the Continental Congress.

Madison's service in the Continental Congress shaped his continental outlook. Careful study of the Articles of Confederation convinced him that Congress was supreme and that it had implied powers that it had failed to exercise. In 1781, he proposed to amend the Articles "to compel the states to fulfill their federal" requisitions. Although this radical and centralizing proposal lost, it reflected his efforts to minimize state power. Congress, thought Madison, must have power to tax and regulate commerce; fundamental steps must be taken to make the national government effective. These were the bolder objectives toward which he had been moving for many years when he teamed up with Hamilton in Annapolis.

In sharp contrast to Madison, Hamilton was a self-made man who rose from obscure beginnings to prominence by natural talent alone. Born on the British island of Nevis in the Caribbean in 1757, Hamilton knew hardship and poverty as a youth. But his intellectual ability caught the attention of Hugh Knox, an American preacher in the West Indies. Knox sent Hamilton, age sixteen, to America in 1773 to study in King's College (now Columbia) in New York. Hamilton was impatient, impetuous, and impulsive—an activist in thought and deed. He fought in the Revolutionary War, became General Washington's aide-de-camp, and displayed superb administrative skills. After the war, he started a successful law practice.

Despite the differences of personality and background, or perhaps because of them, Hamilton reached the same nationalist conclusions as Madison. Being foreign born, and having spent his formative years in the Continental Army, Hamilton had no divided loyalties between state and nation. He thought in terms of the nation, not the states, and was unhampered by narrow localisms and sectional prejudices. His first clear exposition of the need for a constitutional convention shows up in a seventeen-page letter dated as early as September 1780. In this extraordinary document, written when he was only twenty-three years old, Hamilton said it was impossible to govern through thirteen sovereign states, that Congress lacked sufficient power, and that the "only one remedy" is to "call a convention of all the states" as soon as possible.

For the next seven years, Hamilton kept driving and pushing for a convention. He wrote letters, made speeches, and published a series of newspaper articles with the significant title "The Continentalist." The crying need, Hamilton urged, was for a government suited, not to "the narrow colonial sphere in which we have been accustomed to move." Rather, he wished for "that enlarged kind suited to the government of an independent nation." Although not a member of the New York state legislature, in 1782 he persuaded it to pass a resolution urging a convention. Elected to Congress that same year, Hamilton drafted a similar proposal, but with no success.

Both Madison and Hamilton, these two very different men, were delegates at the Philadelphia Convention in 1787, but Madison was far more effective there than Hamilton. Madison was the chief architect of the Virginia Plan, which would form the basis for the Constitution. He was constantly engaged in the debates, at the same time keeping careful notes that are our most complete record of what happened in Philadelphia. Hamilton, unlike Madison, was irregular in attendance and unpersuasive in argument. Revealing his fear of democracy, Hamilton tried unsuccessfully to get the convention to adopt a lifetime presidency.

The Madison-Hamilton partnership continued after the Philadelphia Convention. Its most notable product was *The Federalist Papers*, a series of newspaper essays aimed at securing ratification of the Constitution. Composing that collection of essays, which long ago achieved the status of a classic, marks the time of closest collaboration between the two men. After *The Federalist Papers*, Madison and Hamilton each pushed for ratification in their home states, which ratified only by small margins.

In time, the Madison-Hamilton relationship cooled and eventually they split along political lines. They clashed during Washington's administration when Madison aligned himself with Jefferson and Hamilton led the Federalists. Although Madison later became a champion of decentralized government, during the period of *The Federalist* he supported a strong central government, just like Hamilton.

Their later differences should not hide or obscure Madison's and Hamilton's basic agreement on priorities and tactics in the national crisis of the 1780s. They both went on to other achievements. But if they had both died in summer of 1788, we might still think they had accomplished their greatest work—and had accomplished it as a team. For a few brilliant years, the odd couple of Madison and Hamilton worked in historic harmony.

4

SHAYS' REBELLION

The next big step toward our Constitution, what some regard as the most decisive event of all, came three months after the Annapolis Convention. In December 1786, a ragtag little army of discontented Massachusetts farmers helped make the Constitutional Convention of 1787 a reality. Daniel Shays and two thousand armed followers marched to attack the federal arsenal in Springfield, Massachusetts. This agrarian protest known as Shays' Rebellion frightened moderates as well as property owners and produced a sense of urgency for a constitutional convention. It convinced them of the need for drastic measures against what looked like anarchy.

The high point of Shays' Rebellion came in December 1786 with the attack on the Springfield arsenal. It was a disaster for the farmers. A larger army of volunteers from the Boston area met the farmers at Springfield and routed them. Within a month, the Boston army had completely crushed the Shaysites. The leaders were caught and sentenced, some of them to death.

Tradition has viewed Shays' Rebellion as a violent insurrection by an unruly mob with extreme radical views. According to tradition, Shays had as many as twelve thousand disciplined men under arms who planned to march on Boston, loot the Bank of Massachusetts, recruit more rebels in New Hampshire and Rhode Island, and then march southward. The general impression at the time was that the Shaysites intended to abolish all debts and redistribute all property equally. This general impression was created by a letter in October 1786 from General Henry Knox, superintendent of war under the Confederation, to George Washington—a letter widely circulated and published in newspapers.

This general impression is false, fabricated by Knox. Although armed bands in 1786 did stop several courts from functioning and farmers did meet to draw up statements of grievances, their aims were far from radical. The farmers wanted tax reforms, paper money, and "stay" laws to postpone foreclosures. They protested, among other things, the cost of government, efforts to pay off the state debt at par, the cost of court proceedings, and the location of the state capital in Boston. Later, about two or three thousand rebels were organized into military companies and started to drill. Exactly what they intended to do remains a mystery because the rebellion was crushed so quickly.

Just because it was a military failure does not mean Shays' Rebellion was an ineffectual gesture. On the contrary, Shays' Rebellion—in some ways an earlier version of the Occupy Wall Street movement—had significant and longlasting political consequences. It was a major factor in the calling of a constitutional convention. Creating fear, it crystallized sentiment as nothing else had done, and hastened the decision by Congress and several states to approve and name delegates to the Philadelphia Convention.

Shays' Rebellion added new impetus for a constitutional convention. To many wealthy and solid citizens, the farmers' revolt (as misdescribed by Knox) conjured visions of impending anarchy and a serious threat to property. Reacting with acute fear and shock, and in part recoiling from what they saw as the excesses of democracy, the aroused commercial and propertied classes pushed to convene a convention to form a stronger national government. Shays' Rebellion affected the deliberations in Philadelphia, and the ratification debates afterwards.

Thus was born the controversial idea of Shays' Rebellion as the cause of a conservative counter-revolution that culminated in a property-oriented Constitution that strengthened the rulers' power at the expense of the people's participation in government—the American Thermidor described by Charles Beard in his famous, iconoclastic and influential 1913 book *An Economic Interpretation of the Constitution*.

The true effects of Shays' Rebellion, however, are more complicated and confusing, reflecting the contradictions, complexities and tensions of American history and political thought. To better understand Shays' Rebellion, we need to think of it in terms of economics and law.

The protesters were neither rabble nor a mob, but country farmers under strong economic pressures. Daniel Shays and many of his followers were officers and veterans of the Continental Army who had fought the British and returned to find their farms heavily in debt. They thought they had recently fought for true independence, not to exchange one master overseas for a financial master at home. Even Alexander Hamilton, often regarded as a leader of the anti-democratic forces, noted in *Federalist* No. 6 that, "If Shays had not been a desperate debtor, it is much to be doubted whether Massachusetts would have been plunged into a civil war."

Shays' Rebellion was a preview of certain recurring economic struggles. It was an agrarian protest by debt-ridden farmers against merchants, investors, note-holders and large landowners. In this sense, Shays' Rebellion reflects struggle: conflict between debtors and creditors, poor and rich, the lower classes and the upper classes. Precisely this class aspect is what scared many Americans in the mid-1780s and still scares them now. Today, in the wake of Occupy Wall Street, we still hear the conservative politicians' battle cry of "class warfare," and liberal columnists complaining about growing economic inequality and the power of money crowding out effective democracy, the tiny top (the one percent) against the broad bottom (the ninety-nine percent).

The farmers' economic protest eventually produced legal change. They won decisively at the polls. In the spring of 1787, Massachusetts voters chose as governor John Hancock—he of the big, bold signature on the Declaration of Independence—running on a platform of amnesty for the rebels, by a margin of three to one over Governor James Bowdoin, rigid opponent of the Shaysites. The voters also elected a new legislature with only one-fourth of the members who had sat in the old, unresponsive one. This new legislature not only passed many of the reforms sought by the Shaysites, but, moreover, pardoned the rebel leaders.

These results of the democratic process suggest that Shays' Rebellion can be seen as a reaction to a legislature that did not represent the sentiments of the people. America had just won a war in response to such legislative tyranny. Against this background, Shays' Rebellion was perhaps an understandable abuse of republican liberty, which was greeted not only with chagrin but also with relief by many sympathetic Americans.

For example, Thomas Jefferson, on hearing of Shays' Rebellion, made this famous and oft-quoted comment to James Madison: "A little rebellion now and then is a good thing . . . It is a medicine necessary for the sound health of government . . . God forbid we should every twenty years be without such a rebellion . . . The tree of liberty must be refreshed from time to time with the blood of patriots and tyrants. It is its natural manure."

Law and legal change are at the heart of Shays' Rebellion. It was, after all, the *courts* that the Shaysites closed down as one way to protect the debtors from the penalties of the law. The Shaysites regarded law, courts, and lawyers as symbols of economic oppression. These down-and-out farmers saw lawyers as "savage beasts of prey" who moved "in swarms." Shays would whip up crowds with attacks on courts and lawyers, accusing them of being in league with rich Eastern creditors. He would attack the rapacity of attorneys, pointing out that at the ridiculously high fees they charged, only the rich could hire them. These complaints have a familiar, timeless ring to them. We still hear them.

Shays' Rebellion is more than a catalyst of the Constitutional Convention. It is as relevant today as it was over two hundred twenty-five years ago, and not just because many Americans today face economic problems reminiscent of those that beset Shays' followers. It stands for basic attitudes toward economic struggle and legal change.

It bears on how we interpret the Constitution. To some, Shays' Rebellion may reveal a conservative aspect of the Framers' original intent. To others, Shays' Rebellion may mean that the Constitution should not be interpreted as a document of the elite but in Daniel Shays' spirit of economic justice, responsive democracy, and law that is neither oppressive nor rigid nor beyond reach of the common man.

Shays' Rebellion is, in short, a complex symbol of different, competing strains in the American experience. But as Justice Robert Jackson wrote in a 1943 Supreme Court flag salute case, "A person gets from a symbol the meaning he puts into it, and what is one man's comfort is another's jest and scorn."

5

THE BIG-STATE VIRGINIA PLAN

Five months after Shays' Rebellion, the actual Constitutional Convention got off to a slow start. On Monday, May 14, 1787—the date set for the Constitutional Convention—no more than ten delegates showed up. Only two states, Virginia and host-state Pennsylvania, had quorums. Milling about the chamber where the Declaration of Independence had been signed eleven years earlier, these few delegates could only chat, renew old acquaintances, make new ones, and exchange some preliminary views. Unable to conduct real business, they adjourned until the next day.

It was an inauspicious beginning. Some delegates and observers must have wondered to themselves: "What do you do if you call a constitutional convention and no one comes?"

They came, but slowly, from the North and South, by coach and on horseback. Due to the lack of delegates, no formal business took place during the first week. But delegates continued to drift in. Finally, on Friday, May 25—eleven days after its scheduled starting date—the Convention had quorums from a majority of seven states, enough to start work.

May 25 was taken up with preliminary matters. The delegates unanimously elected George Washington as president of the Convention. Madison noted that the credentials of the delegates from little Delaware prohibited anything but equality of votes among the states under any new government. This ban foreshadowed a major tension throughout the Convention, one that would persist even until now. Then the delegates appointed a committee to prepare rules.

After adjourning for the weekend, the delegates reconvened on Monday, May 28. They spent all that day and part of the next considering and adopting rules. They agreed, among other things, that seven states should form a quorum, and that all decisions were to be made by a majority of the states fully represented. They also agreed that the deliberations should be secret, while at the same time they rejected a rule about recording votes in the minutes. The delegates wanted a free hand to resolve their differences without the glare or disinfectant (depending on your point of view) of publicity.

Later on Tuesday, May 29, more than two weeks after the Convention was supposed to start, the delegates at last got down to substance. It started with a three-to-four-hour speech by well-born Edmund Randolph, governor of Virginia. Randolph, only thirty-three years old, exuded youth, energy, prestige, and the advantage of association with the most powerful families. He already had quite a record: at twenty-three a member of the Virginia convention to adopt a state constitution, a former attorney general, a delegate to the Annapolis Convention, and a distinguished speaker. This was the man said by Madison in his notes to have "then opened the main business."

Randolph began by blending humility with state pride. "He expressed his regret," notes Madison, "that it should fall to him, rather than those who were of longer standing in life and political experience, to open the great subject of their mission." "But," Madison goes on, "as the convention had originated from Virginia, and his colleagues supposed some proposition was expected from them, they had imposed this task" on Randolph. With the preliminaries behind him, Randolph then launched into the substance of his long speech, splitting it into two parts.

The first part focused on the crisis in the country, the need for adequate government, and the defects of the Articles of Confederation. An adequate federal government, said Randolph, ought to secure the country against foreign invasion, prevent dissensions among the states or seditions within them, provide for general benefits and "various blessings" that individual states could not accomplish alone, be able to defend itself against encroachments by the states, and be "paramount" to the state governments. He then showed how the Articles of Confederation did none of these things and that the result was "the prospect of anarchy from the laxity of government everywhere."

Having thus laid out the problem, Randolph used the second part of his speech to offer a solution, the basis of which he said "must be the republican principle." Randolph's remedy consisted of fifteen "resolutions." A key element in Randolph's plan drew on Montesquieu's theory of separation of powers. Randolph proposed a national government composed of three branches: a national legislature, a national executive, and a national judiciary.

Of these three branches, the national legislature had, in Randolph's plan, the most power. As conceived by Randolph, it would have the power to elect the national executive and members of the national judiciary. The national legislature would itself have two houses with representation in both houses based on population (thus favoring the large states over the small states). The first house (the representatives) would be elected by the people; the second house (the senators) would be elected by the first house. The appointment of representatives according to population would prove a sticking point.

To check and balance the national legislature, Randolph said there should be a "council of revision." This council would be composed of the national executive and some members of the national judiciary. Together they would have the power to veto acts of the national legislature.

The heart of Randolph's plan was supremacy of the central government. State laws "contravening in the opinion of the national legislature the articles of Union" would be subject to a veto by the national legislature. This meant that Congress would have the power to void state laws as unconstitutional. Federal force could be applied to any state "failing to fulfill its duty under the articles [of Union]." State governments would have to support the "articles of Union."

Other, less controversial aspects filled out Randolph's remedy. He provided for admitting new states, amending the "articles of Union," and guaranteeing a republican form of government to each of the states.

Randolph's long speech offered the first complete plan of government to the Convention. History calls it by various names: the Virginia Resolves, the Randolph Plan or, more often, simply the Virginia Plan. It formed the basis for discussion and debate throughout the Convention and ended up in large part as the basis for the final document. It lacked details, of course, and many issues were left out, but the main lines of thought were clear. And every delegate knew, despite Randolph's disclaimer that he was merely seeking to "correct" and "enlarge" the Articles of Confederation, that he was proposing bold and great innovations.

The voice may have been the voice of Randolph, but the words were the words of Madison, his fellow Virginian. According to some historians, the Virginia Plan undoubtedly was written by Madison. It corresponds closely with documents Madison wrote on the eve of the Convention.

Actually, the whole distinguished Virginia delegation may have had a hand in shaping the plan. The Virginia delegates had all arrived on time for the opening session on May 14. During almost two weeks of official inactivity after the opening date, the Virginia delegates already in Philadelphia prepared systematically for the Convention. They frequently met and talked at a tavern called the India Queen, which became a headquarters for Convention delegates. Wisely, the Virginia delegates used this time to draft a plan for a new government that could be ready for the Convention.

By doing so, the Virginia delegates set the agenda, defined the issues, and drew the intellectual battlefield for the Convention. They knew that the first plan presented to the Convention might have an advantage over any that came later. And they were right.

6

THE SMALL-STATE NEW JERSEY PLAN

Two hundred twenty-five years after the fact, we tend to think of the Constitutional Convention and its end product as inevitable, as things that had to be. Longevity, familiarity, success, political rhetoric, and many other factors have accustomed us to the Constitution as it is, without serious thought to what it might have been. Looking in our collective rearview historical mirror, we tend to frame events as inexorable, implying that America was always destined to have the Constitution it has. In this respect, we are too apt to adopt the so-called "Whig interpretation" of history, which sees history as inexorable, as the history of progress, and regards the past in terms of the present.

But we need to understand the past in its own terms. Just because things turned out "well" tells us nothing about why they turned out as they did. We need to see the different paths open to those who came before us to explain how and why they chose one over the another. We need to recognize that the outcome was not inevitable.

A keen appreciation of this chanciness, this uncertainty of history comes from considering what happened more than two centuries ago in Philadelphia. The fundamental nature of the Constitution we know and honor was by no means a foregone conclusion.

In proposing the bold, centralizing Virginia Plan on May 29, 1787, the Virginia delegation seized the initiative at the Convention. The Virginia Plan immediately gained ground and seemed headed for apparently quick success. After some debate, the Convention referred it to the Committee of the Whole, which adopted it in somewhat altered form on June 13. But success for the Virginia Plan was not to be so easy, or so smooth.

The small states bridled. For two weeks after Randolph had offered the Virginia Plan, the delegates from the small states had argued against what they saw as a growing trend toward centralization and control by the large states. They feared what would happen if, as called for by the Virginia Plan, representatives of the lower house were elected by the people instead of by the state legislatures. The small states foresaw that they would be completely out-voted in a national legislature by a few large states if seats were apportioned according to taxes paid or the number of the state's free inhabitants. These long simmering fears suddenly came out into the open.

The Virginia Plan forced the delegates to think hard about whom they represented: the whole people of the United States or this or that particular state. For reasons of personal experience or largeness of mind, some of the most esteemed delegates—like Washington, Franklin, James Wilson, Madison and Hamilton—thought of themselves as citizens of America rather than having first duties to their individual states. But others acted on the opposite premise, reflecting the local prejudices and local interests of sectionalism. These differing loyalties caused problems for the Convention, just as they would throughout American history.

The small states found an eloquent champion in William Paterson of New Jersey. Paterson was a former attorney general of New Jersey, with a reputation for brilliance. In his early forties at the time of the Convention, Paterson, like Madison, was physically small, only five feet two inches tall. His modest demeanor cloaked considerable learning and speaking ability. He was a much respected figure, and would later sit on the U.S. Supreme Court from 1793 to 1806.

On Saturday June 9, Paterson spoke about how proportional representation struck at the existence of the lesser states. He reminded the Convention of its limited mission: that it was authorized only "for the sole and express purpose of revising the Articles of Confederation." If the Virginia Plan is adopted, he said, "We shall be charged by our constituents with usurpation . . . The people of America are sharpsighted and not to be deceived. The idea of a national government as a contradistinguished from a federal one never entered into the mind of any of them."

Paterson became more defiant as he continued. He referred to the threat that, if the small states would not agree to any plan, the large states might confederate among themselves. His response was: "Let them unite if they please, but let them remember that they have no authority to compel the others to unite." New Jersey, he said, will "never" agree to the Virginia Plan, adding that he would "rather submit to a monarch, to a despot, than to such a fate."

Paterson's angry outburst must have disheartened those who came to Philadelphia to forge a united nation. Paterson seemed to be splitting the Convention, and subverting its goal. James Wilson of Pennsylvania, speaking right after Paterson on June 9, put his finger on the basic problem. "If no state will part with any of its sovereignty," said Wilson, "it is in vain to talk of a national government." But the large states were in the majority and held to their course. Four days later, the report of the Committee of the Whole on the revised Virginia Plan galvanized the small states into an organized counter-attack.

The mounting rebellion by the minority of small states quickly took concrete form. On June 14, one day after the report of the Committee of the Whole, Paterson asked for and obtained a day's recess so that he could prepare a "purely federal" plan, as distinguished from the Virginia Plan, to put before the Convention. Paterson used the brief adjournment to huddle with a group of small-state delegates, including David Brearly, also of New Jersey, Roger Sherman of Connecticut, Luther Martin of Maryland, and John Lansing Jr. of New York (a large state delegate with small-state anti-nationalist attitude), to clarify their thinking. The next day, Friday June 15, Paterson offered to the Convention an alternative known ever since as the New Jersey Plan.

The essence of the New Jersey Plan was to strengthen Congress under the Articles of Confederation. The plan's most striking feature was a one-house legislature, as previously existed. A unicameral legislature met with approval from Benjamin Franklin, who compared a bicameral system to a snake with two heads: "One head chose to go on the right side of the twig, the other on the left side, so that time was spent in the contest; and before the decision was completed the poor snake died with thirst."

The unicameral legislature proposed by Paterson also met the needs of the small states regarding representation. According to Paterson, the representatives in Congress were to be elected by the states regardless of population or wealth. Each state, quite apart from size, would therefore have one vote in Congress. Equality for the small states, their primary concern, could be preserved.

In certain other important respects, the New Jersey Plan resembled the Virginia Plan. Both plans called for adding a federal executive and judiciary to the legislature, although under the New Jersey Plan Congress would elect a plural executive and the executive would choose a judiciary with curtailed jurisdiction. Like the Virginia Plan, the New Jersey Plan gave Congress the right to tax and to regulate commerce. Most significantly, even the New Jersey Plan included an important provision for the supremacy of the central government. It made acts of Congress and treaties "the supreme law of the representative states," binding on state courts.

When Paterson finished speaking, the Convention adjourned until the next day, Saturday June 16, to allow supporters of the New Jersey Plan to work on their supporting arguments. Saturday's debate touched the obvious themes. Supporters of the New Jersey Plan objected to the Virginia Plan on the familiar grounds that the Convention had no authority to propose it, that the people would not accept it, and that it would be difficult to put into operation. Advocates of the Virginia Plan disagreed. James Wilson asked, rhetorically, why a national government would be unpopular. "Has it less dignity? Will each citizen enjoy under it less liberty or protection? Will a citizen of Delaware be degraded by becoming a citizen of the United States?"

At noon on Saturday June 16, the Convention, without voting on either plan, adjourned to Monday June 18. Would the Virginia Plan, in the interests of the united people, prevail? Or would the winning one be the New Jersey Plan, built on the interests and sovereign rights of the separate states? The outcome was uncertain. As of that Saturday, no one could be sure what the final result would be.

7

HAMILTON'S LONG SPEECH

Defying everyone's expectations, the next working day of the Convention—Monday, June 18, 1787—was not devoted to the pros and cons of the Virginia and New Jersey Plans. It turned out to be the most curious day of the entire Constitutional Convention. True, June 18 was neither the first nor the last day of Convention business. Nor was any important vote taken on that day. Yet, if we could pick one day to have been a fly on the wall of the State House in Philadelphia, it would be that day, June 18, 1787.

Tension was building. The contest between the big-state Virginia Plan and the small-state New Jersey Plan had rubbed the delegates' nerves raw. The stage was set for high drama in a play that as yet had no ending. Everyone expected partisan debate, compromise, or disintegration, but no one knew which. In fact, no one anticipated what actually did happen.

What happened was a total surprise, an unexpected event that still vexes students of that era. Instead of a debate about the pros and cons of the two plans, the Convention heard an extraordinary six-hour speech on the nature of government. This uninterrupted monologue, the longest speech of the Convention, has earned many descriptions, ranging from "notorious," "monarchical," "indiscreet," and "extremist," to "audacious," "energetic," "bold," "brutally frank," and "radically nationalizing," to "masterful and compelling" and "some of the most profound observations on government ever uttered by an American." The speech was, in sum, a controversial event of the first magnitude.

The speaker was Alexander Hamilton. At age thirty, he was one of three delegates from New York, the only one favoring a strong government. As a result of his foreign birth and service in the Continental Army, Hamilton was not limited by a narrow state outlook and had a vision of a single, strong, unified nation. His broad, continental view, unhampered by sectionalism, drove him. His restless ambition and daring had already made him famous, distrusted by some, and not altogether popular. One delegate described Hamilton's manners as "tinctured with stiffness and sometimes with a degree of vanity that is highly disagreeable." His speech on June 18 did not increase his popularity.

Hamilton spoke in support of a powerful central government that minimized, even trivalized, the states. He "particularly opposed" the New Jersey Plan because he was "fully convinced" that "leaving the states in possession of their sovereignty" was no answer. He personally favored doing away with the states altogether, but proposed only to reduce them to mere subdivisions of the central government, something no one else had even considered, let alone suggested. He went so far as to call for the national government to appoint the government of each state. Hamilton's plan left almost no power to the states except over local affairs.

As if Hamilton's radical anti-state views were not enough to startle his listeners, his plan revealed what many saw as a strongly anti-democratic cast of mind. Hamilton had contempt for the common people and criticized both the Virginia and New Jersey Plans as too democratic. Hamilton proposed that the national executive be elected for life and have absolute veto power. Hamilton was a monarchist; he thought the chief magistrate "ought to be hereditary." To offset "popular passions" that "spread like wild fire and became irresistible," Hamilton also proposed life tenure for senators. These ideas, drawing heavily on the unpopular British model, had obvious monarchical and aristocratic elements.

Along with specific anti-democratic proposals, Hamilton made general comments of the same tenor. "We need to re rescued from democracy," he said. "I am not much attached to the majesty of the multitude." "The voice of the people has been said to be the voice of God," remarked Hamilton. "It is not true in fact . . . Can a democratic assembly, who annually revolve in the mass of the people, be supposed to steadily pursue the public good?" Hamilton even ended his speech on a crescendo of anti-democratic sentiment. "The people," he said, "begin to be tired of an excess of democracy. And what is even the

Virginia Plan, but democracy checked by democracy, *or pork still, with a little change of the sauce?*"

Despite its transparent anti-democratic attitude, Hamilton's speech also has a perceptible leitmotif of republicanism. Hamilton defended his plan as republican so long as government officials were chosen by a process of election "originating with the people." His suggestion that the lower house be elected by universal manhood suffrage went further toward democracy than the other plans or even the final product. He favored checks and balances to offset the vices of democracy. "All communities divide themselves into the few and the many. The first one the rich and well born, the other the mass of people . . . . The people are turbulent and changing; they seldom judge or determine right." Hence the need for checks and balances. Worrying whether republican government could be established over so great an extent of land, Hamilton said, "We ought to go as far in order to attain stability and permanency, as republican principles will permit."

Whatever critics may say, none could fail to acknowledge the high intellectual level of Hamilton's speech. It was the first Convention speech to explore in depth the philosophical underpinnings of government. Dealing with the tension between states and nation, Hamilton classified the "principles of civil obedience" under five headings: interest, opinion, habit, force, and influence. He intended to show that, as things stood in America, each of these basic supports of stable government was biased toward the states. This discussion, at once theoretical, practical, and insightful, especially when buttressed by Hamilton's survey of ancient and modern confederations, stands as a monument to our understanding of the foundations of government.

When Hamilton finished speaking, the delegates sat stunned and silent. Hamilton's speech was too high toned, centralized, and even monarchical for the delegates; it was out of tune and unacceptable. Hamilton, in the words of John Roche, "was simply transmitting on a different wavelength from the rest of the delegates." Completely taken aback, they adjourned for the day without arguing over or even discussing what Hamilton had said. Nor did they discuss his plan on any other day. They admired his eloquence but remained unconvinced. As another delegate said three days later, the "Gentlemen from New York" had "been praised by everyone" by had "been supported by none."

Yet Hamilton's long speech had an impact. Hamilton also raised the intellectual level of the debates, paving the way for dazzling speeches by others. His speech focused the debates on the relationship between the states and the national government. Indeed after the Convention resolved the representation issue, it followed Hamilton's basic idea by granting huge powers to the new central government.

The speech's other impact was on Hamilton's reputation. It did much to create and solidify Hamilton's persona as an enemy of the people. Hamilton himself later said the speech was full of "propositions made without due reflection." History has stressed his anti-democratic attitude while overlooking his reference to the *"excesses* of democracy" and his reliance on republican principles as he understood them. His notorious later comment, "Your People, sir, is a great beast" did not help either. Thus has this complex man comes down to us as an elitist and an aristocrat.

Hamilton's reputation has in fact waxed and waned over time. He has been depicted as a demigod or a monster. Everyone acknowledges his brilliance in understanding the rising system of credit and finance, and his great skill and competence and far-sightedness as America's first secretary of the treasury. No one doubts his intelligence or industry. A superb organizer and tactician, he feared chaos and disorder. Hamilton sought to build a powerful national government that could ensure the young nation's security and drive it toward economic greatness.

But his arrogant, prickly and thin-skinned personality was a problem, as he easily made many political and personal enemies with his cutting comments and criticisms, in one case leading to the famous and tragic duel with Aaron Burr that resulted in Hamilton's death at the age of forty-eight. Hamilton is buried on Trinity Churchyard, located, appropriately enough, at the top of Wall Street. Looking at his grave, one can only imagine what other accomplishments and controversies would have filled his life if he had lived longer.

And throughout our history, Hamilton has been mainly identified with banks and financial interests and big cities and strong, centralized national power. He became a symbol of Wall Street, a spokesman of the business economy, and led the Federalist Party in its opposition to the more beloved Jefferson (who was in France during the Constitutional Convention) and his ideas of yeoman farmers and decentralized government. More recently, Ron Chernow's best-selling 2004 biography of Hamilton has done much to foster a more positive public perception of Hamilton. But it will take a lot of work to undo centuries of bad press.

Why Hamilton spoke as he did when he did in the Convention still puzzles historians and biographers. One popular theory holds that Hamilton, knowing his own proposals had no chance of prevailing, intended them to offset the New Jersey Plan, which greatly frightened him. To prevent a compromise that would seriously reduce the powers of the national government, Hamilton supposedly used his radical proposals to shock the delegates back to their senses. This is an interesting and plausible theory, but based on nothing more than inference and speculation.

An equally interesting and no less plausible theory is that Hamilton was venting his pent-up frustration and anger at the humiliating role he was forced to play as minority member of the New York delegation. The other two delegates from New York nullified Hamilton's role by out-voting him every time. Such lack of power and influence must have chafed at Hamilton's ambition, especially regarding a cause—the Constitutional Convention—he held so dearly. Hamilton did not attend many convention sessions after that, so that he who more than anyone else was instrumental in assembling the Constitutional Convention played no part in the laborious task of hammering out the actual wording of the Constitution.

The most obvious possible explanation is to take Hamilton's speech at face value. There is no reason to assume that he meant anything but what he said. He was disclosing to the Convention his sincerely held personal views, based on much thought and research, of the kind of government required by the American crisis. If—as seems likely—Hamilton knew in his heart that his own views could not carry the day, he may have considered his speech as an appeal to the future, a way to send his ideas down through time in the hope that later generations would be convinced and prefer them to the view held by the majority at the Convention.

We are one of those later generations.

8

THE GREAT COMPROMISE

The next day, June 19, the delegates—abashed, embarrassed, and startled by Hamilton's strange tirade—ignored it and returned to the real and pressing problem of either choosing between or reconciling the differences between the big-state Virginia Plan and the small-state New Jersey Plan. That controversy was the main event, the issue that overrode all other issues at the Convention, and an issue that is with us still. Soon after the meeting started on June 19, Madison, not known as a great orator, took the floor. Without mentioning Hamilton or his six-hour speech of the day before, Madison of the big state Virginia attacked the New Jersey Plan. He dissected the New Jersey Plan and revealed its flaws by a series of pointed rhetorical questions.

Madison's speech had the desired effect. It ended the New Jersey Plan. After he finished talking, Rufus King of Massachusetts called the question: Was the Virginia Plan better than the New Jersey Plan? The outcome was not even close. Voting by states, the result was seven to three for the Virginia Plan, with Maryland split. Thus was the New Jersey Plan soundly rejected, dead in the water, never to be raised again in the Convention. Some historians think that this complete rejection of the confederacy form of government, coming so close on the heels of Hamilton's speech, must have owed something to what Hamilton said.

The defeat of the New Jersey Plan did not mean that the Virginia Plan won. But the Virginia Plan did become the basis for discussion, although the final form of the Constitution was still uncertain. Much of the Virginia Plan would be changed before the final document emerged. The result would be a better charter of government.

Despite the defeat of the New Jersey Plan, the small states were not yet finished. They were not giving up. Still fearing domination by the large states, the small states drew a new line in the sand over representation in the national legislature. Rather than furiously fight the extensive power to be granted to Congress, they insisted on each state having equal representation. For their part, the large states wanted proportional representation based on population. The core issue before the Convention became: How was America to be represented in Congress—by population or equally, state to state?

The battle lines were drawn. For about a month, the two sides quarreled so badly that it appeared there would be no solution— and no United States. The Convention seemed to be at a stalemate, with some delegates even threatening to go home in frustration. Compromise was not in the air. Neither side would give in. Reading accounts of that month in 1787, one is reminded of current congressional impasses.

Disheartening as this confrontation was, it demonstrated a salutary process that itself taught an important and lasting lesson in democracy. The delegates talked and talked, airing all views. Debate continued. Both sides had their say. Madison and others thought state equality of representation was an unjust principle. But the small states felt the need to protect themselves against the large. One small state delegate said the large states "[i]nsist . . . they will never hurt or injure the lesser states, I do not, gentlemen, trust you!" But the delegates knew that unless a solution was found, the Convention would end in failure, which no one wanted. The answer was an imaginative, practical one.

The creative solution proposed earlier by Connecticut and passed on July 16, 1787, stipulated that the national legislature would consist of two houses: a Senate and a House of Representatives. In the Senate, the upper house, all of states would be represented equally with two senators. In the House, states would be represented based on population, which would give the large states the advantage. This is the measure that became known as the Great Compromise.

The Great Compromise was the key to the success of the Constitutional Convention. Without it, the Convention would have foundered. It was a close call at that, as many of the delegates recounted. But, as with any compromise, not everyone was happy. "Perhaps not a single delegate in the Convention was fully satisfied with the compromise," writes Carl Van Doren in *The Great Rehearsal*. "It was the creation of the corporate mind of the assemblage, reconciling differences, coming to such general agreement as was possible."

In general though, the small states were happier; the large states felt beaten and tried to regroup. But after a day they abandoned the effort. Meanwhile, the little states, having been mollified and now feeling more secure, became more flexible and willing to give on many other issues. After agreeing on the Great Compromise, the rest of the drafting process, while obviously important, was relatively easy.

What is the takeaway from this episode? We still live with the Great Compromise, although there have been some changes in how we select our legislators. We now take for granted what was then hotly debated. And yet there are times today when we feel the Senate, with its basic structure and its internal rules (for example, filibusters), can override the wishes of the majority of Americans. On occasion, this counter-majoritarian strain rankles. But, as the Great Compromise demonstrates, we do not have a pure democracy.

Another lesson has to do with human nature and psychology. July 16, 1787, the date delegates passed the Great Compromise, was a Monday. This is significant because the delegates had a weekend to calm down and relax from their labors and strife. The weather was also cooler and more comfortable. The combination of these factors, coming after weeks of hostile and heartfelt argument, must have improved the frame of mind of the delegates. Compromises and settlements are perhaps better reached after a break in the arguments, when nerves are not so frayed and tempers not so hot. As professional mediators know, applied psychology is an important part of "getting to yes."

9

THE NOT-SO-GREAT COMPROMISE: SLAVERY

Not every compromise is good, much less great. Compromise can create problems. By its nature, compromise gives no one all that they want. Under the pressure of getting something done or breaking a particular logjam, both sides need to give something up. In the negotiating process, moral values and principles may get sacrificed on the altar of expediency. That is exactly what happened with slavery.

In some ways, the Constitutional Convention revealed deep fissures in the idea of America and demonstrated that the fundamental conflict was not between large and small states—which had been resolved by the Great Compromise—but between North and South, between slave and free states. The most telling and lasting moral criticism of the Constitutional Convention concerns its not-so-great compromise with slavery.

The Constitutional Convention did not abolish slavery; it allowed slavery and the slave trade to continue. It was not until the Civil War that the Thirteenth Amendment in 1865 finally accomplished that fundamental goal. From the summer of 1787 until today, critics have assailed the slavery compromise as the result of a failure of nerve, a loss of moral courage, and a lack of ingenuity in dealing with the problem. It is the evil spirit flapping its dark wings over the cradle of our country's birth.

The Convention's compromise with slavery shows up in what the original Constitution says and what it does not say. Nowhere does the original Constitution prohibit slavery. Nowhere, in fact, does the word slavery even appear in the text. Such conspicuous and telling omissions were by no means accidental; they were studied efforts that led later generations to claim that the original Constitution condoned slavery.

Although the Convention avoided the word slavery, it did find euphemisms to use in three separate provisions. First, as part of the Great Compromise in mid-July 1787 relating to legislative representation, the Convention agreed to apportion congressional delegates on the basis of all "free persons" and "three-fifths of all other persons." By this calculation, slaves were somewhere between property and people.

Second, during the last week in August, the Convention granted broad power to Congress to regulate trade, but denied it power until 1808 to prohibit "the migration or importation of such persons as any of the States now existing shall think proper to admit." The final express constitutional provision relating to slavery is known as the Fugitive-Slave Clause and requires the return to the owner of "any person held to serve or labor in one state" who escapes to another state.

The Constitution's threefold compromise with slavery has produced a profound national sense of cognitive dissonance, a term psychologists use to describe conflicting feelings held simultaneously. On one hand, America professed allegiance to noble ideals of freedom, equality, and human dignity drawn from natural law. Indeed, even as the Philadelphia Convention discussed its compromise with slavery, the Confederation Congress in New York passed the Northwest Ordinance on July 23, 1787 prohibiting slavery in the territories covered. On the other hand, the Convention let continue, under protection of law, the institution of slavery, which stood for the very opposite of freedom, equality, and human dignity. This inherent contradiction was the nation's birth defect.

Some freedom-loving delegates voiced their objections. On August 22, 1787, while the Convention debated the issue, George Mason of Virginia spoke out to condemn "the infernal traffic" in slaves. "Every master of slaves is born a petty tyrant," Mason declared, and with haunting prescience went on: "They bring the judgment of heaven on a country. As nations cannot be punished in the next world, they must be punished in this. By an inevitable chain of causes and effects Providence punishes national sins by national calamities. I hold it essential to every point of view that the General Government should have power to prevent the increase of slavery."

Other delegates at the Convention endorsed those sentiments. Luther Martin of Maryland insisted that a clause tolerating the slave trade would be "inconsistent with the principles of the revolution and dishonorable to the American character." Oliver Ellsworth of Connecticut proclaimed, "In a moral light we ought to go further and free those already in this Country." To John Dickinson of Delaware, the trafficking in slaves was "inadmissible on every principle of honor."

The ratification process evoked some similar remarks. Especially in New England, the ratifying conventions expressed much dislike of the Constitution taking slavery for granted and permitting it to continue. One delegate in Massachusetts feared that citizens of his state would become "partakers in other men's sins." A New Hampshire delegate felt the same way: "We will not lend the aid of our ratification to this cruel and inhuman merchandise, not even for a day."

Decades later, the same criticism became even louder and more strident. In the 1830s and 1840s, abolitionists like Wendell Phillips and William Lloyd Garrison referred to the Constitution as a "covenant with death," "a pact with the Devil," and held public burnings of it. Phillips even wrote a book entitled *The Constitution: A Pro-Slavery Compact*. The abolitionists found a conflict between the Constitution and "natural" or "higher" law.

One Massachusetts judge with abolitionist sentiments resigned, saying: "The oath to support the Constitution of the United States is a solemn promise to do that which is a violation of the natural rights of a man, and a sin in the sight of God . . . I will withdraw all profession of allegiance to it [*i.e.*, the Constitution], and all my voluntary efforts to sustain it."

This tradition of criticism found eloquent support in 1987 in Supreme Court Justice Thurgood Marshall, the first African-American to serve on the Court. Lest the Constitutional Bicentennial become "little more than a blind pilgrimage to the shrine of the original document," Marshall, the great-grandson of a slave, urged all of us to develop a "sensitive understanding of the Constitution's inherent defects," chief among which is its compromise with slavery. The compromise, according to Marshall, reflected the Founders' "ability to trade moral principles for self-interest" and "set an unfortunate example." For this reason, Marshall did not "find the wisdom, foresight, and sense of justice exhibited by the Framers particularly profound."

Such persistent, deep, and stinging criticism of our basic charter of government cannot be brushed aside, ignored, or minimized. The criticism touches an exposed nerve in our national history. It subjects the symbol of our form of government to careful scrutiny rather than fawning worship. And it calls on us, as Marshall asks, to keep perspective on the political process that the Constitutional Convention was.

And a political process based at least in large part on economic self-interest is what it was. The delegates from Georgia, North Carolina and South Carolina would not join the Union if the Constitution prohibited the slave trade because those states "cannot do without slaves." Some delegates thought slavery in America would end in time of its own accord. According to Rutledge, "Religion and humanity had nothing to do with this question. Interest alone is the governing principle with nations . . . . If the Northern States shall consult their interest, they will not oppose the increase of slaves which will increase the commodities of which they will become the carriers." A South Carolina delegate claimed that importing slaves would benefit the "whole Union" because "the more slaves, the more produce to employ the carrying trade. The more consumption also, and the more of this, the more of revenue for the common treasury." The people of the southern states, said Rutledge of Virginia, "will never be such fools as to give up so important an interest."

In the end, the disagreement was resolved by an economic trade-off. The delegates from New England would not vote to prohibit the slave trade if Georgia and South Carolina would not insist on a two-thirds vote in Congress to pass laws regulating foreign commerce. The fateful compromise resolved the last major conflict facing the Convention.

It is easy, in a sense, for us to take the higher moral ground two hundred twenty-five years later and criticize the Framers for not banning slavery outright at the outset. But is such criticism realistic? Were there practicable alternatives to the slavery compromises made by the Convention? Without in any way condoning slavery, we can recognize that it is at a minimum open to question, given the economic and political realities of the day, whether a constitution could have been signed and the Union formed, with a ban on slavery. It took a long and terrible ordeal, a Civil War seventy-five years or so afterward at a cost of more than half a million lives, to resolve that issue. And it is equally uncertain whether in the 1780s, spent by a long war of independence and disrupted by commercial disputes, the non-slave states could have or would have or should have waged a civil war to resolve the slavery issue. Political reality has to be reckoned with. "A little practical virtue," said delegate William Paterson, "is to be preferred to the finest theoretical principles, which cannot be carried into effect."

Today, there is even an argument, advanced by an eminent liberal scholar, that the Constitution should have been totally silent on the subject of slavery. The late John Hart Ely, former law clerk to Chief Justice Earl Warren, argues in his important 1980 book *Democracy and Distrust* that, as a matter of basic constitutional theory, the Founders should have avoided saying anything, either pro or con, about slavery. Ely's point is that the original Constitution was principally—even overwhelmingly—dedicated to concerns of process and structure and not the identification and preservation of specific substantive values. Inasmuch as fundamental values may change over time, writes Ely, attempts to freeze substantive values (*e.g.*, protecting slavery, Prohibition, a balanced budget) do not belong in a constitution.

Ely's constitutional theory is far from universally accepted. Rather, it is highly controversial. Tradition, conceded by Ely, has viewed the Constitution as "an enduring but evolving statement of the general values." But Ely thinks that this tradition—and the subjective nature of judicial review based on it—are wrong. According to Ely, the Constitution leaves choice and accommodation of substantive values almost entirely to the political process. Ely takes seriously what Justice Oliver Wendell Holmes said in his famous 1905 dissent in *Lochner v. New York* about a constitution being "made for people of fundamentally differing views."

Two other primary conclusions emerge from considering the Constitution's compromise with slavery. The first conclusion is to see that particular compromise, obnoxious as it seems to us today, as part of the continuing problem of racism in American life. We Americans live, and will forever live, with the legacy of slavery. Issues such as affirmative action, income and wealth inequality, inner-city problems, de facto segregation, disparity in school quality, and lack of equal opportunity all stem, to a greater or lesser extent, from slavery and racism. We are, as Mark Twain put it in *Pudd'nhead Wilson*, "the heirs of two centuries of unatoned insult and outrage."

The second conclusion is to be wary of simplistic theories of constitutional interpretation based on so-called original intent. As the slavery compromise shows, constitutional interpretation is an intractably complex problem. How do we ascertain the intent of drafters when what they drafted was a compromise? In such circumstances, is there such a concept as one original intent? And of what relevance is original intent anyway, centuries after the fact? It is complicated.

Neither conclusion justifies the slavery compromise on moral or ethical grounds; on those grounds, the Framers are guilty of the accusations against them. But each conclusion takes account of the compromise as part of a *political* process, a pragmatic process that at its best tries honorably to reconcile or balance competing or completely opposed views of human welfare, and that may be the most important thing for us to remember.

10

THE ORIGINAL DEBATE OVER ORIGINAL INTENT

Compromise often creates vagueness and ambiguity. The language of a constitutional clause or a legislative statute that results from compromise may have different meanings even to those who made the compromise. Drafters may seek refuge in ambiguity, but different drafters may have voted for the proposition for different reason. Each may have thought that his or her differing intent was expressed in the agreed-upon text, which makes the search for intent complicated.

Events leading up to the Constitutional Convention of 1787 throw new-old light on our current ongoing debate over original intent and the Constitution. That debate is about whether judges should interpret the Constitution according to what it originally meant to the Framers or as a living document that has evolved. Who would have thought that such a debate goes all the way back to the beginning, indeed, even before the Constitution was drafted?

I

The resolution by the Continental Congress authorizing the Philadelphia Convention has been the subject of the longest-running debate about the Framers' original intent. From the start, serious questions have arisen about whether the delegates in Philadelphia acted beyond the scope of their authority in drafting a new charter of government. Were the delegates supposed to merely revise an old government or create a totally new one?

After the Annapolis Convention in September 1786 went beyond its stated authority and called for a national convention, Congress failed to respond for several months. But when Congress finally did something, it restricted the role of the delegates. Meeting in New York, Congress on February 21, 1787 "resolved" that "on the second Monday in May next a Convention of delegates who shall have been appointed by the several states be held at Philadelphia *for the sole and express purpose of revising the Articles of Confederation*" (emphasis added).

The limiting, tentative language used by Congress suited the temper of the times. Congress said nothing about a new constitution. The forthcoming meeting in Philadelphia was a very uncertain venture. It was not known at the time as a *Constitutional* Convention. If it were, if the stated purpose was to write a new "constitution," many delegates would not have attended.

Nowhere is this attitude better illustrated than in some of the Anti-Federalist literature published soon after the Philadelphia Convention. One famous Anti-Federalist article, "Letter from the Federal Farmer" dated October 8, 1789, described the outcome of the Philadelphia Convention as "a bold step," which is "usually followed by a revolution or a civil war." "Had the idea of a total change been stated," continued the polemic, "probably no state would have appointed members to the convention. The idea of destroying, ultimately, the state governments, forming one consolidated system, could not have been admitted."

Even after Annapolis, according to the same Federal Farmer, "still not a word was said about destroying the old constitution, and making a new one. The states still unsuspecting, and not aware that they were passing the Rubicon, appointed members to the new convention for the sole and express purpose of revising and amending the confederation—and, probably not one man in ten thousand in the United States . . . had an idea that the old ship was to be destroyed, and he put to the alternative of embarking in the new ship presented, or of being left in danger of sinking—The States, I believe, universally supposed the convention would report alterations in the confederation."

James Madison was quite sensitive to this widely voiced charge that the convention had exceeded its powers and disregarded the mandate of Congress. He devoted all of *Federalist* No. 40 to a careful lawyer-like defense of the Convention against the accusation. His defense is only half successful.

The less successful half of *Federalist* No. 40 deals with, of all things, the question of original intent. First, Madison underscores the language of Hamilton's Annapolis report calling for a convention "to devise such further provisions as shall appear to them necessary to render the Constitution of the federal government adequate to the exigencies of the Union." Then Madison focuses on Congress's resolution concluding that it sought a "firm national government" capable of meeting the current problems and that the Convention could change the Articles of Confederation to meet those needs.

Madison then poses a hypothetical. "Suppose, then, that the expressions defining the authority of the Convention were irreconcilably at variance with each other, that a *national* and *adequate government* could not possibly, in the judgment of the convention, be effected by *alterations* and *provisions* in the Articles of Confederation." Faced with such a tension, Madison asks which of the two concepts should prevail. Was it "of most importance to the happiness of the people of America that the Articles of Confederation should be disregarded, and an adequate government be provided, and the Union preserved"? "Or that an adequate government should be omitted, and the Articles of Confederation preserved"? To state the question as Madison does is, of course, to answer it.

Having posed and answered his hypothetical, Madison dismissed the hypothetical as unnecessary. The apparently contradictory instructions, says Madison, are not "absolutely irreconcilable to each other." Inasmuch as the Convention was expressly authorized to make alterations and add new provisions, where, Madison asks, is "the boundary between authorized and usurped innovation; between the degree of change which lies within the compass of *alteration and further provisions* and that which amounts to a *transmutation* of the government?" To Madison, the answer "is that the great principles of the Constitution proposed by the Convention may be considered less as absolutely new than as the expansion of principles which are found in the Articles of Confederation." But even here, Madison admits that the "degree of enlargement . . . gives to the new system the aspect of an entire transformation of the old."

After this point, Madison's argument in *Federalist* No. 40 takes a different turn. Up to now, Madison has been defending what the convention did in terms of its authorizing documents. That defense analyzes the relevant language, raises and disposes of a hypothetical conflict and ultimately concludes that the conflict does not exist because the continuum between alteration and transmutation is hard to mark. If that were the most that could be said—or all that Madison did say—in defense of the Convention's authority, that authority would be questionable at best. But there is more to be said, and Madison started to say it.

Toward the end of *Federalist* No. 40, Madison virtually concedes the charge of unauthorized conduct by the Convention. He admits "the liberty assumed by a very few deputies from a very few states, convened at Annapolis, of recommending a great and critical object, *wholly foreign to their commission*" (emphasis added). So that the Anti-Federalists "may be disarmed of every pretext," Madison grants "for a moment that the Convention were neither authorized by their commission, nor justified by circumstances in proposing a Constitution for their country." And again he assumes "they had violated both their powers and their obligations in proposing a Constitution." These apparent concessions do not, however, end the matter.

Madison clinches his argument by citing ratification. He winds up by appealing to his audience to forgive the Convention in its small trespasses and to judge the Constitution on its own merits. Exactly here is where Madison stands on most firm ground. The Convention's "powers were merely advisory," Madison points out. It had no real or final power for establishing a Constitution. The Convention "planned and proposed a Constitution which is to be of no more consequence than the paper on which it is written, unless it be stamped with the approbation of those to whom it is addressed."

Ratification saved the Constitution's legitimacy. As Madison says, "This reflection places the subject in a point of view altogether different." Whatever the scope of the Convention's authority, the American people through their state conventions ratified what the Philadelphia Convention had done. Ratification pardoned any disobedience of orders.

Not everyone agrees. According to historian Robert Brown, writing in 1963, "Whether or not the Convention was legal under the Articles of Confederation is open to question . . . . There is no doubt, however, that what the Constitutional Convention finally proposed was illegal under the Articles. The Constitution was not an amendment to the Articles, and it was not to be ratified by the legislatures of every state. In this sense, we could say the Convention was staging a political coup." Another historian, E. James Ferguson, described the Constitution as the product of "extra-legal procedures."

This history has a bit of irony for us today. As we consider today's issues of original intent, it is ironic to recall that the Constitution itself was born of an alleged violation of original intent. If the delegates had not had the audacity to violate Congress's instructions by making constitutional changes "adequate to the exigencies" of the time, we might still be living under the Articles of Confederation. There is food for thought here, particularly for the debate about judicial activism and restraint and the quest for original intent.

II

That debate took on new life and veered off in a new direction in 1985 when U.S. Attorney General Edwin Meese proposed what he called "a jurisprudence of original intention." Meese was reacting to what he regarded as decisions by the Supreme Court that "have been more policy choices than articulations of long-term constitutional principles." Instead of reading their policy preferences into the Constitution, the justices—according to Meese—should "go back to the original intent of the Framers" and "resurrect the original meaning of the constitutional provisions."

This originalist quest, a fertile source of controversy and confusion, has since gathered many conservative adherents. According to Supreme Court nominee Robert Bork, "only by limiting themselves to the historic intentions underlying each clause of the Constitution can judges avoid being legislators [and] avoid enforcing their own moral predilections." Supreme Court Justice Antonin Scalia puts it slightly differently. "What I look for in the Constitution is," he explains, "the original meaning of the text, not what the draftsmen intended . . . . [T]he Great Divide with regard to the constitutional interpretation is not that between Framers' intent and objective meaning, but rather between *original* meaning (whether derived from Framers' intent or not) and *current* meaning."

Viewed sympathetically, the search for original intent and meaning can be seen as no more than a needful search for standards in the age-old tension between law and discretion, between a government of laws and a government of men. Lack of standards and guidelines creates unpredictability, uncertainty, and subjective judicial policy-making, *i.e.*, judicial activism. Such complaints have long been a loud refrain of Supreme Court critics. The cure they propose is judicial restraint by resort to supposedly more objective principles, such as original intent. From this perspective, one can at least understand the jurisprudential desire for standards.

Much can be said in favor of relying on original intention. Such reliance asks a historical question: What was the original intent? It tries to avoid making a political judgment that imports individual value preferences. It accords with what educational theorist E.D. Hirsch Jr. referred to in *Validity in Interpretation*, a book on literary criticism, as the "sensible belief that a text means what its authors meant." Hirsch, and many originalists, think that the author's intent is the "only compelling normative principle that could lend validity to an interpretation."

But, as Scalia seems to recognize, we have to be careful, especially in constitutional law, to search for certainty and objectivity in original intent beyond the language actually used in the Constitution. Original intent may appear to be objective, when in fact such supposed objectivity is mere illusion and a mask for equally subjective policy-making.

As a general matter, the language used in a statute or a constitutional provision is the best evidence of the intent and meaning of such language. To divine the original intent, we traditionally look first to the words of the Constitution. The actual language used—the language ultimately agreed upon—is by far the most important factor in ascertaining intent. It is objective.

If the words are unclear—as frequently happens—then comes the quest for intent beyond the language used. This is particularly so when we try to determine what the Framers would have done had they considered a problem that they failed to consider or did not even exist at the time. But once we get beyond the actual text in question, problems arise that should make us skeptical, or at least wary, of relying on original intent.

Originalists, for example, still have to deal with what literary critics call the "Intentional Fallacy." According to that fallacy, as famously described by Professors W.K. Wimsatt and Monroe Beardsley, an author's intention is a highly uncertain guide to the meaning of what the author wrote. Thus, the Framers' desire to communicate a particular meaning is not necessarily the same as success in doing so, especially where the final language is compromise language. The text represents the actual performance. Any special attempt to divine intention would equate private wish with public accomplishment and would confuse the final language with its origins. What is most important is not what the Framers meant, but what they said.

Even in the ordinary situation, legislative history is a tricky source. Not every legislator will have a precise understanding of the meaning of the statutory language, or will feel compelled to put such understanding on the record. Nor will every legislator correct every contrary interpretation offered by another legislator. Legislation is often the product of compromise, so that a statute may embody more than one intent.

These problems are compounded by constitutional interpretation. Ordinary tasks associated with routine legislative history are inapplicable to ascertaining constitutional intent. In addition to the problems of ascertaining what the drafters intended is the problem as determining what the *ratifiers* intended. The reason for these differences flow from the special process of creating the Constitution and its amendments through ratification.

Ratification by the states makes the quest for constitutional intent especially difficult. The original Constitution and all later amendments had to be ratified by a certain number of the states to become effective. In vivid contrast, a garden variety statute is proposed, debated, altered and passed by one legislative body. But the Constitutional Convention of 1787 merely *proposed* the Constitution, and, under Article V of the Constitution, later Congresses merely proposed amendments. By ratification, the states—not Congress—made the Constitution and amendments into law.

The mechanics of Constitution-making mean that constitutional intent depends in large part on the views of those voting to ratify. Their views are as important, if not more important, than the views of those proposing the constitutional language. Yet rarely if ever are the views of ratifiers considered in determining constitutional meaning.

Everyone quotes the Framers of the original Constitution and the drafters of amendments, but who quotes from the state ratifying conventions?

Once the views of ratifiers in many states are considered vital, the whole process of determining intent fans out in scope. It means that for the intent behind any particular constitutional wording, one must consider what the Framers *and* the ratifiers said and did. As John Ely writes in *Democracy and Distrust*: "That gets to include so many different people in so many different circumstances, however, that one cannot hope to gather a reliable picture of their intentions from any perusal of the legislative history."

Equally important, many of the relevant records are unavailable. Some have simply not survived. Others are incomplete. It is difficult even to attempt to infer intent from legislative history if the history itself is not all there. For this reason, the Framers' meaning may be inaccessible and therefore beyond knowing for sure.

None of these observations means intent is irrelevant to constitutional interpretation. As Wimsatt and Beardsley recognize, "poetry differs from practical messages, which are successful if and only if we correctly infer the intention." But that only points up the importance of the constitutional language used as the best evidence of intent. What the Framers proposed and what the ratifiers voted is what they meant. The wording itself is the most important factor, and far more reliable than safaris into the jungle of legislative history. For the truth is that the legislative history of many crucial constitutional provisions, such as the Fourteenth Amendment, for example, is in unusual disarray.

The call for "a jurisprudence of original intention" has provoked and should provoke debate. It raises two fundamental questions. First, how do we ascertain such original intention? Second, why should such original intention—even if ascertainable—necessarily govern us more than two hundred twenty-five years later under far different conditions.

The originalist program has to be scrutinized from another perspective. A "jurisprudence of original intention" is supposedly meant to replace "subjective judicial policy-making." But given the vast difficulties of determining original intent, is not the alleged objectivity of the original intent a delusion? And if such objectivity is illusory, may not originalist jurisprudence be a disguise for equally subjective policy choices and personal value judgments by judges? Such a theory of interpretation is akin to the Affective Fallacy, by which critics interpret poetry according to the emotional effect it produces in them. As applied to constitutional interpretation, the outcome of either Fallacy, the Intentional or the Affective, is that the constitutional or statutory text tends to disappear.

III

Taken literally, the originalist approach might possibly mean that the Constitution itself is null and void. The "sole and express purpose" of the Philadelphia Convention was to "revis[e] the Articles of Confederation." That was the explicit limited authority granted to it by Congress. The Convention obviously—and thankfully—went far beyond its authority. Moreover, the ratification process in the Constitution (requiring only nine states) violated the unanimity for rule for revising the Articles of Confederation. Could someone argue, based on original intent, that the resulting Constitution was therefore illegal? The Anti-Federalists thought so. A few modern historians think so.

There are important lessons to be learned from this long ago experience in constitutional interpretation by the people who actually wrote the Constitution. The practicalities of the situation, the actual exigencies of government, the problems of the real world may occasionally override strictly faithful and liberal interpretation. That is exactly how the Framers themselves behaved. Just as Hamilton did not think the Annapolis Convention should be cabined by its instructions, so too the Framers did not think themselves bound by the limited literal scope of Congress's resolution merely to revise the Articles of Confederation. Their contemporary construction of the congressional resolution did not slavishly follow its original intent. Lucky for us. Originalism ought not to be a fetish. We need the ability to see through such legal thickets to moral daylight beyond.

11

THOSE MACHIAVELLIAN FRAMERS

Niccolo Machiavelli is one those rare historical figures whose very name has come to stand for certain qualities—in his case political cunning. Ever since he wrote *The Prince* in 1512—a how-to primer for rulers—his name has been synonymous with ruthlessness, duplicity, and bad faith. To label someone as Machiavellian has for centuries meant that such a person would use any means, however lawless or unscrupulous, to establish and maintain himself or herself in power. In light of his bad name, Machiavelli is not someone we ordinarily think of in connection with the framing of the U.S. Constitution. We should think again.

Machiavelli has another, lesser known but much brighter side. Coexisting with his dark side is a most attractive aspect that makes him in some sense the intellectual godfather of the Framers' best work. In one of the greatest reversals of modern intellectual fashion, Machiavelli the bad has in recent years become Machiavelli the good. The amoral and ruthless political theories of *The Prince* represent only part—the darker part—of his thinking. Machiavelli's other writings reveal a fundamentally noble and appealing line of thought about government that served as a beacon for the Founders.

These other writings by Machiavelli examine the nature of republics and republican values. In essence, he discusses whether and how people can govern themselves, how republics come into being, and how they might be maintained. This was a vital problem for Florentine political thinkers of his time. Machiavelli lived in Florence at the height of the Renaissance, and breathed its bracing and exhilarating air. He looked into the idea of republicanism, which had started in ancient times and, with his help, reached profound political expression in Renaissance humanism.

In *The Discourses, The Histories,* and *The Art of War,* Machiavelli explores in detail the republican form of government. He focuses on modern republics as well as ancient ones. In these humanist discussions, he delved into what is called classical republicanism, and in doing so inspired the men who founded our nation.

Classical republicanism has at its core certain important concepts. It stresses political virtue as a life of disciplined public duty, values military service by citizen-soldiers, worries about how such virtue will be corrupted, and periodically re-educates the people about the ideals of public duty and the original ideals of the republic.

Central to republicanism as expounded by Machiavelli is the concept of "virtue." By "virtue," republicanism means the demands imposed on the idea of true citizenship. "Virtue" is a celebration of citizenship and requires the people's direct participation in civic affairs. But such political activism is not enough.

"Virtue" is an attitude of simplicity, frugality, self-control, and duty to the public good. "Virtue" requires true citizens to subordinate their private interests to the public good. "Virtue," in this republican (*i.e.,* Machiavellian) sense, is a political ideal that makes moral ideas and culture more important than material interests and power.

Political virtue includes military service. In *The Art of War,* Machiavelli (not Sun Tzu) looks into the republican citizen's obligation to bear arms. He greatly fears a mercenary armed force composed solely of professionals. A soldier who is nothing but a soldier, says Machiavelli, is a menace to all other social activities. A part-time soldier—a citizen called to arms—with a home and an occupation of his own is Machiavelli's ideal. He thought that loss of liberty and corruption of the body politic occurred when citizens expected from others what they should have expected from themselves as citizens.

Machiavelli might have some interesting, no doubt critical, things to say about America's all-volunteer military. Based on his comments in *The Art of War,* Machiavelli would not approve. Ending the draft and the disappearance of the citizen-soldier would strike Machiavelli as a mistake. Separating the military from the citizenry would make Machiavelli nervous. Reliance on a totally professional military would distress Machiavelli. He would view it as evidence of a loss of "virtue."

When "virtue" disappears, according to Machiavelli, a republic declines. With most if not all republics, he says, time weakens the moral fiber of the citizens. This moral decay comes about with commerce and economic development, which bring in their train wealth and luxury. Such commerce makes the citizen pre-occupied with his self-interest and indifferent to the public good. Commerce "corrupts" the citizens and makes them surrender to their base material appetites.

What the Framers did in Philadelphia over two hundred twenty-five years ago can be seen as a continuation of Machiavelli's classical republicanism. Indeed, classical republicanism is an important theme in contemporary scholarship on early American ideas and culture. The leading advocate of this theme is J.G.A. Pocock, a historian of political thought at Johns Hopkins University, whose exciting 1975 book *The Machiavellian Moment* has already become a classic.

According to Pocock, the "last great pre-modern efflorescence" of the Machiavellian tradition "took place in the American colonies," and "the American Revolution and the Constitution in some sense form the last act of the civic Renaissance." Even after the passing of the Founders, says Pocock, one can find in American history proof of "the Americanization of virtue."

This Machiavellian thesis stirred the intellectual waters. It was the main target of John P. Diggins's important 1984 book *The Lost Soul of American Politics*. Diggins accepts Pocock's description of Machiavelli's classical republicanism but offers a different explanation for the main themes in American culture.

To Diggins, liberalism rather than classical republicanism is the key to explaining America. Liberalism, Diggins argues, means ideas derived from Locke and Calvin, the realities of interest politics, the value of protecting property as central to American thought and politics, and the importance of materialism and commerce. In rejecting the Machiavellian thesis, Diggins says, "the idea of political virtue had ceased to have relevance and meaning in America."

The debate over republicanism and liberalism may never be resolved conclusively. Evidence exists to support both competing explanations. Obviously, interest politics (what Madison famously called factions in *Federalist* No. 10) and property rights were, as Diggins points out, crucial concerns of the Framers. But, at the same time, it would be inaccurate as well as a slur on the Founders to attribute to them entirely ignoble motives, bereft of any ideals of political virtue inherited from Machivelli's classical republicanism. Ideals of political virtue did motivate to a large degree men like Washington, Jefferson, Adams, Madison, and Hamilton.

From this point of view, to call the Framers "Machiavellian" is to pay them a high compliment. It is not the infamous Machiavelli of *The Prince* on whom we draw, but the noble and zealous republican Machiavelli of his other works. To be Machiavellian in this brighter sense is to believe in liberty and in the capacity of people to govern themselves, to celebrate citizenship and advancing the public good, and to guard against corruption and material interests. Only when the ideals of political virtue cease to inspire will the rehabilitated label "Machiavellian" be disparaging.

Another reason exists for thinking of Machiavelli in connection with a look at how the Constitution came about. He believed in periodic revitalization as the way to avert the process of corruption so fatal to republics. When citizens become so corrupted that they forget the original ideals of the republic, they are incapable of practicing citizenship. Revitalization comes about by returning to first principles from the moment of the republic's creation and recapturing the concept of civic virtue.

Is not thinking about the Constitution a Machiavellian (in the complimentary sense) revitalization, a return to original principles, a re-education of the people about the ideals of public duty?

12

THE CONVENTION AND PARTIAL VERDICTS

Quite apart from the text of the Constitution and any amendments, the Philadelphia Convention itself has something important to teach us about trial procedure. The Convention's actions on May 29, 1787 in adopting two rules and rejecting a third shed light on the proper understanding of modern trial procedure relating to what are known as partial verdicts. One rule, called the rule of "mutability," gave the Convention the right to reconsider votes already taken by a majority. Young Spaight of North Carolina suggested the rule: "The House may not be precluded, by a vote upon any question, from revising the subject matter of it when they see cause." Throughout the summer of 1787, the Committee of the Whole frequently invoked the rule of "mutability" and reconsidered issues already voted on.

To make this first rule more effective, the Convention rejected a proposed rule authorizing delegates to call for recorded votes on every issue. Rufus King of Massachusetts led the opposition to the recording rule because, he said, it would be binding to delegates and confusing if they later changed their minds. Some of Rufus King's concerns also led to the more general rule of secrecy that enveloped the Convention. The blend in adopting the "mutability" rule, rejecting the recording rule, and adopting the secrecy rule allowed the Convention to consider, debate, take tentative votes, and then reconsider its provisional stand, without recording its votes or being subject to publicity until it completed all its important business.

The Convention's actions on these three rules can be recast in terms of trial procedure. Think of the Convention as a jury, and decisions on various issues as verdicts. Viewed this way, the Convention allowed itself the freedom to take partial verdicts without recording them, subject to reconsideration before a complete final verdict at the end of secret deliberations before discharging itself. On the last day of the Convention, Ben Franklin gave a good explanation for the three rules. He said, "I have lived long, I have experienced many instances of being obliged by better information, or fuller consideration, to change opinions even on important subjects, which I once thought right, but found to be otherwise."

How much of the Convention's approach, one might reasonably ask, survives in our current law of partial verdicts? With respect to a complete, unitary, nonpartial verdict, which resolves at once all issues of guilt or innocence, civil liability and damages, the Convention's approach survives pretty much intact. The unanimous rule is that a complete verdict becomes final only on jury discharge. This rule means that the discharge of the jury, not the recording of its verdict, determines the finality of a complete verdict.

This finality cut-off is important. Jurors are allowed to repudiate a complete verdict between recording and discharge. As to complete verdicts, a jury can change its mind any time before it is finally discharged.

A different rule applies to partial verdicts. A partial verdict is generally understood as a decision by a jury, before its deliberations are fully completed, on less than all the issues presented to it. After rendering such a partial decision, a jury resumes its deliberations on the remaining issues.

This partial verdict procedure can raise troublesome issues. For example, the "difficult and novel" question in *United States v. Hockridge*, decided in 1978 by the U.S. Court of Appeals for the Second Circuit, was whether a partial verdict in a criminal case could be impeached by the voluntary and spontaneous testimony of a juror before the jury's discharge. The Court of Appeals held in *Hockridge* that a duly recorded partial verdict is as final as a complete verdict after discharge.

Hockridge's holding illustrates the interplay of three rules considered by the Constitutional Convention. On one hand, the jury deliberations in *Hockridge*, like the debates at the Constitutional Convention, were secret. On the other hand, because the partial verdict in *Hockridge* had been recorded, it could not be modified or impeached even though deliberations still went on. The ghost of Rufus King—the successful opponent of the Convention's recording rule—must have smiled when the *Hockridge* decision was circulated in Framers' heaven. For, in effect, the *Hockridge* rule subverted the Convention's "mutability" rule, significantly undercut the value of partial verdicts, and departed from the Framers' view of deliberative decisionmaking.

If partial verdicts are held final for all purposes, then at least some of the perceived advantages of partial verdicts will be purchased at a price. Finality may prematurely freeze a jury into a partial verdict that the later course of deliberations reveals to be unwise. As the same Court of Appeals later stated in 1981 in *United States v. DiLapi*: "There is a risk that some jurors might mistakenly permit a tentative vote to become an irrevocable vote and forgo the opportunity to gain new insights concerning the evidence in one defendant's case from consideration of the same evidence as it bears upon the other defendants." Thus, a partial verdict should be likened only to an early estimate of guilt or innocence, an estimate subject to revision in light of further deliberation.

Absolute finality of partial verdicts violates common sense and experience with provisional hypotheses, particularly in deliberative decisionmaking groups, such as constitutional conventions. Such hypotheses often undergo change as more investigation, more light, and more discussion take place. For example, appellate judges often have formed initial positions following oral argument, only to change their positions after more reflections or after reading draft opinions for the majority and the dissent. The tentative decision made by appellate judges in conference following oral argument resembles a partial verdict, and that decision is subject to change before publication of the formal written decision.

The same reality applies to jury verdicts. Certainly votes taken in the jury room before being returned in court are preliminary. One court has noted with insight that this "applies particularly where more than one count has been submitted to the jury, for continuing deliberations may shake views expressed on counts previously considered."

Where there is nothing in the jury instructions to indicate that a recorded partial verdict is unchangeable and immutable forever, jurors might well think a partial verdict was entirely nonfinal. To correct this possible misimpression, the court in *DiLapi* ruled that any instruction on partial verdicts "should advise the jurors that any verdicts they choose to report will not be subject to later revision." Such a clear instruction might go far toward the prevention of freezing tentative votes. At a minimum jurors would know what they are doing. But the trouble with *DiLapi* rule is that it may discourage partial verdicts.

Absent such a clear instruction as to finality, partial verdicts must, as the Constitutional Convention regarded its own preliminary votes, be considered in the nature of tentative, working hypotheses subject to change before the jury's discharge. Therefore, if they are allowed at all, they must be regarded only as assumptions that are not immutable until the jury is discharged. As the same appellate court said about journalists in another case too, the juror, the judge and the Framer "must formulate his views, and at every step, question his conclusions, tentative or otherwise." This approach is the only rational approach fully consistent with scientific method, whose hallmark is a readiness to abandon theory when the facts so demand.

Changes in our early hypotheses indicate that we are progressively realizing the ideal, since they arise from corrections in previous observations or reasoning, and such correction means that we are in possession of more reliable facts. In science, law or any intellectually honest discipline, we select that hypothesis most probable on the factual evidence; it is the task of further inquiry to find other factual evidence that will increase or decrease the probability of such a theory. Applying any hypothesis involves some risk, for it may not be in fact applicable. "Opinions are at best provisional hypotheses, incompletely tested," wrote Learned Hand to Oliver Wendell Holmes in 1918.

Viewing partial verdicts as tentative, working hypotheses is a self-corrective process that makes possible the noting and correction of errors by continued application of itself before the jury discharge. This is what Ben Franklin was referring to on the last day of the Convention.

The Constitutional Convention's lesson about partial verdicts opens up a new mode of constitutional interpretation. *How* the Framers formulated the Constitution, what procedural rules they accepted and rejected may tell as much about "original intent" as what they said in debate or wrote in the text. Professor Charles Black argued that the "structure" of the Constitution is an important guide to interpreting it. Now we can start thinking about interpreting the Constitution in light of the procedural rules and understandings used at the Convention by the Framers themselves.

13

A WRITTEN CONSTITUTION

At some point during a study of the drafting of the Constitution, we have to ask ourselves some basic questions: What is so special about a *written* constitution? What difference does it make to have a written rather than an unwritten constitution? Do we really have a written or an unwritten constitution?

Justice Hugo Black, in his little book *A Constitutional Faith*, declared, "It is of paramount importance to me that our country has a written Constitution. This great document is the unique American contribution to man's continuing search for a society in which individual liberty is secure against governmental oppression." Black was echoing earlier sentiments expressed by another great Supreme Court justice.

"A written constitution," wrote Chief Justice John Marshall in the landmark 1803 case of *Marbury v. Madison*, is "what we have deemed the greatest improvement on political institutions." In the same case, Marshall went on to point out that in America "written constitutions have been viewed with so much reverence."

Marshall's comments in *Marbury* are intriguing. On one hand they beg the question. They assert without demonstrating the value of a written Constitution. On the other hand, he was making the case for judicial review, that is, the power of a court to void an act of Congress as unconstitutional. He argued that not to have judicial review would, in his words, "subvert the very foundation of all written constitutions." Yet the doctrine he was creating—judicial review—would eventually produce claims that we have an unwritten constitution.

Which is it? As the king says in "The King and I," "Is a puzzlement!"

Part of the puzzle is easy, for Marshall was surely correct about the high regard in which Americans of his day held written constitutions.

Constitution-writing rooted in American colonial history had become a fever in America. Written constitutions, writes Bernard Bailyn in his brilliant book *The Ideological Origins of American Revolution*, "had existed, had been acted upon, for a century or more." The thirteen colonies had originated and carried on under basic written documents, namely, royal charters.

With the advent of the Revolutionary War, each of the colonies drafted its own state constitution. Thus, by 1787, Americans already had a long tradition of wanting and needing written constitutions. They were our basic instruments of government and gave rise to the notion of "American constitutionalism" referred to by Justice Black. To Americans, wrote Tom Paine in *The Rights of Man*, a constitution was "the political Bible of the state," with every family having a copy and every government official carrying a copy in his pocket (as Justice Black did) to consult.

But more than tradition, experience and form were involved. Eighteenth-century Americans saw the primary function of a written constitution as a means to mark out the boundaries of government and as a vitally important way to limit government and erect defensive bulwarks against misuse of power. Written constitutions allowed the people not to have to "trust" government. Words have meaning, and a written constitution embodies the ultimate power of words, the magical power of language. Americans were preoccupied with written restraints on political, especially legislative, power. The English system, under which Americans had chafed, had imposed no limits on Parliament. As a result, Americans viewed expressly written documents as the best security against what the Massachusetts House of Representatives in 1768 called "the danger of an indefinite dependence upon an undetermined power."

What emerged in 1787 from this background was a new American idea of constitutions. A constitution was a single written document that became a fundamental law, superior to statutory law as well as common law, and emanating, at least in theory, from the people. It is not a contract with the government, it creates the government. The special authority and importance of a constitution is enhanced and acquires permanence if embodied in some fixed written document. The U.S. Constitution is a written superior law set above the entire government against which all other law is to be measured. This is certainly Marshall's constitutional theory in *Marbury*.

Ultimately, this novel American idea of a written constitution—"constitutionalism"—went viral. Over time many other countries, especially new ones, adopted it. The genuine virtues of a written constitution continue to attract people all over the world, so much so that today we speak of this phenomenon as global constitutionalism. This concept of constitutionalism may be the single most important, most widespread, most long lasting result of the Constitutional Convention.

The differences between a written and unwritten constitution are often obvious. An unwritten constitution, like that of England, is "something grown"; a written constitution, like ours, is said to be "something made." In commenting on England's unwritten constitution, in which everything depends on legislative power, Edmund Burke said a country's constitution "is made by peculiar circumstances, occasions, tempers, dispositions, and moral, civil and social habitudes of the people, which disclose themselves only in a long space of time." In contrast, American constitutional law depends on the interpretation of a basic written text or document. With a written constitution, the document is the touchstone for analysis.

Differences also arise in flexibility and adaptability. An unwritten constitution, unhampered by an old outmoded text, may appear to be more flexible and adaptable to changing conditions. A written constitution can be more rigid, especially where amendment is, as in our system, difficult. Such differences may be good or bad, depending on the changes sought and one's point of view.

Flexibility or rigidity leads to issues familiar to American constitutional law. A written constitution raises the basic problem of majority rule in a democracy. Should a current democratic majority be prevented from carrying out its wishes by a prior majority that favored a particular constitution? And then there is the related issue of accountability. Is it not anti-democratic for non-elected judges to use judicial review to prevent a majority from acting? Such questions do not arise in precisely this way where there is no written constitution.

But such differences can be overdrawn. Interpreting a written constitution inevitably involves flexibility, growth and development. This is especially so where the written constitution, like ours, uses vague phrases. Expressions like "due process" and "equal protection" are glittering generalities. For a written constitution to survive, those who live under it must cultivate flexibility and practicality as an attitude. Even with a written constitution, a nation depends on tradition, experience, wise judges, able administrators and sensitive legislators—many of the things referred to by Edmund Burke—to give concrete meaning to the basic charter. In America, our real constitution is not a piece of yellowing parchment in the National Archives, but a combination of the words on the actual document together with our entire national history.

We are becoming more and more aware of this phenomenon. Two of our leading constitutional scholars have recently drawn attention to it. In 2008, Harvard law Professor Laurence Tribe published a book entitled *The Invisible Constitution* and in 2012 Yale law Professor Akhil Reed Amar published *America's Unwritten Constitution*. Both books are important and stress the limited use of the actual text of the written Constitution in the way we live and are actually governed. Even with a written constitution, then, it depends on how it is interpreted.

A crucial part of that national history is the role of the Supreme Court in interpreting and applying the written Constitution. Ever since *Marbury*, the institution of judicial review has produced in effect a constitutional common law. Court decisions authoritatively explain and interpret the Constitution, much as talmudic commentators authoritatively explain and interpret the Torah. The ongoing nature of such constitutional interpretation shrinks the differences between a written and unwritten constitution, John Marshall and Hugo Black to the contrary notwithstanding.

This process is what gives rise to phrases like "a living document," a "continuing constitutional convention," and Chief Justice Charles Evans Hughes's famous remark that, "We are under a Constitution, but the Constitution is what the judges say it is." At one point near the end of the 1963 Supreme Court Term—a Term with major cases that pushed constitutional doctrine far in many areas—journalist Anthony Lewis passed Solicitor General Archibald Cox a note asking "How does it feel to be at the second American Constitutional Convention?"

All of this is highly relevant to the current debate over the role of the Framers' intent in constitutional interpretation. Those who call themselves "originalists" stress the written nature of the Constitution and the inherent limits on interpreting such a written constitution. Doubtless they agree with Thomas Jefferson's comment, "Our peculiar security is in possession of a written Constitution. Let us not make it a blank paper by construction." If the 1987 Bork confirmation hearings were any indicator, however, the "orignalist" approach is far from commanding universal acceptance.

Indeed, the existence of a written or an unwritten constitution is no guarantee of particular results. Some countries, Russia and China come to mind, have impressive written constitutions that in practice afford little or no protection for civil liberties. Other countries, notably England, long had no written constitution but have a bright history of civil liberties. English common law has achieved more than many empty promises in national charters. This comparative look leads to the conclusion that individual freedom may depend less on pieces of paper and more on the spirit and hearts of people.

Surely this was the view of Judge Learned Hand in his memorable 1944 speech called "The Spirit of Liberty." In that speech, given during World War II, Hand said, "I often wonder whether we do not rest our hopes too much upon constitutions, upon laws and upon courts. These are false hopes; believe me, these are false hopes. Liberty lies in the hearts of men and women; when it dies there, no constitution, no law, no court can ever do much to help it. While it lies there, it needs no constitution, no law, no court to save it."

And yet, false hopes or not, a written constitution does help to instill and preserve the spirit of liberty. Such a document draws attention to national values, goals and ideals above partisan politics. It is an indispensable tool for interpreting legislation and seeking legal review of governmental actions. As Chief Justice Marshall foresaw, the combination of a written constitution and judicial review establishes a frameowrk for giving practical effect to a superior fundamental law and, going beyond Marshall's vision, for protecting the rights of the minority against a temporary majority.

The benefits of a written constitution are therefore real. They are what make a written constitution so special. As Alexander Hamilton wrote in *Federalist* No. 83, "The establishment of a Constitution, in time of profound peace, by the voluntary consent of a whole people is a prodigy." And that is one reason why we venerate the Constitution.

14

THE LIBRARY EXHIBIT ON THE CONSTITUTION

The best exhibit mounted during the 1987 Bicentennial of the Constitution was entitled "Are We to Be a Nation? The Making of the Federal Constitution," and was put on at the Gottesman Exhibition Hall of the New York Public Library at Fifth Avenue and Forty-Second Street. The exhibit was nothing less than spectacular. Drawing on many sources, it displayed prints, portraits, cartoons, maps, documents, manuscripts, newspapers, pamphlets, books and sculpture related to the key people and events involved in the making and adoption of the Constitution. Such an exhibit, which is unlikely to be assembled again in our lifetimes, is in some ways a major art exhibit, comparable to exhibits of Van Gogh or Vienna-1900. Perhaps those comparisons are not strong enough. Given its uniqueness, the Library Exhibit may be more properly compared, in terms of its importance, to the famous 1913 Armory Show of modern art, which people still write about.

But of course the broader theme of the Library Exhibit made it about more than art alone. It went beyond art to combine history, culture, law and political science. The blend worked. The cross-current and mixture of disciplines—recognizing that life rarely is cabined neatly—added a depth and a reality to the exhibit.

Most of all, the Exhibit breathed life into the Bicentennial. Each of the items on display was intriguing in itself; together they conveyed an overwhelming sense of living history, national purpose and continuing debate that made the writing of the Constitution seem more real and human. The concreteness of the items on display stimulated the mind to make a chain of mental associations that enhanced our understanding of the Framers and what they were about.

At the Exhibit, for example, were several paintings, drawings and sculptures of the leading Founders. These likenesses focused the mind of the viewer by giving face and body to these Founders. One of the most affecting was a bust of Alexander Hamilton. Like Rembrandt's vision of Aristotle contemplating the bust of Homer, we stood and contemplated the bust of Hamilton, meditating on this unusual man's large role in laying the foundation of our government. The sculptured head encouraged a certain communion, a deeper understanding and empathy between minds separated by two centuries.

This heightened sense of communicating through time to the minds of the Framers grew even more when stimulated by the documents on display (which we did not even know existed). We saw a few pages of James Madison's original notes of the convention debates and our thoughts flew unbidden to the past, to that hot summer of 1787. We thought of Madison, sitting at his front-row desk at the Convention, faithfully transcribing on these very sheets. We wondered if one of the other delegates said to Madison, borrowing what William Henry, Duke of Gloucester, said to Edward Gibbon in 1781 on receipt of Volume II of *The Decline and Fall of the Roman Empire*: "Always scribble, scribble, scribble, eh, Mr. Madison?"

Nearby were other treasures. Here were Hamilton's notes in his own hand for his famous six-hour speech at the Convention on June 18, 1787. There were John Jay's handwritten drafts of some of his contributions to *The Federalist*. A few steps away were rare copies of the minutes and report of the Annapolis Convention of 1786.

We looked at these original documents and our minds were transported. We imagined these long dead men dipping their quill pens into ink and writing their thoughts on paper that has survived. Their thoughts, more than two hundred and twenty-five years old but still very much alive, the continuity of it all were the major themes. It is as if the heart and mind and soul of America were on display.

These feelings were not confined to original handwritten documents. The same emotions arose from studying the printed pages of the newspapers in which the individual numbers of *The Federalist* originally appeared. One looked at these newspaper pages from 1787 and got a better sense of the polemical debate over ratification. It was a good antidote to the way we usually read *The Federalist* today: as a collection in book form of classic essays on government. Seeing it set in newspaper type made more vivid the uncertainty of ratification and disabused us of any notion that the Constitution was preordained or that it had to be.

Organized more or less chronologically, the Library Exhibit went beyond just the Constitutional Convention. It put the Convention in context, taking us from the Revolution to Washington's first term as President. It was divided into seven groupings, each with a different, self-contained theme. The groupings were sensible and allowed the visitor to assimilate the exhibit in small doses and to ponder the meaning of each section.

One section of the Exhibit was a nice surprise. Called "The Great Confluence," it was an excursion into intellectual history and described the American experiment in government in the context of various strains of Western thought. It went into our eclectic use of thinkers like Montesquieu and Locke, and even ancients like Plutarch and Tacitus. It explored the "problem" of America in European thought and demonstrated how several contemporary European thinkers criticized what Americans were doing. The Exhibit illustrated how Franklin, Jefferson and John Adams (especially with his book defending the Constitution) led a vigorous and successful campaign for American's intellectual independence from the Old World.

As is now common with large art museum exhibits, the Library Exhibit offered an accompanying book similar to a fine art show catalogue. Bearing the same title as the Exhibit, the Library's book was written by Richard B. Bernstein with Kym S. Rice and was a substantial, first-rate volume for the Bicentennial. Lavishly illustrated with pieces from the Exhibit, it was clearly and finely written, comprehensive and sophisticated.

The extraordinary Bicentennial Exhibit was housed in an appropriately symbolic setting—the main branch of the New York Public Library. The Library's magnificent *beaux arts* structure lent majesty to the display. The immense main lobby, the high vaulted ceilings, the gleaming marble columns and walls of the Gottesman Exhibit Hall added a fitting mood of grandeur, as if the Library itself were a physical monument to the values underlying the Constitution. And, of course, in a sense it is.

The symbolic link between the Library and the Bicentennial was far deeper than physical. A library, with its leathery cliffs of books, is a repository of knowledge, the history of the human race, its traditions, culture, hopes, aspirations and errors, and a great library available free to the people is a premise of our constitutional theory. And a free library open to the public is a great democratic institution. The Founders knew that the best pillar of good government was an informed and educated populace, what Jefferson called "the diffusion of knowledge among the people." "No other sure foundation can be devised," added Jefferson, "for the preservation of freedom and happiness." Nor is it mere happenstance that Benjamin Franklin in 1730 set up the first lending library in America.

The vital and living bond between the constitutional Bicentennial and the New York Public Library is carved high up on the wall in the Library's main lobby. There, only a few steps from the exhibit in the Gottesman Hall where Jefferson, Franklin & Co. were honored, an anonymous workman long ago inscribed, in letters too large and noble to be missed by anyone who looks up rather than down, the following sacred promise from the past to the future: "THE CITY OF NEW YORK HAS ERECTED THIS BUILDING TO BE MAINTAINED FOREVER AS A FREE LIBRARY FOR THE USE OF THE PEOPLE."

"The people," "free," "forever"—those are the key words in that inscription. They capture the essence not only of the Library, but also of the Constitution.

15

CHANGING PUBLIC PERCEPTIONS

The drafting of the Constitution was only the beginning. It had to be ratified and quickly amended to include the Bill of Rights. Then it had to be interpreted and applied by each branch of the government. The Constitution in practice over the span of the nation's history, with the courts assuming the important power to declare federal and state statutes unconstitutional—judicial review—breathed life into the written document. But America's view, its notion, of its founding charter has not always been the same.

Ever since 1787, the framing of the Constitution has occupied an important but variable place in American consciousness. Immediately after the signing, the boisterous ratification process made the Constitution itself the object of controversy, with serious arguments, powerfully made, for and against. For most of the nineteenth century, American culture revered the Constitution with colorful imagery. But about a hundred years ago, a significant shift occurred in American attitudes toward the Constitution. Historians began to regard the Constitutional Convention as a conservative counter-revolution against the radicalism of the Revolution and the ideals of the Declaration of Independence. By now, though, the pendulum has swung partly back to the point where Americans can have a more balanced and realistic view of their creation myth.

We Americans venerate our Constitution, and this national attitude of reverence is understandable. It is our founding document; it set the whole machine in motion. This one document contains our fundamental, supreme law and embodies a plan of government that we live by and has so far stood the test of time. We keep it enshrined on display, for all to admire and view in awe, in a a marble temple in our capital city. To say some law or government action is unconstitutional is to utter the most severe political criticism possible, is to brand the action un-American. The Constitution is a unifying abstraction, a symbol, commanding loyalties and surviving strife.

As a result, the Constitution has throughout American history often been a topic for fulsome ceremonial praise. We celebrate it, we commemorate it, often with sweeping rhetorical, self-congratulatory flourishes, even bombast, to the point where the Constitution has acquired the status of the central myth of our political culture. The framing of the Constitution is a historical fact, but its origin has become legend. Yet myths and legends are not lies, they are a type of poetry and metaphorical.

"Constitution worship" and the "cult of the Constitution" led to the Constitution being called, for example, "the most wonderful instrument ever drawn by the hand of man" and "our Ark of Covenant." It comes down to us a having been fashioned and given to the people by a race of classic heroes, even demigods, an Olympian gathering of wise and virtuous men who stood splendidly above all faction, ignored petty self-interest, and concerned only with the freedom and well-being of their fellow citizens, their work product a supreme and transcendent effort of disinterested statesmanship, issuing forth in a miraculously perfect charter of government. Hence we traditionally capitalize the letter "F" in Framers and Founders.

Although such uncritical views are not entirely false, neither are they historically sound. The legendary hero is the founder of something, so our Founders are legendary heroes in the sense that they founded a new country. But such unalloyed reverence toward the framing of the Constitution did not last forever. Events and experience dispelled the supernatural mists that envelop the Constitutional Convention, and the role of the Constitution in popular culture has changed over time. Americans wanted another freedom; they wanted freedom from illusion.

The aura of its semi-divine origin came under attack as an old fashioned, immensely oversimplified, and rather dewy-eyed view of the Framers. Abolitionists surely did not praise the Constitution's toleration of slavery. Nor, for their part, did slave-holding states regard the Constitution as anything more than a voluntary and loose confederation of sovereign states from which they could withdraw anytime they wished or nullify national laws with which they disagreed. Other criticisms arose until, around the beginning of the twentieth century, worship of the Constitution came to an end as a whole new, revisionist approach swept the field, at least temporarily, based primarily on the work of historian Charles Beard.

In 1913, at the height of the Progressive Era, Beard published a book in the reforming spirit of his time that would ever after alter the way Americans thought about the framing of their Constitution. Beard's explosive *Economic Interpretation of the Constitution*, building on the work of J. Allen Smith, was based on the premise that "economic elements are the chief factors in the development of political institutions." He studied the financial and property holdings of the Framers and analyzed the Constitution in light of his findings. He concluded that the Constitution was an economic document and the product of class conflict and economic self-interest favoring the rights of private property and the propertied class in the new government. The Framers, asserted Beard, were hard-fisted conservatives looking out for their own vested interests, which they thought were insufficiently protected by the Articles of Confederation.

The Constitution, according to Beard, was also an undemocratic document. It was, so his argument went, framed and ratified by an undemocratic minority for an undemocratic society. No popular vote had called for a constitutional convention and property qualifications for voters meant that, contrary to the first three words of the Preamble ("We the People"), the people did not ratify the Constitution. Beard asserted that only one-fourth of males were eligible voters, and only one-sixth voted to ratify.

In Beard's iconoclastic thinking, the Constitution itself reflected the Framers' distrust of local government and popular rule. Shays' Rebellion had made conservatives afraid of social radicalism and the chaos and anarchy it foreshadowed. Supposedly fearing and despising democracy, the Framers chose a strong central government with many checks and balances as a way to limit democratic majorities.

Beard's startling thesis, in short, is that the Constitution was an economic document framed by an unrepresentative minority employing undemocratic means to protect personal property rights by establishing a national government responsive to their needs and able to thwart the populist majorities in the states. In this analysis, republicanism had yielded to oligarchy. Based on Beard's revisionist approach, the Constitutional Convention has since been occasionally described picturesquely as a counter-revolutionary junta, a Thermidorean reaction, a conspiracy by a reactionary group, that led to a *coup d'état* by eliminating the Articles of Confederation (which embodied the democratic principles of the Declaration of Independence) and replacing them with the Constitution, symbolically repudiating the democratic gains of the Revolution.

The Beard thesis, as it came to be called, held great sway for decades. An extraordinary turnabout, it upset the creation myth and legend, but, with its economic analysis, it seemed to many to have the ring of truth and to lift the veil from an event up to then shrouded in patriotic oratory. When *An Economic Interpretation* was republished in 1935, at the height of the economic hardship and dislocation of the Great Depression, Beard's message appeared even more relevant, accurate, persuasive, and in tune with the times. It was generally accepted by historians as the more or less correct explanation of what had occurred. And with some modification, that view has been widely shared or taken seriously ever since. What had started out as a new unconventional, unorthodox theory had itself become old orthodoxy and received wisdom.

But, as often happens, the intellectual tide turned. The Beard thesis itself became the "old interpretation" and was the object of critical scrutiny. Although the light of the constitutional myth may have been dimmed by Beard, the torch of its attraction still glowed. On one level, the Beard thesis met opposition because cherished myths die hard. Critics thought Beard oversimplified what happened by stressing economic facts to the exclusion of everything else and by ignoring the Framers' patriotic sincerity.

This was the position, for example, of Justice Oliver Wendell Holmes, who said he read Beard's "ignoble" book "without much profit" and thought it was a "stinker" and "humbug" because it encouraged "the notion that personal interests on the part of the prominent members of the Convention accounted for the attitude they took." Holmes could not "easily believe" Beard's argument that "the Constitution primarily represents the triumph of the money power over democratic agrarianism and individualism." Rejecting the "economic origin of the Constitution," Holmes said, "It doesn't need evidence that the men who drew the Constitution belonged to the well-to-do classes and had the views of their class." But Holmes felt deeply that "some men have emotions not dependent on their pocketbooks" and that the "real dominant motive" behind the drafting of the Constitution was patriotism. "Belittling arguments always have a force of their own," Holmes wrote to his English friend Frederick Pollock about Beard's book, "but you and I believe that high-mindedness is not impossible to man."

Other critics assailed Beard on his own terms. In his 1958 book *We The People*, Forrest McDonald attacked Beard's economic approach and concluded that Beard was wrong on his facts. To McDonald, Beard was rigidly simplistic. McDonald found no significant class differences among those for and against the Constitution. The fundamental conflict during the Convention was not "class," but between slave and free states, between North and South. "It is impossible," wrote McDonald, "to justify Beard's interpretation"; Beard's thesis "is entirely incompatible with the facts."

As for Beard's political approach, Robert Brown in 1963 concluded that the Constitution was essentially a democratic document framed by democratic methods for a democratic society. The state constitutions had property qualifications for voters, and the Articles of Confederation gave each state one vote (like the Senate). The Constitution needed ratification and, says Brown, "most men were voters." Ratification was not a close thing. The debates, which show a "great deal of democracy," do not support Beard. Of course economic factors are important in all constitution-making, but most Americans at the time were middle class, neither wealthy nor poor. (Compare to today with growing disparity in wealth and income.) The Constitution and the government it created were designed to do many things, not just protect property rights. As a result, "we cannot assume, as we have in the past, that the Constitution was adopted undemocratically in an undemocratic society and that it was put over on the people as a sort of *coup d'état* or conspiracy by holders of personal property."

So where does this debate leave us? Some believe that Beard's ideas have been partially if not wholly discredited. Others, while not accepting Beard's thesis in its entirety, think his idea that the Constitution reflected economic interests of the large property holders who wrote it has survived much research and, in the words of Jackson T. Main, "any book that challenges it ought to be examined with a cautious and skeptical eye." After all, Alexander Hamilton himself had stressed self-interest as the mainspring of human action, that the "vast majority of mankind is entirely biased by motives of self-interest." Professor Main thought McDonald's facts were incomplete and his conclusions wrong and "absurd." Still others reassert, as Holmes did, love of country and the national interest as the motivation behind forming a powerful nation to replace squabbling states.

Certainly we can say that blind veneration of the Constitution prevented Americans from achieving a realistic understanding of their government, their Constitution and how it came to be. Perhaps the time has come to raise the Framers from immortality to mortality. Perhaps the Framers hammered out a pragmatic compromise that would both bolster the national interest and be acceptable to the people, a patchwork sewn together under pressure of time and events by a group of extremely talented democratic politicians.

The debate over the Beard thesis has a larger dimension. All revolutions have their Thermidors. The term comes from the fall of Reobespierre and the end of the Reign of Terror on the ninth of Thermidor of Year II of the French Revolution (July 27, 1794). According to Crane Brinton in *The Anatomy of Revolution*, a Thermidorean reaction is "a convalescence from the fever of revolution." Professor Brinton explains, "In some sense the phenomenon of reaction seems almost inevitably a part of the process of revolution." Revolutions, adds Brinton, "end in a return, not to the *status quo ante*, but to an equilibrium, a state of 'normalcy' recognizably related to that of the old regime."

These comments apply to the American Revolution, which was one of the four revolutions (English, French, Russian and U.S.) analyzed by Brinton. In the United States, "the decade of the 1780s displays in incomplete forms some of the marks of Thermidor." The process leading up to the ratification of the Constitution reflected a move away from the radicalism of the Revolution and a return to quieter, less tumultuous times. The outcome of the Constitutional Convention meant that equilibrium had been restored and generally accepted and that the Revolution was truly over. But in all revolutions, including ours, a series of lesser revolutions follow in which the forces present in the initial one are worked out, for example, Shays' Rebellion, the Whisky Rebellion, the ascent of Thomas Jefferson and Andrew Jackson, and the long trial of the Civil War.

Viewing the Beard thesis from this perspective also gives us a vantage point on current world events. As we look around the globe and see various governments overthrown, we should not be surprised by the different course of such revolutions. It is not easy to go from a society held together vertically—from the top down—with an iron fist to a democratic society governed horizontally by communities themselves writing their own social contracts for how to live together as equal citizens. It is hard to go, in journalist Thomas Friedman's words, "from Saddam to Jefferson—from vertical to horizontal rule—without falling into Hobbes or Khomeini." Usually a tyrant emerges, an unconstitutional ruler brought to power by revolution (*e.g.*, Crommell, Napoleon, Stalin) together with repression. But America did it in 1787 without a tyrant and without repression and with, at worst, the mild and incomplete Thermidor represented by the Beard thesis.

In the end, the argument probably defies resolution. The legend is extraordinarily durable. Yet to eliminate entirely the role of economic motive in the political affairs of the time is as doctrinaire and as unnecessary as Beard's overstatement of it. Beard's ideas persist. The full story of the Constitution and its ratification probably remains to be written. The entire subject of the Constitution and its creation has become a little murky. Each generation forms its own conceptions of the past in accord with its own values and needs. All beginnings are unfathomable.

PART TWO

CIVIL LIBERTIES

A big reason why we cherish the Constitution is because it protects our freedom. Civil liberties are the crown jewels of our Constitution. But, oddly enough, they were not in the original version that emerged from the 1787 Convention. One of the main grounds of the Anti-Federalists in opposing ratification of the Constitution was exactly that—the absence of a bill of rights. A constitution was not the only thing people wanted in writing. Many people also wanted a written bill of rights.

The authors of *The Federalist Papers*, particularly Hamilton in No. 84, responded that no bill of rights was necessary because the Constitution did not give the central government the power to do anything to interfere with such rights. "For why declare that things shall not be done which there is no power to do?" Hamilton went further and said that a bill of rights would not only be unnecessary but "would even be dangerous." In a subtle line of reasoning, Hamilton explained that, "They would contain exceptions to powers which are not granted" and thus "afford a colorable pretext to claim more than were granted." Hamilton's argument lost.

The opposition to the lack of a bill of rights was so great that the supporters of the Constitution, in order to secure ratification, had to agree to accept amendments protecting civil liberties. And so the first ten amendments to Constitution were quickly drafted and passed and made part of the Constitution in 1791, within two years of the ratification of the Constitution. Those ten amendments, our Bill of Rights, together with certain later amendments, are where we find the textual home of our precious civil liberties.

Freedom of speech, freedom of religion, privacy and the like are the subject of this next group of essays.

16

"AREOPAGITICA" REMEMBERED

A few years ago, in 2009, we observed the four-hundredth anniversary of the birth of poet John Milton, and we Americans who value freedom of the mind should remember it. For it was Milton who, in addition to his undying poetry, wrote one of the greatest and most eloquent defenses of free speech. That defense took the form of a pamphlet written in 1644 in opposition to a law passed by Parliament restricting what the press could print.

Milton called his pamphlet "Areopagitica." He took the title from the hill in ancient Athens, Areopagus, where the democratically elected supreme court of that fabled city-state met. Milton thought the title appropriate because in the pamphlet he was comparing Parliament, to whom he was appealing, to the ancient Greek court.

Milton's famous pamphlet is like many classics and coffee table books. It is often talked about but rarely read. That is a shame. Just as we ought to reread the Gettysburg Address on Lincoln's birthday and the Declaration of Independence on July Fourth, we should once a year look at the actual text of "Areopagitica." We will surely be inspired.

Milton's words themselves, written almost one hundred fifty years before our First Amendment, are powerful and still ring loudly in our mind's ear. Those of us who like to read will be moved, even overjoyed. "For books are not absolutely dead things," wrote Milton, "but do contain a potency of life in them to be as active as that soul whose progeny they are; nay, they do preserve as in a vial the purest efficacy and extraction of that living intellect that bred them."

As for censorship, Milton called it a "kind of homicide." This is so, he explained, because, "who kills a man kills a reasonable creature, God's image; but he who destroys a good book, kills reason itself."

How can government decide what we should or should not read? "Read any books whatever come to thy hands," wrote Milton, "for thou art sufficient both to judge aright and to examine each matter."

But then Milton surpassed himself with language and thoughts that thrilled me when I first read them five decades ago in college. He may have been writing about freedom of thought but he was really advocating a vigorous, fearless philosophy of life. "I cannot praise a fugitive and cloistered virtue, unexercised and unbreathed, that never sallies out and seeks her adversary, but slinks out of the race, where that immortal garland is to be run for, not without dust and heat."

Milton was not done. "That which purifies is trial," he added, "and trial is by what is contrary." A motto for lawyers, if there ever was one.

He is bold and unafraid. "What some lament of, we rather should rejoice at." Disagreement is acceptable, even welcome. "Where there is much desire to learn, there of necessity will be much arguing, much writing, many opinions; for opinion in good men is but knowledge in the making."

With the majestic language one might expect from the author of "Paradise Lost," Milton endowed truth with invincibility. "And though all the winds of doctrine were let loose to play upon the earth, so Truth be in the field, we do injuriously, by licensing and prohibiting, to misdoubt her strength. Let her and falsehood grapple; who ever knew Truth put to the worse, in a free and open encounter?" Now, three hundred seventy years later, and in an age of spin, some of us might recall a few instances where truth lost, at least temporarily, a battle with falsehood. But Milton's thought and expression make us feel good.

Milton anticipated the core of First Amendment theory. "Give me the liberty," Milton proclaimed, in cadences foreshadowing Patrick Henry, "to know, to utter, and to argue freely according to conscience, above all liberties." This is the soaring essence of the preferred freedoms doctrine, which holds that freedom of speech is, as that other master of the English language Benjamin Cardozo once wrote, "the matrix, the indispensable condition, of nearly every other form of freedom."

So let us Americans take a moment to think about John Milton, the blind poet whose stirring words in "Areopagitica" about freedom of speech echo so resonantly more than four centuries after his birth. To help get in the right mood, go see and contemplate the mesmerizing dark painting in the main building of the New York Public Library of Milton, blind, dictating "Paradise Lost" to his daughters. The painting conveys the strength of Milton's mind and the courage of his soul. Milton's powerful and forceful imagery, and his piercing and vivid expression, appeal to the best within us and set the stage for considering our civil liberties.

17

ELOQUENCE, REASON AND NECESSITY: *GITLOW v. NEW YORK* IN A NEW AGE OF TERRORISM

Famous law cases often have strange, checkered careers. They may represent what Oliver Wendell Holmes called "the felt necessities of the time," but those necessities change as times change. Consider, for instance, the fates of the *Dred Scott* decision (slaves are property, not citizens), of *Plessy v. Ferguson* (separate but equal facilities are constitutionally permissible), and of *Bowers v. Hardwick* (criminal statutes against consensual adult homosexual activity are constitutional). All three of those landmark cases were reversed eventually, as public and legal attitudes toward slavery, segregation and same sex relations changed.

Law students with busy schedules and heavy reading assignments rarely have the time to go behind such famous judicial opinions in their casebooks. But it would be good to do so, to dive into the warm stream of life, to understand the plate tectonics of legal change. Such a plunge is how we learn about the drama of the characters strutting briefly on the law's stage: the personalities of the main actors, their passions, despair and triumphs, the issues that moved them, the historical setting of the disputes, and the links to our own local courts, local history, and current events.

Revisiting a law school staple decades later, with the benefit of many years of law practice and life experience, gives us an opportunity to do what we could not do in law school. Taking, in our maturity, a second, harder look at an old casebook assignment may reveal aspects of it we either missed or did not appreciate the first time around. We may, the second time around, gain new insight and discover psychological reasons that give us more understanding. This is especially true when the political climate that gave rise to the old case seems to be resurfacing. A good example is the, by turns, celebrated, notorious, controversial but ever so instructive case of *Gitlow v. New York*.

Gitlow at First Glance

We first meet *Gitlow* in our law school course on constitutional law, and it is an unforgettable encounter. Decided by the U.S. Supreme Court in 1925, *Gitlow* is one of the Red Scare free speech cases that arose shortly after World War I and the Russian Revolution. In 1920, amid widespread public hysteria, a state court jury in Manhattan convicted twenty-nine-year-old Benjamin Gitlow of advocating criminal anarchy because he helped publish a pamphlet in favor of "revolutionary Socialism" and the ultimate overthrow of the existing government by class struggle and "mass political strikes and revolutionary mass action." Although the pamphlet had no practical effect or consequence, Gitlow's conviction was affirmed by every court he appealed to, including the U.S. Supreme Court. Free speech paid a steep price.

Since then, however, *Gitlow* has been largely discredited. The Supreme Court appears to have eroded it to the vanishing point. By 1969, the Court seemed to repudiate *Gitlow* in all but name. That 1969 ruling looked, at least on the surface, as if it relegated *Gitlow* to the dustbin of history—but one still wonders. *Gitlow* might well be regarded as a historical curiosity, a legal relic from a bygone time, were it not for current events.

Why *Gitlow* Matters

Gitlow matters to us today. It is one of those rare cases that, due to their timing and the issues involved, provide both a window on history—history past and history in the making—as well as a glimpse into the future. And the more we think about *Gitlow*, the more we find out about it, the more relevant it becomes, the more psychological truth it demonstrates, the more modern parallels we see, and the more lessons it has to teach us, in our anxious post-9/11 terrorist-obsessed world. *Gitlow* deserves another look, today, if only as a warning and a cautionary tale.

One significant positive legacy of *Gitlow* is its role in applying the Bill of Rights to the states. Before *Gitlow*, the conventional legal wisdom held that the Bill of Rights bound the federal government only, but not the states. *Gitlow* was the first case to say otherwise. It did so briefly, without fanfare, and almost in passing. "For present purposes," the Supreme Court wrote, "we may and do assume that freedom of speech and of the press . . . are among the fundamental personal rights and 'liberties' protected by the due process clause of the Fourteenth Amendment from impairment by the States." Almost unnoticed at the time, that nonchalant dictum—"we . . . assume"—began the gradual, decades-long, all-important, far-reaching process of "selective incorporation" that made the Bill of Rights apply to the states.

Gitlow is also important because it is a provocative milestone along the road to our modern, more liberal approach to free speech. It achieved this special status through the law of unintended consequences. The majority opinion in *Gitlow*, written by Justice Edward Sanford, relied on what has become known as the "bad tendency" test, which made speakers and writers liable for the reasonable, probable outcome of what they say, regardless of how likely it is that their words would actually cause an overt criminal act. The Court distinguished between "abstract 'doctrine' or academic discussion having no quality of incitement to any concrete action," on one hand, and "utterances inimical to the public welfare, tending to corrupt public morals, incite to crime, or disturb the public peace," on the other. Even more subject to punishment, ruled the Court, are "utterances endangering the foundations of organized government and threatening its overthrow by unlawful means." Whether the utterances were likely to actually persuade anyone to do anything illegal was beside the point.

The "Bad Tendency" Test

The basic idea behind the "bad tendency" test was to reduce or eliminate the possibility of future criminal acts by prohibiting speech that might lead people to commit such acts. It was an effort, in the Supreme Court's words, to "suppress the threatened danger in its incipiency." Colorful metaphors caught the concept. The Supreme Court compared it to "extinguish[ing] a spark without waiting until it has enkindled the flame or blazed into a conflagration." One of the judges on the New York Court of Appeals said it was an attempt to "nip in the bud" the danger of anarchy. An appellate brief filed by the Manhattan District Attorney claimed, "the time to kill a snake is when it is young." But whatever the metaphor, the "bad tendency" test was an effort to criminalize speech that was not itself a criminal act.

The "bad tendency" test, a low point in free speech jurisprudence, is what made *Gitlow* infamous and even ludicrous. The bad tendency test made *Gitlow* a bad precedent. As a law student, one read the case in horror and disbelief and wished the Supreme Court would have, to paraphrase its own formula, arrested the *Gitlow* doctrine in its incipiency. But a bad precedent can be a good catalyst for change; the worse the precedent, the more likely the reaction and change. Although a few Supreme Court cases have followed it, the overwhelming modern trend of First Amendment law in the High Court has come to reject it.

Unintended Consequences

In reality, by its excesses and overreach, *Gitlow* became an agent of change, precipitating a long term reaction, really a transformation in First Amendment law, favoring the more tolerant positions taken in dissents by Justices Oliver Wendell Holmes and Louis Brandeis. But the path has not always been straight. During the McCarthy era of the Cold War, when Americans feared an international Communist conspiracy, the "bad tendency" test again occasionally found its way into judicial opinions dealing with subversive advocacy. But the predominant shift away from *Gitlow*'s rationale was and is real. By 1969, the Supreme Court seemed to bury *Gitlow* once and for all.

Holmes's Eloquent Dissent

Important as the Supreme Court's *Gitlow* opinion is in the development of constitutional law, some of us really remember *Gitlow* not so much for what the majority did but for what one great dissenting justice said. We remember *Gitlow* because of the brief, impassioned, Olympian, and wonderful dissent of an elderly Civil War veteran named Holmes. That stirring opinion by eighty-four-year-old Oliver Wendell Holmes, joined in by Louis Brandeis, still rings in our mind's ear more than forty-five years after reading it for the first time. Holmes disagreed with the majority's description of Gitlow's left wing polemics as a "direct incitement" that "may kindle a fire" and lead to a "conflagration."

"Every idea is an incitement," insisted Holmes. He went on: "It offers itself for belief and if believed it is acted on unless some other belief outweighs it or some failure of energy stifles the movement at its birth. The only difference between the expression of an opinion and an incitement in the narrower sense is the speaker's enthusiasm for the result. Eloquence may set fire to reason." Eloquence, which Holmes himself often displayed, may also set fire to a law student's (and a lawyer's) enthusiasm and ignite the flame of intellectual passion.

"It is manifest," Holmes added, with a nod to his fledgling "clear and present danger" test, "that there was no present danger of an attempt to overthrow the government by force on the part of the admittedly small minority who shared" Gitlow's views. According to Holmes, "whatever may be thought of the redundant discourse before us, it had no chance of starting a present conflagration. If in the long run the beliefs expressed in proletarian dictatorship are destined to be accepted by the dominant forces of the community, the only meaning of free speech is that they should be given their chance and have their way." As far as Holmes was concerned, Gitlow's pamphlet was not advising an "uprising against government at once" but at "some indefinite time in the future."

These fearless, tolerant, inspiring, almost poetic passages from the still sharp and remarkably fluent pen of the aging but intellectually and emotionally secure Union war hero is, for some of us, what really makes *Gitlow* a memorable landmark in the law and in our outlook on life. Like the stalwart and reliable soldier he was in the Civil War, Holmes stayed at his judicial post on guard duty protecting the Constitution and our freedoms. His bravura performance in *Gitlow* is part of what made us want to study, and then spend our life practicing, law.

The Underlying Drama

Memorable and motivating as Holmes's *Gitlow* dissent is, however, neither it nor the majority opinion reveals the true drama, the intense conflict of forces, in the case. Buried and often hidden in judicial opinions in most important cases lurks a clash of policies, principles, and personalities, against a background of historical and political movements and economic interests. The individual parties, the lawyers, and even the judges, are real and complicated people, with strengths and weaknesses, and driven by powerful forces or self-destructive foibles. And their disputes are located in a particular time and place. Context counts. As in *Gitlow*, the full case name and date sometimes give the geographical and temporal location: New York 1925.

But that bare reference in the caption of the Supreme Court case hardly explains the depth and importance of New York's connection to *Gitlow*. Nor does it explain why and how *Gitlow* affects our thinking and attitudes today. These are connections worth exploring, intrinsically interesting, and full of intense relevance for our own beleaguered time, beset as it is by new threats of terrorism and the problem of how to respond.

Much more than a case name forever yokes together *Gitlow* and New York. Simply put, they are inseparable. It is impossible to truly understand and explain *Gitlow*, to grasp how and why it came about, to fathom why it is still germane, without knowing at least a little about the political atmosphere of New York in the early part of the twentieth century.

Those were unsettled times, in New York and elsewhere. By the late 1800s, unbridled capitalism and industrialization had generated great inequalities in income and wealth and harsh working conditions, which led to frequent labor unrest punctuated by violence. Socialism and anarchism spread in Europe, producing more violence and even assassination attempts on heads of state. In 1886, after a demonstration for the eight-hour workday, a bomb thought to be set by anarchists exploded in Haymarket Square in Chicago, killing seven policemen and causing a riot. One of the most horrifying successful assassinations took place in New York State, in Buffalo, in 1901, when an anarchist shot and killed President William McKinley.

Quickly reacting to the McKinley assassination, the New York Legislature in 1902 passed a law that made it a felony to advocate the "doctrine that organized government must be overthrown by force or violence . . . or by unlawful means." That criminal anarchy statute came about because New York authorities felt frustrated by their inability to prosecute the real perpetrators of the crime, anarchist orator Emma Goldman (whose lectures the assassin had attended) and her like, for the McKinley murder. The purpose of the criminal anarchy statute was to outlaw dangerous doctrines before any consequences occurred or were likely to occur. It was passed to supply a basis for future prosecutions of people like Emma Goldman and Ben Gitlow.

After the 1902 law was enacted, the troubling economic and social situation in America only got worse. Labor strikes and associated violence multiplied. A political assassination ignited World War I, which the U.S. entered in 1917, and our government stifled and punished dissent over the war effort and the draft. Then, later in 1917, came the violent Russian Revolution, which encouraged and energized leftists in America, in particular New York. As the main entry point for European immigrants, New York was home to a disproportionate number of Socialist intellectuals, activists, and even anarchists. The combination of violent Bolshevik success in overthrowing the Czarist government and heightened political consciousness amid economic hardship here proved combustible. In those days "class warfare" was more than an election campaign sound byte.

The next few years saw more agitation, protests, polemics and even occasional bombings. The turning point was 1919. In June of that year, a bomb apparently planted by an anarchist exploded on the doorstep of the U.S. Attorney General Mitchell Palmer. Other explosions occurred that month around the country at the homes of judges and other prominent men. The post office stopped a wave of mail bombs aimed at members of President Wilson's cabinet, U.S. senators, and others (including justices of the Supreme Court). Race riots upset Washington, D.C. and Chicago. Members of the International Workers of the World fired on a parade in Washington state. A general strike in Seattle, national coal and steel strikes, and a police strike in Boston led a long list of ugly labor disputes. In 1920, a bomb exploded outside the J.P. Morgan Bank building on Wall Street killing twenty-nine people and leaving pockmarked damage to the outside of the building still visible today.

This growing wave of unrest, coming as it did on the heels of the Russian Revolution, frightened people and became known as the Red Scare. In late 1919 federal and state authorities raided homes and meeting places in fifteen cities in search of communists and anarchists. Attorney General Palmer, who had his eye on the 1920 Democratic presidential nomination (he did not get it), grabbed headlines as he cracked down on American radicals. With his name forever linked to these "Palmer Raids," he chillingly described the "blaze of revolution . . . sweeping over every American institution of law and order . . . burning up the foundations of society." To Palmer, "there could be no nice distinctions drawn between the theoretical ideals of the radicals and their actual violation of our national laws." Reflecting this turmoil, in 1920 thirty-one states passed laws against sedition, anarchy, and criminal syndicalism. The government seized and deported immigrants, and put American citizens on trial for treason.

New York breathed this same highly charged air. In 1919 the New York Legislature formed a Committee to Investigate Subversive and Seditious Activities, which became known as the Lusk Committee (after its chair, Senator Clayton Lusk). The Committee's work was spearheaded by its special counsel, Archibald Stevenson, a self-styled expert on Bolshevism. Stevenson saw the up-to-then unused 1902 criminal anarchy law as a means to prosecute socialists, communists, and anarchists. The Lusk Committee obtained search warrants and, months before Palmer, raided several left wing offices and organizations in New York. This was the frenzied, tense climate in New York when Ben Gitlow took center stage.

Gitlow's Arrest

Gitlow was arrested in November 1919 at a celebration in New York of the second anniversary of the Russian Revolution. He was twenty-eight years old and a member of the National Council of the Left Wing Section of the Socialist Party, which soon became the Communist Labor Party. He was arrested, along with hundreds of others in raids on seventy-three "Red-Centers" in New York, for violating the state's 1902 criminal anarchy law for publishing in July 1919 a polemical tract called the "Left Wing Manifesto" that, according to the authorities, advocated violent overthrow of the government. It was the first time the criminal anarchy statute had been invoked. Stevenson convinced the Manhattan District Attorney to prosecute Gitlow on the theory that the dangerous tendency of the words alone, and nothing more, were enough under the criminal anarchy law.

Gitlow's "Left Wing Manifesto," about six thousand copies of which were distributed, was a fairly typical example of Communist rhetoric. Gitlow neither wrote nor edited it. He was the business manager of a magazine called *Revolutionary Age*, which had published the Manifesto in July 1919. In typical overheated, Communist polemical style, the Manifesto reviewed the rise of socialism, condemned "moderate Socialism" for relying on democratic means, and advocated a "Communist Revolution" by a militant socialism based on antagonism between classes. It referred favorably to mobilizing the "power of the proletariat in action" through mass industrial revolts, political strikes and "revolutionary mass action" for the purpose of destroying the parliamentary state and replacing it with Communist Socialism and a dictatorship of the proletariat.

Despite its aggressive, disputatious bombast, the Manifesto had no practical consequences. As was admitted by the prosecution at every stage, and by every court, the Manifesto produced no real world response from its targeted audience or from anyone else. It led to no action of any kind by the working class. In actuality, there was, as the Supreme Court itself conceded, "no evidence of any effect resulting from the publication and circulation of the Manifesto." The only consequence and response was the prosecution of Gitlow and his colleagues.

By the time he was arrested, Gitlow had already been involved for years with leftist politics in New York. Raised in Manhattan's Lower East Side, Gitlow was the son of Russian Jewish immigrants, both of whom were ardent socialists. Young Gitlow, like many others of his time, place and background, was beguiled by the siren song of socialism. With its promise of transforming the world, better living and working conditions, economic and social equality, and redistributed wealth, socialism had a great appeal amid the excesses and hardships caused by capitalism. After graduating from

Manhattan's Stuyvesant High School, Gitlow joined the Socialist Party in 1909 when he was eighteen years old. In 1917, Gitlow was one of seven Socialists elected to the New York State Assembly. (He did not win re-election.)

Gitlow thought that social and political change through democratic means would be too slow and uncertain. Inspired by what happened in Russia, he favored more vigorous and direct action, and was part of the "Left Wing Faction" of the Socialist Party. In June 1919 he took part in a meeting in Chicago to discuss forming a Leninist-style party, and became a founder of the American Communist Party. The "Left Wing Manifesto" was the public explanation for the militants' break with the more staid old Socialist Party.

With the public jittery to begin with, the Manifesto's language only aggravated antagonism toward Gitlow, as he learned almost immediately. A week after his arrest, Gitlow appeared (along with another defendant, Jim Larkin) in Magistrates' Court to see if grand jury action was warranted. William McAdoo, the chief magistrate and a former New York City police commissioner, not only ruled that the grand jury should act, but wrote a vitriolic opinion excoriating Gitlow and Larkin as "guilty as charged," and as "mad and cruel men," "positively dangerous men." McAdoo set the tone for the rest of the case by quoting from the Manifesto and interpreting it as implicitly calling for force and violence as part of a "militant uprising of the red revolutionists."

"Are we to lose ourselves," asked McAdoo, "in legal subtleties and nice disquisitions and historical references, and bury our heads in clouds of rhetoric about liberty of speech?" That question has often been asked in times of stress. According to McAdoo, the criminal anarchy law was a "preventative measure . . . intended to put out a fire with a bucket of water which might not later on yield to the contents of a reservoir."

The Trial

At his trial in January and February 1920, Gitlow had a pretty good lawyer. His defense counsel was none other than Clarence Darrow, probably the most famous trial lawyer in American history.

Ever since the Pullman Railroad Strike in 1894, Darrow had made a national reputation for himself by devoting his practice to unpopular clients and causes, always on the side of working men and women against large corporate employers or the state. Darrow's legal work for the labor movement often supplied him with clients accused of anarchism and violence. His own political sympathies as well as his independence of mind made him a perfect choice for Gitlow's case. But the Gitlow trial was not one of Darrow's better efforts.

Even the skillful Darrow could not get Gitlow off. Darrow could not overcome the fear and hostility generated by Gitlow and what he stood for. Three weeks earlier, the New York State Assembly, reflecting the public's mood, had expelled all the Socialists elected to it.

If thorough preparation is the key to success at trial—and it usually is—Darrow did not follow that advice in the *Gitlow* case. Parachuting in at the last minute, he met Gitlow for the first time only the night before the trial began. Previously, Gitlow had been represented by other lawyers. At that eve-of-trial meeting, Gitlow told Darrow that if Darrow called him as a witness he would "affirm and defend every communist principle in the Left Wing Manifesto." Hearing Gitlow's adamant position, Darrow persuaded his client not to testify (and thereby avoid cross-examination), but agreed to ask the judge if Gitlow could make a speech to the jury. "Well," said Darrow, "I suppose a revolutionist must have his say in court even if it kills him."

As a result, Gitlow in effect presented no defense. Darrow made no opening statement, called no witnesses on Gitlow's behalf, and did not let Gitlow take the stand. Darrow stipulated that Gitlow was responsible for publishing and circulating the Manifesto. This unusual, minimalist trial strategy resembled the successful approach used in another famous, perhaps the most famous, New York free speech trial. In 1735, when John Peter Zenger went on trial for seditious libel, his lawyer Andrew Hamilton had done the same thing. Hamilton admitted publication, called no witnesses for the defense, but argued that Zenger committed no crime. The gambit famously worked for Zenger, but not for Gitlow.

Despite Darrow's stipulated concessions, Gitlow's prosecutor, Alexander Rorke, called witnesses anyway. One of them testified to Gitlow's actions and was promptly arrested for her beliefs as soon as she stepped off the stand. Rorke also read the entire Manifesto to the jury. Darrow told the trial judge that the Manifesto would probably put the jury to sleep, while the prosecutor said it would make their hair stand on end. Rorke thundered that *Gitlow* "would make America a red ruby in the red treasure chest of the Red Terror."

The judge, Bartow Weeks, was obviously partial to the prosecution. He had recently tried other anarchist cases, during which he took over questioning of defendants and debated them over communism and Marxist theory. In an unusual ruling, however, Weeks allowed Gitlow to address the jury, presumably because he thought, correctly, that Gitlow would only make matters worse for himself. The prosecutor did not object.

Gitlow mounted his courtroom soapbox and delivered a spirited, unrepentant, unremorseful, rambling defense of his views, frequently interrupted by Judge Weeks. "I am a revolutionist," Gitlow declared. "No jails will change my opinion." "[T]o bring about socialism, capitalist governments must be overthrown . . . . I ask no clemency."

He got none. The jury convicted him in less than three hours and Judge Weeks sentenced him to the maximum five-to-ten years at hard labor. This was the result in spite of one of Darrow's trademark stirring summations.

In his closing argument, Darrow described Gitlow as a harmless "dreamer" whose ideas posed no threat, were protected by the First Amendment, and stood in the American tradition. Darrow asked the jury to separate the "sense" from the "nonsense" in the Manifesto. The famous lawyer argued that the Manifesto was too abstract to cause criminal acts. There was "not a word" in the Manifesto, proclaimed Darrow, "inciting anyone to violence, not a word inciting anyone to unlawful activity." But, Darrow went on, revolution is a treasured part of American history, part of our heritage, and advocating it should not be punished.

Darrow must have known that his pitch would not work. He did not even wait around for the verdict. By leaving early, Darrow missed hearing Judge Weeks compliment the jury on the "intelligence" of their verdict and say, "There must be a right in organized society to protect itself." So Darrow was done with the case and Gitlow went off to Sing Sing, where he would stay pending appeal unless granted bail.

No Bail Pending Appeal

To obtain bail pending appeal, Gitlow had to file with the court a petition for a certificate of reasonable doubt. Other lawyers (Swinburne Hale and Charles Recht) who had previously been involved in the case filed the petition a month and a half later. Then a respected recent former Republican governor of New York, Charles Whitman, entered the picture on Gitlow's behalf. Somehow Gitlow retained Whitman to write the brief in support of the petition, and Whitman did a creditable job.

Whitman's main argument was a lawyer's argument. He explained that Gitlow had been prosecuted under a law aimed at anarchists, not communists, and that the Manifesto advocated replacing one existing government with another—the dictatorship of the proletariat. Therefore, argued Whitman, there was reasonable doubt about the conviction.

Gitlow's choice of ex-governor Whitman was a good one. It illustrates the value of the personal qualities of the advocate. It was a smart decision for a communist like Gitlow to get a well-respected and conservative lawyer to represent him. Nonetheless, Judge John McAvoy denied Gitlow's bail request, although Whitman's legal argument would surface again on appeal.

The Appeals

Gitlow had no luck on appeal. Whitman, like Darrow, dropped out of the case. Gitlow reverted back to his prior lawyers Hale and Recht. Recht, who had been involved in the case from the start, wrote the first appeal brief and Hale made the oral argument—to no avail.

In 1921 a five-judge panel of the Appellate Division affirmed unanimously. After quoting extensively from the "Left Wing Manifesto," Judge Frank Laughlin, writing for the court, said the Manifesto was "not a discussion of ideas and theories" but advocacy of doctrine, and "the doctrines advocated are not harmless. They are a menace." To Laughlin and many others, Gitlow threatened their security and challenged their values. Laughlin's entire opinion illustrates the nervousness and clouded judgment surrounding the *Gitlow* case.

The McKinley assassination had scarred Judge Laughlin. He had lived for decades in Buffalo, where McKinley was killed, sitting as a judge there until 1901, the year of the assassination. In that year, Laughlin was designated to the Appellate Division in Manhattan by then Governor (and vice-president-elect) Theodore Roosevelt, who became president on McKinley's death.

With this personal history, Laughlin described Gitlow's "plan and purpose" in acid terms. According to Laughlin, Gitlow "contemplate[d] the overthrow and destruction of the governments of the United States and of all the States . . . by immediately organizing the industrial proletariat into militant Socialist Unions . . . compelling the government to cease to function" and then setting up a proletarian dictatorship. And, yet, even Laughlin had to admit that Gitlow did "not expressly advocate the use of weapons or physical force in accomplishing these results." But, wrote Laughlin, "their aims and ends cannot be accomplished without assassination, violence and bloodshed."

One particular passage in Laughlin's appellate opinion stands out and sounds like something from an anti-immigration stump speech in today's political campaigns. Americans, Laughlin wrote, should "be on their guard" against a movement that "may undermine and endanger our cherished institutions of liberty and equality." The danger could be averted, said Laughlin, if "immigration is properly supervised and restricted," so that the "propaganda of class prejudice and hatred— by a very small minority, mostly of foreign birth," will not "take root in America." These "pernicious doctrines," Laughlin went on, should be rejected by "God-fearing, liberty-loving Americans." It is, unfortunately, easy to imagine something similar being said today on the campaign trail, though, one hopes, not in a judicial opinion.

A year later, Gitlow, this time with the help of the American Civil Liberties Union, fared no better in the highest state court, the New York Court of Appeals. Five of the seven judges there voted to affirm, with only Judges Cuthbert Pound and Benjamin Cardozo dissenting. Like the Appellate Division, Judge Frederick Crane's opinion focused on and quoted at length from the Manifesto, concluding that it "advocated the destruction of the state and the establishment of the dictatorship of the proletariat" by means of mass strikes. It found the criminal anarchy law constitutional because freedom of speech does "not protect the violation of liberty or permit attempts to destroy that freedom." Crane, it was later said at his memorial service, "never lingered in legal technicalities," but supposedly used "common sense, always with respect for the moral and social implications, to control the determination and application of the law."

In a separate opinion, Chief Judge Frank Hiscock, known for his doctrinaire legal philosophy, found the jury justified in rejecting the view that the Manifesto "was a mere academic and harmless discussion of the advantages of communism and advanced socialism and a mere Utopian portrayal of the blessings which would flow from the establishment of those conditions." Hiscock regarded it as a "justification and advocacy of action," even though he too agreed "there is no advocacy in specific terms of the use of assassination or force or violence."

Hiscock also blithely swept aside any constitutional objection. "We shall spend no time in discussing the proposition urged upon us that this statute is unconstitutional" as a violation of the First Amendment. Hiscock's judicial opinions, according to the mini-biography of him in the 2007 volume *Judges of the New York Court of Appeals*, were said to "reflect the attitudes of the time."

Perhaps the most curious opinion of all was the dissent. Written by Judge Pound, with whom Cardozo silently joined, the dissent makes for strange reading. Whatever we may think of the two majority opinions, we understand their motivations, which are transparent. The dissent is another story, one more puzzling.

Pound and Cardozo voted to reverse not on First Amendment grounds, but on the surprising, narrower ground, previously articulated by Governor Whitman, that Gitlow did not violate the criminal anarchy law because he was not advocating anarchy. According to the dissent, advocacy of revolution—change of government by unlawful means to substitute another form of government (*e.g.*, dictatorship of the proletariat)—is not advocacy of anarchy, which is the total absence of government. Citing Tolstoy, Kropotkin and Marx for support, the dissent developed this line of argument, ending on a high note: "Although the defendant may be the worst of men; although Left Wing socialism is a menace to organized government; the rights of the best of men are secure only as the rights of the vilest and most abhorrent are protected."

One has to wonder if this odd dissent was a lawyerly way to protect free speech indirectly. Reading the dissent, one gets the distinct impression that Pound and Cardozo, drawing on Whitman's legal theory, made a technical argument to avoid a larger, more fraught First Amendment issue. After all, Pound had a reputation as a strong supporter of the right of the people to criticize their government. Pound found "nothing in our [criminal anarchy] statute which makes it a crime to teach such revolutionary doctrines and advocate such a change in our form of government, except as such teaching amounts to a breach of the peace." Today's reader might well wish that the noble and philosophically-minded Cardozo himself had weighed in and given his views on the *Gitlow* case. Later, as a Supreme Court justice, Cardozo would hail freedom of speech as the wellspring of most other freedoms. In hindsight, *Gitlow* seems like a missed opportunity for Cardozo.

Following the adverse ruling by the Court of Appeals, Gitlow would have received a pardon from Governor Al Smith if Gitlow had dropped any further appeal. As a matter of principle and at the cost of his immediate freedom, Gitlow pressed on. Now represented by lawyers from the ACLU, Gitlow pursued his appeal to the U.S. Supreme Court, with negative results. He lost seven to two.

Common Timeless Theme

A common thread runs through all stages of the *Gitlow* case, from Magistrate's Court up to the Supreme Court, and it is evergreen. That timeless theme is how to decide when, if ever, it is appropriate to punish subversive speech. At what point can the government step in? When does allowable advocacy become unacceptable incitement? Are there any such circumstances that justify abridging freedom of subversive speech? How do we balance free speech and national security?

Gitlow gave one answer, an answer that met with approval at the time but has since been largely rejected. *Gitlow* answers "yes, you can nip revolution or anarchy in the bud by forbidding speech that might have a dangerous tendency to encourage people to violent acts at some unspecified time in the future." That answer, however upsetting to free speech advocates in ordinary times, is more attractive in times of public stress, anxiety and fear, as our history demonstrates. The impulse behind *Gitlow's* "bad tendency" test—public fear and anxiety—grows and ebbs.

During the Cold War, a second Red Scare gripped America, and McCarthyism was its worst expression. Federal statutes modeled on New York's criminal anarchy law became the basis for prosecuting American Communists for advocating noxious doctrines. In those cases, most of which affirmed criminal convictions, courts wrestled with many of the issues posed by *Gitlow*. Various legal tests were used, most of them trying to adapt or modify *Gitlow* in light of the more tolerant attitudes expressed in dissent by Holmes and Brandeis. Some Supreme Court opinions from that era indicate that those dissents had in fact become the precedents to be followed and that the rationale of *Gitlow* had been repudiated.

As the '60s unfolded, protests about civil rights and the Vietnam War again brought to the fore the hot button issue of limits on speech and advocacy. The issue seems to have been settled in 1969 with the Supreme Court's unambiguous and unequivocal ruling in *Brandenburg v. Ohio*. In that case, the Court held that advocacy could not be constitutionally prohibited or punished unless it was advocacy (1) "directed to inciting or producing imminent lawless action" and (2) "likely to produce such action." The Court took pains to say it was announcing a rule more speech friendly than even the clear and present danger test. The *Brandenburg* rule would have led to a different result in *Gitlow*.

But, curiously, *Gitlow* has never been expressly overruled. Even in *Brandenburg*, where the Court did explicitly overrule a famous prior decision that relied on *Gitlow's* rationale, it did not come right out and say it was overruling *Gitlow*. It is hard, however, to read *Brandenburg* without concluding that *Gitlow* was silently overruled and is no longer good law. But one can never be absolutely sure.

On the other hand, it is also possible *Gitlow* may just be hibernating. It is just possible that *Brandenburg's* conspicuous failure to expressly overrule *Gitlow* was intentional, that the omission was not inadvertent, but the product of some compromise among the justices in the opinion-drafting process. Supreme Court precedents, even those that have been disregarded, have a strange way of hanging around, waiting to come back to life. *Gitlow* may only be resting until the right conditions—fear and anxiety—make it serviceable again, a sleeping giant ready to wake up when summoned. And we now have widespread public fear and anxiety.

Striking Parallels

Striking parallels exist between today's climate of anxiety and fear and the political climate surrounding the *Gitlow* case. To paraphrase the opening of another manifesto very familiar to Ben Gitlow, today a new specter is haunting America—the specter of terrorism. That specter may confront the ghost of *Gitlow*, if it has not already done so. Ever since the terror attacks of 9/11, New York and the rest of the country have felt an extreme but understandable anxiety and fear about the new face of terrorism, with predictable and traditional results.

From legislation like the U.S. Patriot Act to prosecutions of Muslim clerics who advocate jihad, from indefinite detentions to warrantless searches, from extraordinary rendition to drone strikes to kill U.S. citizens labelled as dangerous without judicial review of the decision, from denial of habeas corpus to enhanced interrogation techniques (that is, torture), today's government antiterrorism policies resemble what happened around the time Ben Gitlow was arrested. To protect national security, government understandably wants to stop trouble before it starts, before it is too late. But that creates serious civil liberties issues. In this context, our context, the jury is still out on which precedent will ultimately prevail—*Gitlow* or *Brandenburg*. Despite our forever strong attachment to the ideas expressed in Holmes's *Gitlow* dissent, *Gitlow*'s repressive shadow still looms, if only because it reflects deep-seated psychological needs.

This is the larger, ever timely, reason why *Gitlow* is significant for us today. *Gitlow* vividly illustrates what happens when anger and anxiety, fear and frustration, and a genuine feeling of being threatened, become widespread and grip people's hearts and minds. *Gitlow* is part of a pattern that we see over and over again. The insecurity bred in America by the Russian Revolution abroad and by violence at home produced here a emotional response of repressive statutes, prosecutions and court decisions. Pearl Harbor led to the internment of innocent

Japanese-Americans. Fear begets repression, and often overreaction. Then it was the Red Scare; today, after 9/11, it is radical Islam.

In 1951, *Gitlow* figured in *Dennis v. United States* when the Supreme Court considered the prosecutions of the leaders of the American Communist Party. Some justices in *Dennis* indicated that time had undermined *Gitlow* and the clear and present danger test had become the law. But the same justices then distinguished *Gitlow* on its facts and affirmed the convictions in *Dennis*.

A cynic or a skeptic might say that *Dennis* paid lip service to the clear and present danger test, but then came to the same result as in *Gitlow*. It seems that one judge's clear and present danger is another's vague and far-in-the-future unlikely hazard. The end result may be the same, but at least *Dennis* requires analysis of facts and circumstances, and is not the rubber stamp of the legislature it would be under *Gitlow*.

The *Dennis* approach influenced the final ruling from the New York Court of Appeals on the *Gitlow* criminal anarchy law. In 1967, that law again came before the New York Court of Appeals in a case arising from the 1964 Harlem riots. In that case, *People v. Epton*, Judge John Scileppi wrote for the Court of Appeals that "the Supreme Court's view of the First Amendment's protection of speech has been altered drastically since *Gitlow* was decided." All the judges on the Court of Appeals agreed that the Holmes-Brandeis dissent represents "today's law." The Court in *Epton* stated that the statute as interpreted by *Gitlow* was unconstitutional but, citing *Dennis*, ruled it would be constitutional if the government could demonstrate an intent to bring about violent acts and that there was a "clear and present danger" based on circumstances.

Epton recognized that circumstances change. The Court of Appeals there stated it had interpreted the same statute in 1922 "in light of the prevailing conditions of that time and in accordance with the current understanding of First Amendment freedom." But the passage of time has led to a "clearer understanding of the scope of constitutional protection of speech." These statements mean that different "prevailing conditions" and a different "understanding of First Amendment freedom" could bring about a different result.

Thus did wise old Holmes eventually have a double victory in *Gitlow*. Not only has his admirable *Gitlow* dissent become the law (and was even strengthened by *Brandenburg*), but his early reference to public policy considerations—the felt necessities of the time—has won the day, and applies to our own day, when we are more aware of the impact of pressures, passions and fears on the law.

The *Gitlow* cycle continues. If law responds to the felt necessities of the time, as Holmes said, the question always is, which necessity is felt to be at the moment more pressing, civil liberties or the community's safety? John Milton referred to "necessity" as "the tyrant's plea," and sad experience has taught us why. But one still hopes civil liberties and security can be reconciled, so that civil liberties can be preserved without sacrificing safety and security. One hopes we are enlightened enough, have traveled enough in time, and recall our own national experiences, to avoid hysteria. Sharing this hope, President Obama, in his first inaugural address, rejected "as false the choice between our safety and our ideals." *Gitlow* was one such false choice. As Obama explained, "Those ideals still light the world, and we will not give them up for expedience's sake."

A Twist of Fate

The destinies of Ben Gitlow and the New York criminal anarchy law were oddly, and eerily, intertwined. Time diminished and undermined both. Political developments and his own change of heart had made Gitlow the man a threat no longer. In 1925, the same year as the Supreme Court's decision in his case, Gitlow, after serving three years in prison, was pardoned by Governor Smith. In 1924 and 1928 Gitlow was the Communist Party candidate for president. In 1929 Gitlow became General Secretary of the Communist Party of the U.S. Later that year, after a personal meeting and disagreement with Stalin, Gitlow was removed from his leadership position and then expelled from the party. By 1939 Gitlow had, like Whittaker Chambers, become a government informer and fervent anti-Communist, testifying at length and naming names before the House Un-American Activities Committee. He wrote two memoirs.

Developments in First Amendment law have made the 1902 statute constitutionally moribund as a practical matter, although, like the infamous Alien and Seditious Acts, no court had ever officially declared it unconstitutional.

In an ironic twist of fate, both the man and the law expired within twenty-four hours of each other. Ben Gitlow died in New York at age seventy-three on July 19, 1965. One day later, the New York Legislature, without mentioning Gitlow's death, repealed the old law. Some will say the timing was just a coincidence. Others will say there is no such thing as coincidence.

18

THE GREAT DISSENT

Holmes's 1925 *Gitlow* dissent was not his first or even necessarily his most memorable statement of freedom of expression. His ideas on that issue had been creatively fermenting for years. They found their most vivid, moving and forceful form six years earlier in a case that foreshadowed his *Gitlow* views. Holmes's dissent in that earlier case has won many fervent admirers who value civil liberties and has been the subject of much commentary.

Have you ever finished reading a good book about a familiar subject and, admiring the book so much, said to yourself, with envy, "I wish I had written that myself"? It recently happened to me as I, satisfied beyond expectation, finally read the last page and put down *The Great Dissent*, by Thomas Healy, a law professor at Seton Hall. *The Great Dissent*, published in 2013, is an amazing, terrific, brilliant, extraordinary book. Such adjectives are not hyperbole, they are accurate and well deserved.

On its face, the book is about Justice Holmes's classic hymn to freedom of speech in his dissent in the 1919 Supreme Court case of *Abrams v. U.S..* That opinion—"the most important minority opinion in American legal history" according to Healy—is the "great dissent" of the book's title. Every lawyer remembers it; like Holmes's dissent in *Gitlow*, his dissent in *Abrams* too was one of the highlights of the first year of law school; it too kindled or reaffirmed one's desire to be a lawyer.

Abrams was a case under the repressive Espionage Act passed during World War I, which prohibited anything—including speech—that supposedly interfered with our war effort. In 1918 Jacob Abrams and several other Russian immigrants threw down some leaflets from the roof of a loft in Manhattan's garment district. The leaflets did not oppose the war with Germany. They opposed American intervention in the Russian Revolution and, toward that end, urged workers not to produce arms for that purpose. The government claimed, however, that the war effort against Germany would thereby be hampered. After a trial before a hostile judge, Abrams and his co-defendants were convicted, and he was sentenced to twenty years in prison. (In 1921 the government commuted the sentences and deported the defendants to Russia.)

Amid lingering war-time hysteria and fear of Bolshevism, the Supreme Court affirmed the convictions over the memorable dissent of Holmes. In what amounted to an eloquent little essay, Holmes dispatched the majority's decision, calling the leaflets harmless and the defendants "puny anonymities." And, then, in the last paragraph of his dissent, Holmes's words really took wing.

"Persecution for the expression of opinions," Holmes started off that famous paragraph, "seems to me perfectly logical." He went on, "If you have no doubt of your premises or your power and want a certain result with all your heart, you naturally express your wishes in law and sweep away all opposition. To allow opposition by speech seems to indicate that you think the speech impotent."

Here is where Holmes's thought made the important, unexpected turn to the future and to the light with what Healy calls "one rich, profound, and unforgettable sentence." "But" continued Holmes, "when men have realized that time has upset many faiths, they may come to believe even more than they believe the very foundations of their own conduct that the ultimate good desired is better reached by free trade in ideas—that the best test of truth is the power of the thought to get itself accepted in the competition of the market, and that truth is the only ground upon which their wishes safely can be carried out." That noteworthy sentence, with its market metaphor, is what Healy and the rest of us celebrate.

Having stated his theory, Holmes proceeded to describe what it meant in law. "That," referring to his preceding sentence, "at any rate, is the theory of our Constitution. It is an experiment, as all life is an experiment." Then he slightly reformulated the "clear and present danger" test he had recently devised as the appropriate legal test. "We should be eternally vigilant against attempts to check the expression of opinions that we loathe and believe to be fraught with death, unless they so imminently threaten immediate interference with the lawful and pressing purposes of the law that an immediate check is required to save the country."

Inspiring words those, especially considering the tense times and context in which they were written. "No one else on the Court could write like this," says Healy. "Only Holmes could translate the law into such stirring, unforgettable language." Reading Holmes gives you the sense of fog lifting. Reading him, you feel windows opening, clouds passing, sunlight and a fresh breeze entering the room. His shimmering, philosophical opinion in *Abrams* strikes Healy as "elusive and oracular, suggesting hidden depths and complexities." Indeed, the well-read Holmes's famous reference to "free trade in ideas" may owe something to his memory of Milton's description, in *Areopagitica,* of truth in a "free and open encounter" with falsehood.

But Healy's book is much more than a rehash of *Abrams. Abrams* is the focal point, but only the focal point. That case is a vehicle, a springboard for a wonderful and stimulating literary/legal performance by Healy, as he "reconstruct[s] the story behind these famous words . . . a story of intellectual exploration and emotional growth." Holmes's dissent in *Abrams*, contends Healy, "gave birth to the modern era of the First Amendment." His words have "worked their way into our collective consciousness" to the point where "we have internalized his words." We become more aware of the silence of the printed word and how inward words have to go in our minds before they come alive. One way to keep in touch with the famous dead is through their words. If their words ring in our ears, we can talk with them in our imagination.

In part, the book is first-rate and original intellectual history, a "retracing of a man's journey toward enlightenment." The subtitle of the book clearly announces its theme: "How Oliver Wendell Holmes Changed His Mind—and Changed The History of Free Speech in America." Healy elaborates on his theme by tracking, step by step, the development of Holmes's evolving attitudes toward the First Amendment, from the conservative "bad tendency" test, to his original "clear and present danger" test first applied conservatively, to the definitive liberal shift in the *Abrams* dissent.

Healy demonstrates and explains the liberal progress, what Healy calls the "transformation," in Holmes's thinking about free speech during, and in the crucial years immediately after, World War I. Healy attributes Holmes's change of mind to an "extraordinary chain of events." Commenting on his own earlier, more restrictive, views, Holmes said, simply and candidly, "I was ignorant." This is a book about Holmes's intellectual career, the tale of his mind. His change of heart about the First Amendment may be an example of Holmes's existential emphasis on the lived human experience being more important than abstract reasoning as a guide to law.

Because of its subject matter, *The Great Dissent* is also in large part the condensed but thrilling story of the changing meaning of one of our nation's greatest badges of liberty and tolerance—the First Amendment. Some subjects are so riveting that we never tire of reading about them. Washington, Jefferson, Hamilton, Franklin; the American Revolution and the framing of our Constitution; Lincoln and the Civil War; and Winston Churchill and World War II are all in this category. We can never get enough of them. So too with the history of freedom of thought and freedom of expression in this country. We enjoy reading the story again and again. It is one of the things that sets us apart from all other countries, that defines the brightest aspect of American exceptionalism.

We never tire too of reading about Holmes and the aura of legend that glows about his name. He is at the heart of this book, and his searching personality, his indomitable spirit, his well-cultivated mind, his liveliness of expression, his zest for life, and his openness to new ideas drive the narrative. The volume revolves around Holmes, his interests, his thinking, his attitudes, and his life. Healy rightly calls him "an inspiring, romantic figure, a sort of philosopher-poet whose intellectual curiosity, dazzling style, and contrarian impulses seemed like a breath of fresh air in the musty world of government and law." With Holmes, we are in contact with an orderly, lucid, well-stocked and ultimately heroic mind.

Woven throughout Healy's narrative are the threads of a subtle biography of the Justice, from his Civil War soldiering to his intellectual achievements to his personal life. Unlike most other books about Holmes, *The Great Dissent* makes the man come alive. Here he is not merely a cardboard talking head, but a thoughtful and emotional man, filled with yearnings and contradictions like the rest of us. Healy presents Holmes in the round. We feel, by virtue of Healy's descriptions, as if we are actually in Holmes's study lined with his thousands of books. Reading about Holmes, especially his inner life, is as stimulating as reading what he actually wrote.

The aging and childless Holmes attracted youthful admirers, and they have a major role in this book. People like English socialist Harold Laski, Harvard law professors Felix Frankfurter and Zechariah Chafee, Judge Learned Hand, and journalist Walter Lippmann pushed Holmes away from his early, crabbed Espionage Act opinions toward the soaring *Abrams* dissent. These figures, in Healy's capable hands, become the subjects of astute mini-biographies as they walk on stage and play their parts in this story. Holmes "saw something in these men that reminded him of himself when he was young: a fire, a curiosity, a disregard for received wisdom."

Healy's thesis is, in essence, that these young admirers with progressive views eventually persuaded Holmes to take a more liberal view of the First Amendment. As Healy points out, Holmes at one time thought the First Amendment only barred prior restraints and in no way prevented punishment after statements were made. And it was none other than Holmes who not too much earlier had written the majority Supreme Court opinions affirming convictions under the Espionage Act, including one of Socialist Eugene Debs.

Such an apparently inconsistent record led journalist H.L. Mencken, another virtuoso of the English language, to take a dissenting view and warn us not to think of Holmes as a liberal. Not quoted by Healy is Mencken's trenchant comment that, "On at least three days out of four during his long years on the bench the learned justice remained the soldier—precise, pedantic, unimaginative, even harsh. But on the fourth day a strange amiability overcame him, and a strange impulse to play with heresy, and it was on that fourth day that he acquired his singular repute as a sage." We still appreciate that fourth day, and it was on one of them that Holmes wrote his *Abrams* dissent.

Healy, to his credit, does not join the ranks of modern Holmes bashers. For the past few decades, it has become fashionable in some intellectual quarters to try to knock Holmes off his jurisprudential pedestal. Misguided iconoclasts argue that Holmes's signature deference to democratically enacted legislation outside the free speech realm meant he believed in tyranny of the majority and a totalitarian view of government. Such claims are arrant nonsense, of course, unfairly punishing Holmes for putting limits on judicial review, and probably stems from one generation's need to tear down and replace the heroes of a previous generation. Healy stands fast in his admiration for Holmes, and if his book smacks of hero-worship, that is just fine with me. Hero-worship is perfectly all right as long as you choose your heroes carefully and wisely. We all need heroes, and Holmes is a good one.

Perhaps the most prominent theme in the book is how change in the law happens. Healy shows us how one well-situated person, prodded by others, can modify his views, express himself eloquently, and thereby alter the course of the law. That is what happened here, and we need to be thankful for it. Nothing about our law's current expansive views of free speech was inevitable. It was—and is—the product of continuing struggle, persuasion, courage and inspiring language by persons of influence. It is "almost as if Holmes had been working toward this moment his entire career, and now in one opinion—in one paragraph—it had all come together in a brilliant expression of constitutional faith."

Another explanation, overlooked by Healy, is possible. Holmes, as Healy reminds us, was a great reader. He devoured books of all kinds, fiction and non-fiction, voraciously and omnivorously, even keeping a list of every book he read. Healy tells us about the ten thousand—yes, TEN THOUSAND!—books in Holmes's Washington house. Holmes was especially drawn to books about ideas: philosophy, literature, history, and art. Might not Holmes's own outsize passion for reading explain, at least in part, his more liberal attitude and tolerant tilt toward freedom of expression? It is hard to imagine an avid reader with a skeptical turn of mind like Holmes being in favor of anyone, in or out of government, telling him what he can or cannot read.

Government tends to exercise such power—Healy's book underscores this—in times of public stress, fear, and frustration. We know from American history and our own post-9/11 experience that war and other perceived threats to national security often lead, even here, to government repression. Whether it takes the form of the Alien and Sedition Acts during the Napoleonic Wars, Lincoln clamping down on Copperheads and anti-war newspapers, Palmer raids during the Red Scare after World War I, McCarthyism after World War II, and anti-protest campaigns more recently, repression of civil liberties comes and goes with the times. As a result, the fight to preserve and protect freedom of expression continues in each generation. We look up to Holmes for lighting the way with such deathless language.

Healy himself knows how to use language. His welcome, lively, non-academic style is accessible, but more than that, it is fluid and well paced. He can really tell a story. For example, here is Healy's word portrait of Holmes starting to draft his *Abrams* opinion: "He picked up his steel-ribbed pen, dipped the rusted tip into his father's inkwell, and added yet another chapter to the long history of the law." And again, when Holmes meets a young federal judge named Learned Hand on a train, Healy describes the scene indelibly: "The face smiled, Holmes smiled back, and the wheels of history began to turn."

That is good writing, something we should all aspire to and admire when we chance upon it. A book on this same subject written by someone else, someone less skilled, might have been a dull, clanking textbook. Crafted by Healy, it reads like a suspenseful historical novel, stimulating and provocative at the same time. I found myself reading it on the train, over lunch hour, and before going to sleep. I could not put it down.

This book, Healy's first, is an auspicious beginning. It is one of the best books ever written about American law, on a par with classics like *Gideon's Trumpet* by Anthony Lewis and *Simple Justice* by Richard Kluger. As Healy says of Holmes, so too we can say of Healy: "Like Lincoln at Gettysburg, he had produced a document that far exceeded his own estimation and would survive long after he was gone" and "he had done it with style." We cannot wait for Healy's next book.

19

ANTHONY LEWIS AND THE FIRST AMENDMENT

Holmes's legacy left an indelible impression on Anthony Lewis, the late columnist for the New York Times. With Lewis's death in 2013, America lost a good friend of civil liberties. A wise person gave me a gift during my first term of law school: *Gideon's Trumpet*, the book by Lewis about the 1963 Supreme Court case of *Gideon v. Wainwright* and the right to counsel. That gift—with its clear but dramatic account of a transforming case of constitutional law—was inspiring. Lewis's book brightened my law school experience, taught me that law cases were more than court opinions, and made me believe that the practice of law could be good, noble and thrilling. But it was not about Holmes or freedom of speech. Those books came later.

I

Twenty-seven years after *Gideon's Trumpet*, Lewis in 1991 did it again. Focusing on one Supreme Court case, he used that case as a vehicle for retelling an important story and for reexamining the profound effects of the case on the law and on society. As before, Lewis chose a case of constitutional law—and he deals with the Bill of Rights. The formula still works.

Make No Law is about *New York Times Co. v. Sullivan*, the landmark 1964 decision that revolutionized the law of libel. In its narrowest terms, the case held that a public official may not successfully sue for defamation relating to his official conduct unless he proves that the statement was made with "actual malice"—that is, with knowledge that it was false or with reckless disregard of whether it was false. The case set forth several subsidiary libel rules as well.

But to think of *Sullivan* as no more than a libel case would be like describing *Brown v. Board of Education* as just another equal protection case. To state the rule of the *Sullivan* case does not start to expound its far-reaching significance. That is Lewis's mission, which he carries out with style and sensitivity.

Even Lewis's choice of subject is unerring. When the constitutional history of our epoch comes to be written, few cases will loom as large and as important as *Sullivan*. Like *Brown* in the civil rights field, *Sullivan* stands out sharply on the constitutional landscape as a case that, in a way, defined America.

"The [*Sullivan*] Court," writes Lewis, "used to the full its extraordinary power to lay down the fundamental rules of our national life. It made clearer than ever that ours is an open society, where citizens may say what they wish about who temporarily governs them." Viewed most broadly, *Sullivan* changed the character of public life in the United States.

Sullivan, like Holmes's dissent in *Abrams*, also marked a turning point in free speech theory. The decision described the "central meaning" of the First Amendment as the right to criticize government free of criminal and civil penalties, such as seditious libel. It began the judicial shift toward the Meiklejohn theory for self-government. In his influential 1948 book *Free Speech and Its Relation to Self-Government*, Alexander Meiklejohn, president of Amherst College, argued that free speech is protected by the First Amendment as essential to self-government in a democratic system. According to the Meiklejohn theory, public discussion of issues of civic importance deserve absolute protection.

As for federalism, *Sullivan* completely redrew the map of the common law of each state in light of the U.S. Constitution. Establishing First Amendment requirements for state common law libel actions, *Sullivan* for the first time made clear that fundamental federal law would control, at least as a minimum, the relevant common law of all the states. Although the facts of *Sullivan* involved libel, the logic of the decision proved in time to encompass any common law cause of action—like invasion of privacy or injurious falsehood— that turned on expression. In this way, *Sullivan* constitutionalized the common law.

Ever sensitive to these large themes, Lewis also laid out the background and history of the case. One might well wonder if

Sullivan would have turned out the way it did if its facts were not so compelling. In some ways, it could be seen less as a libel case and more as a civil rights case. The allegedly defamatory statements occurred in a 1960 newspaper advertisement complaining about racial inequality in Alabama. Some Southern officials came up with his idea to use libel suits as a weapon to prevent publicity, even when truthful, about racial conditions.

Lewis unearthed some telling information. The Alabama trial judge in the *Sullivan* case, Walter Jones, "was a devotee of the Confederacy." In 1961, at a reenactment of the one-hundredth anniversary of the swearing-in of Confederate President Jefferson Davis, Judge Jones administered the oath of office. As a judge, Jones opposed civil rights, even insisting, as unbelievable as it sounds, that seating in his courtroom be segregated.

The odor of the trial proceedings in *Sullivan* wafted all the way up to the Supreme Court. No wonder the $500,000 libel award was reversed without dissent. (The concurring opinions would have given even more protection to the press.)

Make No Law is a book about a case and a process. Lewis notes that "a skillful brief is readable; it should tell a story, sweeping the reader along to a desired end." Oral argument, he observes, is a "direct opportunity" for lawyers to reach the minds of judges, "with an idea, a phrase, a fact." Like any good writer, Lewis anchors abstractions to real, living, breathing people. In this story, his heroes are a lawyer and a judge.

The lawyer is Herbert Wechsler, the Columbia Law School professor who represented the *Times* in the Supreme Court. Lewis describes Wechsler's strategy and tactics in drafting his petition for certiorari and brief on the merits, and in preparing for the oral argument. The *Sullivan* opinion, says Lewis, "owed much . . . to the analytical power of Wechsler . . . Much of the opinion's structure was taken from the brief." We can never learn enough about the choices a successful advocate exercises in presenting a case.

The judicial hero in this book is Justice William Brennan, author of the Court's opinion in *Sullivan*. As Lewis notes in a prefatory acknowledgment, "What Justice Brennan did for all of us when he wrote the opinion in *New York Times v. Sullivan* needs no further comment." (He nonetheless comments on that precise subject for the next two hundred forty-eight pages.) According to Lewis, "The manner of the *Sullivan* opinion was as striking as its substance. It was written in the grand style." Lewis calls it "an opinion with distinctive literary and historical qualities: an opinion so rich in its observations on freedom of expression and libel that on repeated readings one keeps discovering new meanings."

The history and analysis of the *Sullivan* case form the core, but only the core, of this book. To set the stage for the Supreme Court ruling in *Sullivan*, Lewis devotes a number of chapters to tracing the history of free speech in this country. He examines how the "Madisonian premise"—the crucial role of free speech in democracy—has fared over time. These historical sections provide a useful sketch of vital themes in American law and life.

Justice Brennan, the hero of Lewis's book, expressed it well. Journalist Nat Hentoff once asked Brennan: What is the most important amendment to the Constitution? According to Hentoff, "Brennan said the First Amendment, because all the other ones come from that. If you don't have free speech you have to be afraid, you lack a vital part of what is to be a human being who is free to be who you want to be."

What catches the reader more than anything else, however, is the author's attitude, his response to his fundamental theme. For Lewis—and for us—freedom of expression is more than a utilitarian tool of self-government; it is something deeper and more profound, going to the essence of what it means to be human and alive, to think, to believe and express oneself. Nowhere is this better illustrated than in Lewis's discussion of certain free speech opinions of Justices Holmes and Brandeis.

Like Thomas Healy, Lewis also gives Holmes credit for turning the tide in First Amendment law. Lewis credits Holmes's dissent in the 1919 *Abrams* case as the "beginning of the Supreme Court's recognition of the paramount imporant of the First Amendment." He quotes that dissent, in which Holmes spoke about "free trade in ideas" and the need to "be eternally vigilant against attempts to check the expression of opinion that we loathe and believe to be fraught with death." As Lewis feelingly told a lecture audience at the New York Public Library, "I never fail to respond to the words [of Holmes's *Abrams* dissent], so forgive me if I read some of them." In the book,

Lewis points out that Holmes's language "approached poetry in its rhetorical power," and that it makes "the hair rise at the back of the neck."

Lewis has a similar response to Brandeis's concurrence in the 1927 *Whitney* case, part of which he also sets out in the book. A basic document of American freedom, it is worth quoting again: "Those who won our independence believed that the final end of the State was to make men free to develop their faculties; and that in its government the deliberative forces should prevail over the arbitrary. They valued liberty both as an end and as a means. They believed liberty to be the secret of happiness and courage to be the secret of liberty. The believed that freedom to think as you will and to speak as you think are means indispensable to the discovery and spread of political truth; that with them, discussion affords ordinarily adequate protection against the dissemination of noxious doctrine; that the greatest menace to freedom is an inert people; that public discussion is a political duty; and that this should be a fundamental principle of the American government. They recognized the risks to which all human institutions are subject. But they knew that order cannot be secured merely through fear of punishment for its infraction; that it is hazardous to discourage thought, hope and imagination; that fear breeds repression; that the path of safety lies in the opportunity to discuss freely supposed grievances and proposed remedies; and that the fitting remedy for evil counsels is good ones. Believing in the power of reason as applied through public discussion, they eschewed silence coerced by law— the argument of force in its worst form. Recognizing the occasional tyrannies of governing majorities, they amended the Constitution so that free speech and assembly should be guaranteed."

Lewis thinks of Brandeis's "astounding" opinion as "the most profound statement ever made about the premises of the First Amendment in protecting the freedom of speech." I whole-heartedly agree.

How Lewis responds here is the key. He is not reacting simply as a writer admiring well-wrought and powerful language, though that is undoubtedly part of it. He is responding from the soul. Anyone who can read those Holmes and Brandeis opinions without a strong reaction will never grasp the meaning of free expression. Such freedoms depend on strong responses.

For all its benefits, *Sullivan*, as Lewis recognizes, caused problems, too. In the post-*Sullivan* era, libel cases have not disappeared, nor have libel verdicts shrunk. Libel cases still impose heavy burdens on courts and litigants in terms of time and money. From another angle, *Sullivan* may have encouraged a certain occasional arrogance among the media. Lewis evaluates a number of proposed reforms.

To Lewis's credit, he takes a balanced view of the press. Unlike some of his colleagues, who automatically side with the press in every court case regardless of the facts, Lewis candidly admits that, "The press can be destructive, too. It is not always the good guy." Such straight-shooting on Lewis's part enhances his overall credibility, lifting the book beyond the level of special pleading to more fair-minded commentary.

We expect a newspaper columnist to be accessible, and Lewis is certainly and unfailingly that. But such accessibility becomes even more valued when the subject is law and the temptation to slip into technical jargon is great. Lewis resists the temptation. As with *Gideon's Trumpet*, he writes for the layman as well as the lawyer: both will profit mightily from reading *Make No Law*.

Lewis never condescends to the reader, even as he explains legal terms as needed. The non-lawyer is introduced to the world of constitutional lawyers and the Supreme Court. For the lawyer, a familiar world develops more nuances and connections. Lewis writes about the law the way great literary critics and art historians write about their subjects.

Perhaps Lewis's most original contribution in this book is his understanding of how much freedom of expression ultimately depends on optimism. He compares European attitudes to American attitudes on free speech, and noting our greater tolerance, explains the difference in terms of national experiences. Spared the darkest forces that have scarred the European mind, especially in the twentieth century, America is more optimistic than Europe about the efficacy of free speech. "I am essentially an optimist," Lewis told his Library lecture listeners. "I believe we should stick to the optimism of Holmes and Brandeis."

As long as we are blessed with gifted and humane writers like Anthony Lewis, who are sensitive to the true meaning of free expression, optimism is justified. If only we could find more Supreme Court justices with the same qualities.

II

Make No Law, his book about the landmark *Times v. Sullivan* libel case, was in some ways a prelude to Lewis's last book. Lewis, a fearless, freedom-loving civil libertarian, unafraid to challenge those in power when they make mistakes, knows how to inspire with words. His final book-length effort with words before he died only adds to this long list of impressive credentials. *Freedom for the Thought That We Hate*, published in 2013 (the year of his death), is subtitled *A Biography of the First Amendment*. It is part of a series of books called "Basic Ideas," each volume of which consists of "a leading authority" offering "a concise biography of a text that transformed its world and ours." Author and subject here both meet the stated criteria.

Lewis is certainly a "leading authority" on the First Amendment. A Pulitzer Prize-winning journalist, the former *New York Times* columnist wrote about law in accessible language that laypeople can understand and read with pleasure and profit. He was, at the age of eighty, a gifted old hand at his task. *Gideon's Trumpet*, his 1964 book about the right to counsel, is a genuine legal classic. For these contributions, in May 2007 the New York County Lawyers' Association awarded Lewis its Law and Literature Award.

As a "text that transformed its world, and ours," the First Amendment obviously qualifies. The very idea of a guarantee of freedom of expression written into a nation's organic document was revolutionary. Its continuing vitality in practice is still revolutionary, even as it is rare in world history. Not many societies have learned how imperative it is to tolerate "freedom for the thought that we hate," a phrase of Justice Holmes that Lewis takes for his title and that embodies the spirit of the First Amendment.

Unlike some civil libertarians, Lewis never lets his deep emotional attachment to the First Amendment distort his judgment. He is a mature and subtle student of free speech principles and how they operate in a democratic society. He does not interpret the First Amendment in isolation; he looks at it realistically and in context. The result is an important and sensitive perspective.

Lewis's central theme hinges on a two-sided view of the First Amendment. One side is the bedrock importance of freedom of expression. The other side is the occasional need in particular circumstances to balance the values embodied in that freedom against other values. Such recognition is itself the beginning of wisdom in this field.

For all his passionate devotion to the First Amendment, however, Lewis avoids being seduced by its rhetoric and blinded by its cachet. He knows there are limits. He does not elevate the First Amendment into an absolute that always trumps other values that may come into conflict with it. He believes, quite rightly, that such conflicts require careful judgment.

He poses the underlying question thusly. Freedom of speech and of the press is a "fundamental value" in American society. "But is it a paramount value, overriding others when they conflict with it?," he asks. Some people, Lewis warns, "invoke the First Amendment as if those words would settle whatever issue was being debated." Lewis knows that this view, however attractive and seductive to some, is false, misleading and, what is more, dangerous.

The outcome would be dangerous because it would always subordinate other, sometimes equally or even more important values, depending on particular circumstances. The liberties in the First Amendment are "fundamentals of our freedom, but they are not the only essentials of a healthy society." If First Amendment freedoms "succeed in totally overriding" all competing interests, "it would be a terrible victory."

To avoid such a "terrible victory," Lewis favors balancing. "But in truth," Lewis correctly writes, freedom of expression has "never been absolute." In one trenchant sentence that compactly explains much of the sprawling and controversial First Amendment law, Lewis says: "The courts and society have repeatedly struggled to accommodate other interests along with those" protected by the First Amendment.

Those sometimes competing "other interests" easily come to mind. A criminal defendant's right to a fair trial without prejudicial press coverage. National security. An individual's interest in protecting his or her reputation, privacy or emotional well-being. A press privilege for confidential sources versus the needs of law enforcement and compulsory process. Public disorder.

When those other interests conflict with the First Amendment, an automatic knee-jerk reflex in favor of expression can create serious problems, as Lewis demonstrates. He uses two upsetting examples, both from famous privacy cases. In *Sidis v. F.R. Publishing Corporation*, a federal appeals court in Manhattan in 1940 rejected a privacy claim by a lonely, one-time boy genius who, having sought to avoid publicity as an adult, sued *The New Yorker* magazine for a mocking, amusingly contemptuous follow-up article. The court held that the public had a legitimate interest in learning about what happened to the prodigy. Four year later, Sidis, unemployed and poor, died of a cerebral hemorrhage at age forty-six. Lewis calls this case and its aftermath "tormenting."

The other "remarkable" case cited by Lewis in *Time, Inc. v. Hill*, a 1967 case in the U.S. Supreme Court involving a story in *Life* magazine about a Broadway play based on a real family—the Hills—held hostage by escaped convicts. The *Life* story devastated the family, and Mrs. Hill suffered a psychiatric and lasting emotional breakdown, supported by medical testimony at trial. The Supreme Court, however, ruled against the Hills' privacy claim. Four years later, Mrs. Hill committed suicide. (Interesting sidelight: The Hills were represented in the Supreme Court by Richard Nixon, who argued the case.)

Justice Brennan's majority opinion in *Hill* contains a passage that, in Lewis's view, "amounts to a rejection of privacy as an important value." According to Brennan, "Exposure of the self to others in varying degrees is a concomitant of life in a civilized community." Lewis's reaction: "I am a great admirer of Justice Brennan, but I disagree with his conception of a 'civilized community.'"

These two cases—*Sidis* and *Hill*—underscore the real-world consequences of automatic deference to the First Amendment regardless of consequences to countervailing values. Reality requires recognition of competing values and the necessity, even agony, of choice. Sometimes, in the words of intellectual historian Isaiah Berlin, "[E]nds equally ultimate, equally sacred, may contradict each other." Nonetheless we still have to choose, and it is not enough to say the First Amendment always wins.

Even in this superb little book (the text is less than two hundred pages), one important element is missing: the money connection. In the First Amendment field, as elsewhere, it is a good idea to "follow the money." For some time now, big media has effectively wrapped itself in the mantle of the First Amendment. Large corporate publishers of newspapers, magazines and books and even credit rating agencies like Standard & Poors and Moody's sometimes use high-sounding rhetoric about free expression to justify what are often essentially, even obviously, financial choices. Much as politicians can press the patriotism button to cloud the public's mind, so too big media can press the free speech button to befog clear thinking. This tendency begs for more analysis.

Freedom For the Thought That We Hate once again shows how Anthony Lewis can inspire lawyers and non-lawyers alike. We are sorry he is done writing such thrilling books. We need more of them desperately. Running through his impressive body of work is this motivational message for lawyers: Be ashamed to die before you have used your legal skills to strike a blow for freedom.

20

THE FREE SPEECH PARADOX

The balancing discussed by Anthony Lewis leads to problems of choice and even a paradox. In this sense, free speech and taxes have something in common. Our attitudes toward both have long been caught in a persistent paradox. On the one hand, everyone seems at least to pay lip service to the notions of eliminating or reducing tax deductions and to the exalted place given freedom of expression in the First Amendment ("Congress shall make no law . . . abridging the freedom of speech, or of the press"). On the other hand, when it comes actually to deciding which tax deductions to do away with or which speech to protect in specific instances, those same people often want all deductions eliminated except their own, or favor protecting speech except when it affects issues important to them. This tension between theory and practice creates the "free speech paradox."

I

An example of the free speech paradox involves local laws against pornography. Some jurisdictions have passed laws subjecting sellers of pornography to money damages and injunctions. The laws defined pornography as "the sexually explicit subordination of women, graphically depicted, whether in pictures or words." The Mayor of Minneapolis vetoed the bill there, but the Indianapolis bill became law, although a federal court enjoined its enforcement.

This spurt of anti-pornography laws underscores the free speech paradox. Spearheading the drive behind the laws are radical feminists. Feminism is ordinarily associated with liberalism—even extreme liberalism—particularly in its effort to change women's role in society. And liberals are usually thought to put a high value on First Amendment guarantees.

How does a dedicated feminist square her belief in the First Amendment with her outrage at pornography? That is the dilemma, and the essence of the free speech paradox.

Of course, the tension is sought to be minimized or ignored. No doubt the law's sponsors would say there is no conflict. No doubt they would argue there is neither a violation of the First Amendment nor an attempt to inhibit freedom of expression. It is all, so they might argue, a question of balancing.

But such a desultory protests are unconvincing. One cannot ignore the monumental threshold problem of defining pornography with enough precision so as to avoid the constitutional flaws of vagueness or overbreadth. But even aside from the danger of sweeping non-pornographic magazines or literature within a fuzzy definition, there remains a larger, more basic question.

If feminists who proclaim allegiance to the First Amendment seek a law restricting speech *they* object to, what is to prevent any other group from seeking to restrict speech *it* objects to?

Certainly feminists are far from unique in this regard. Society is made up of all sorts of individuals and groups who may find certain kinds of expression false or offensive. For feminists, the buzz word that subordinates freedom of expression is pornography. For government officials, it is national security. Decades ago, groups that insisted on their First Amendment rights of speech, assembly and petition during the civil rights movement tried to prevent speakers on college campuses from discussing the genetic transmission of intelligence. Why? Because such speakers supposedly promoted racism. For Jews, the trigger phrase is anti-Semitism. For Catholics, it is abortion. For those who opposed the Vietnam War, it was considered appropriate to prevent defenders of that war from explaining their position.

To be sure, civility and mutual respect might counsel against such expression. A decent respect for others should discourage slurs and epithets designed to discredit another's race, ethnic group, religion or sex. The resulting distress can be significant. A civilized society should be considerate toward its members.

Important as those social and ethical values may be, however, the fundamental right to free expression must supersede them. If every group could have its way and bar speech it finds offensive or objectionable, there would not be left a whole lot of controversial speech. The First Amendment would have so many holes in it, it would look like a piece of Swiss cheese. If freedom of speech means freedom only for speech we agree with, then freedom of speech has lost its traditional meaning. So defined, freedom of speech is no great fundamental liberty. It would be a promise to the ear, broken to the hope. It would be no freedom at all.

Many of these issues were discussed in 1975 by a Yale student-faculty committee headed by historian C. Vann Woodward that examined "the condition of free expression, peaceful dissent, mutual respect and tolerance." The Committee grew out of incidents at Yale during the 1960s and early seventies involving rights of speakers on campus. The resulting report is a model of clarity and balanced judgment and well exemplifies the tradition of tolerance.

"If expression may be prevented, censored or punished because of its content or because of the motives attributed to those who promote it," stated the Woodward Committee, "then it is no longer free. It will be subordinated to other values that we believe to be a lower priority in a university."

The Yale report goes far beyond the university context. The attitude criticized by it guts our system of freedom of expression. That system depends on a variety of different views being pressed without censorship. The resulting cacophony of voices—the very discordance— is precisely what is healthy about a system of freedom of expression. It fosters debate, criticism, and progress, without censorship.

Once censorship is involved, and make no mistake that censorship is what is involved, the whole system is skewed. Things may be more tranquil, but tranquility is not the proper goal. Montesquieu pointed out in *The Spirit of the Laws*: "A general rule is that, always, in a state which calls itself republican, when absolute tranquility reigns, you can be assured that liberty does not exist there. What is called unity in a political body is a very ambiguous thing: true unity is a harmonious one, through which all the parties opposed as they may appear to us, concur in the general good of the society; like dissonances in music, they concur in the total harmony."

At its core, the free speech paradox is a paradox of ends and means. Freedom of speech is a means, a process. In our system, our widely shared belief in the primacy of free expression is more important than any particular end or objective. Indeed, our overriding commitment to free expression is so important a means or process that it becomes an end or goal in and of itself.

In the words of the 1975 Yale report: "We take a chance, as the First Amendment takes a chance, when we commit ourselves to the idea that the results of free expression are to the general benefit in the long run, however unpleasant they may appear at the time. The validity of such a belief cannot be demonstrated conclusively. It is a belief of recent historical development, even within universities, one embodied in American constitutional doctrine but not widely shared outside the academic world, and denied in theory and in practice by much of the world most of the time."

Every time someone objects to what someone else is saying or printing, and is thinking about censoring it, he or she should be required to recite aloud ten times what Justice Holmes said in *United States v. Schwimmer* in 1928: "If there is any principle of the Constitution that more imperatively calls for attachment than any other," wrote Holmes, "it is the principle of free thought—not free thought for those who agree with us but freedom for the thought that we hate."

Holmes solved the free speech paradox. Taxes, which he viewed as the price we pay for civilization, are another matter.

II

If Americans were asked to identify "the thing that is most unique and precious about the United States," what do you think they would say? High standard of living? Educational opportunity? McDonald's? Hollywood? MTV? For Marjorie Heins, founding director of the ACLU's Arts Censorship Project, the answer is freedom of speech. That answer and the fundamental values it embodies fuel Heins's outstanding 1993 book *Sex, Sin and Blasphemy: A Guide to America's Censorship Wars.*

Her volume—a smooth blend of social commentary, legal scholarship and cogent argument—explains a complex and controversial subject with disarming simplicity and a deep commitment to tolerance. Heins describes her book as a "product of the censorship wars." It canvasses the "different fields of combat" and "explores both the direct and the subtle ways that censorship happens." Ultimately this book, aimed at a general audience, becomes a call to action, with an afterward listing "What You Can Do."

Before finding out what we can do, we should first find out what we mean by censorship. Heins favors a functional rather than a technical definition. Censorship, she writes, "happens whenever some people succeed in imposing their political views or moral values on others by suppressing words, images or ideas that they find offensive." Note the absence of government action in Heins's definition. She is right, of course, because, as she says and as we all know, "censorship can also be accomplished very effectively by private groups."

This is not a book that shrouds the author's point of view in mystery or doubt. And yet, for all her obvious advocacy of civil liberties and her antagonism toward censorship, Heins never lets her book descend to the level of mere polemic. On the contrary, throughout the book runs a tone of reasonableness and imperturbability that will confound even if it fails to convince her true-believing adversaries. Heins admits, for example, that not all forms of censorship are illegal or even wrong.

Within the last few decades, censorship has "become a key word in political debate," says Heins. Following a 1986 federal government report on pornography, we have seen greater use of the criminal law to punish "obscenity," including forays against music lyrics. We have watched the National Endowment for the Arts deny funding to artists whose work was controversial. We have looked on as books have been removed from school libraries and reading lists.

To Heins, these highly publicized skirmishes are mere epiphenomena. The real issues run much deeper and cut to the heart of what many have called an American "culture war." Heins points out that the censorship fights are not isolated or unrelated, but the result of "an explosion of ideological conflict over differing attitudes about sexuality, religion, women's liberation and 'family values.'" She understands that censorship involves "subjects that arouse emotions so powerful that they may interfere with rational thought." They are the subjects we often avoid in conversation: sex, especially homosexuality; religion, especially sacred symbols or perceived heresies; race, especially images connecting race with sex or violence; and patriotism, especially if symbols like the American flag are involved.

The author excels when discussing the political aspects of censorship. With great insight, Heins goes behind the façade of politicians' press releases. "Symbols, words, ideas and images," Heins comments, "were being blamed for social ills." Paraphrasing those politicians, Heins writes ironically, "If only America would rid itself of all those pesky artists, all that crude and irreverent and sometimes violent popular entertainment, surely our social problems would fade away."

Heins returns to this important theme later. Blaming artistic expression for the ills of society, she concludes, is misguided. "Words and images don't cause bad acts. Messages in art are influenced by social conditions and attitudes, not the other way around." She adds: "The reasons for our social ills lie in the real world, not in the world of imagination."

Censorship thus becomes a form of political evasion. "Scapegoating speech is a dangerous excuse for failing to deal with real-world problems," Heins notes. By pursuing an "elusive and falsely oversimplified solution to social ills," we become distracted "from searching for real-world problems." Heins thinks some politicians "prefer to invent and attack demons and scapegoats instead of seriously addressing the tough, massive problems of poverty, homelessness, a stagnating economy, crushing debt, destructive racial divisions, widening economic disparities," among others. Censorship is a diversion from frustration and malaise, a convenient distraction from worsening social conditions.

A censor's mind is a terrible thing to contemplate. What moves someone to try to prevent someone else, especially an adult, from reading a book, seeing a movie or listening to certain music? Political distraction or manipulation is only one possible motivation. Another, often favored by those in power, is to forestall change. A third reason is the impulse to ban or stifle what one finds offensive. Finally we come up against the dark forces, such as an irrational fear of sex or elements of religious faith.

Although Heins's book is non-fiction, one almost wishes some of the censorship incidents in it were imaginary. She recounts the history of the "obscenity" exception to the First Amendment, concluding that the end of such an exception "would be a good start toward defeating censorship." She describes how movies have over the years been censored. She shows how government threats can bring about censorship. She then proceeds to discuss the controversy over warning labels on popular music and criminal obscenity cases against rap groups like 2 Live Crew. Tolerance and intolerance seems to have coexisted throughout our history.

Heins's best chapter is on pornography. It is especially tricky topic for a woman to write about, but Heins does it with clarity and skill. In addition to a fine account of the general issue from a civil libertarian point of view, Heins does not shrink from dealing with strident objections to pornography by Catherine MacKinnon and Andrea Dworkin. Heins sets out the MacKinnon-Dworkin anti-porn position: that pornography "is a major source and cause of women's oppression," is "inherently coercive and degrading," molds the attitudes and actions of men, and constitutes discrimination against women. Heins then lays bare the flaws in the MacKinnon-Dworkin argument.

Heins combines courage and fine legal analysis on an issue that has divided the women's movement. First, Heins argues that MacKinnon and Dworkin "confuse the images in pornography with actual sexual abuse." Next, Heins explains that the "fundamental complaint is the nature of sexual intercourse itself" based on the far from universal view that "even consensual heterosexual activity" is "violent and degrading." Then Heins explains why the anti-porn statutes favored by the MacKinnon-Dworkin faction are a mistake as well as unconstitutional. By censoring sex information, the MacKinnon-Dworkin anti-porn campaign has also "undermined the cause of women's rights." Heins ultimately regards the MacKinnon-Dworkin censorship campaign as "profoundly *anti*feminist" and intolerant.

This book matches forthright and controversial content with forthright and non-controversial style. Clarity and grace, in thought and expression, are Heins's hallmarks. The author, a writer before entering law school, produced a remarkable book that reads easily. Abstract ideas are anchored to concrete examples. But the reader's ease is deceptive; it masks the writer's profound and complex thought patterns, her breadth of learning, and her genuine love of freedom of thought and expression.

Marjorie Heins, a Harvard Law graduate, is the perfect author for this book. Her important post with the ACLU's Arts Censorship Project, relevant as it may be, only starts to reveal the depths of Heins's commitment to the issues. For many years she had divided her professional life, mostly in the Boston area, among teaching, writing and practicing civil liberties law. She has been co-counsel on *Finley v. National Endowment for the Arts* (involving the NEA's efforts to impose "decency" standards), was founding director of the Free Expression Policy Project, served as staff counsel for the Civil Liberties Union of Massachusetts, as chief of the Civil Rights Division of the Massachusetts Attorney General's office, and as editor-in-chief of the *Massachusetts Law Review*. One of her earlier books, *Cutting the Mustard*, described a case she handled for a female Boston University dean allegedly fired for exercising her freedom of speech—her vocal advocacy of affirmative action and her criticism of the university's procedures and criteria for hiring faculty and administrators. Her most recent book *Priests of Our Democracy*, published in 2013, is about academic freedom. Heins has spoken on civil liberties issues, with a calm, steady purpose that discomfits her antagonists.

Sex, Sin and Blasphemy deserves wide readership and great success. It is an expert's clear-eyed and sensible perspective on a basic issue that continues to rend our society. It is a book that Hugo Black and William Douglas and William Brennan would have enjoyed.

III

The late Irving Younger, a dynamic law teacher, judge, and lawyer wrote a provocative essay in 1985 in *Commentary* magazine entitled, "What Good Is Freedom of Speech?" In it he argued that, apart from the First Amendment, the sole defense of free speech is the idea of "sanctuary." By sanctuary, Younger means "the line around some parts of our lives past which the power of the state may not tresspass." A law interfering with free speech thus violates sanctuary and is beyond the state's power to legislate.

For Younger, "There is no justification [for free speech] beyond" the idea of sanctuary. Nothing in the Constitution (other than the First Amendment), either explicitly or implicitly, justifies it. Nothing else in history, philosophy, or political science provides a defense for free speech. Sanctuary, and sanctuary alone, is the key, he says.

The idea of sanctuary advanced by Younger is not, however, what makes his *Commentary* essay provocative; it is his dismissal of other arguments in favor of free speech. His total lack of reference to other parts of the Constitution besides the First Amendment and his failure to relate the idea of sanctuary to existing constitutional and philosophical doctrine are surprising, inexplicable and strange.

Let us start with the Constitution minus the First Amendment. How about the Ninth Amendment, with its protection for unenumerated rights? According to the Ninth Amendment, "The enumeration in the Constitution, of certain rights, shall not be construed to deny or disparage others retained by the people." Or the Privileges or Immunities Clause of the Fourteenth Amendment, which provides that "No State shall make or enforce any law which shall abridge the privileges or immunities of citizens of the United States." Even if it may be debatable whether freedom of speech can necessarily be inferred from those provisions, surely it is extraordinary for them to go unmentioned by Younger.

More extraordinary still, particularly in light of his idea of sanctuary, is Younger's failure to mention the doctrine of substantive due process, which is essentially a concept of sanctuary. Substantive due process refers to those aspects of liberty that government has no right to interfere with. As a legal doctrine, it has had its ups and downs. In the early twentieth century, substantive due process was the basis for "liberty of contract," which led conservative courts to void much progressive economic regulation. Although substantive due process came under strong attack as too subjective, it has been invoked more recently as protection for personal rights. The sorts of rights that find shelter in Younger's sanctuary are substantive due process rights: "Whether and when we marry, what work we pursue, where (if anywhere) we find the solace of the supernatural." Yet the phrase substantive due process nowhere appears in the article.

Reading it, one would have no idea that substantive due process ever existed, or that it and the idea of sanctuary could be criticized as subjective. Nor would an uninformed reader learn anything from the article about "penumbra theory" as a possible justification for free speech.

In 1965, the Supreme Court found an implied right of privacy in the "penumbra" of other explicit constitutional rights. Certainly one could argue that freedom of speech is implicit in the penumbra of other express constitutional rights. As the Supreme Court stated in 1980, "Fundamental rights, even though not expressly guaranteed, have been recognized by the Court as indispensable to the enjoyment of rights explicitly defined." Once again, Younger neglects to mention a possible non-First Amendment argument in favor of free speech.

Penumbra theory is to some extent an argument based on constitutional structure, to which Younger does refer and reject. According to him, to say that freedom of speech would, regardless of the First Amendment, be found anyway to inhere in the nature of American government is to beg the question because it comes to this: given a government in which freedom of speech is necessary, freedom of speech is necessary.

Here Younger is a little too fast on the draw. The structural argument in favor of free speech is neither question-begging nor so easily dismissed. The governmental structure set up by the Constitution, especially in light of the Framers' intent (another factor not addressed by him), support at least a serious non-First Amendment justification for free speech. Indeed, some of the Framers, including Hamilton as the author of *Federalist* No. 84, thought a Bill of Rights unnecessary because government would have no power to interfere with basic rights. But Younger does not deign even to mention that bit of relevant history.

Outside the strictly constitutional realm, Younger is almost cavalier. He dismisses John Milton's glorious defense of freedom of the press in "Aeropagtica" as "incoherent," "tautological," and an "underdone" reasoned argument. "Tautological" is the epithet he also applies to John Stuart Mill's memorable discussion of free speech in "On Liberty." About all that he finds useful and relevant in these great writers is Mill's concept of self-regarding actions, which Younger uses as the springboard for his notion of sanctuary.

Concededly, the notion of sanctuary advanced as a new panacea by Younger is useful, but it is hardly original. On the contrary, it was discussed at length almost sixty years ago in 1958 by the Oxford intellectual historian Isaiah Berlin in his celebrated essay "Two Concepts of Liberty." In that essay, Berlin divides liberty into two types, "positive" and "negative," with negative liberty being what Younger now calls sanctuary. Although no difference exists between Berlin's negative liberty and Younger's sanctuary, Younger fails to give Berlin credit for the idea. This failure is particularly ungenerous since Younger cites and quotes from Berlin's book elsewhere in the article.

Quite apart from lack of originally and stinginess, Younger's treatment misses half of Berlin's message. Positive liberty, as Berlin uses the term, means political rights. It embodies the desire for self-government. Younger fails to see the positive liberty component in freedom of speech.

To defend free speech in terms of sanctuary or negative liberty alone is, then, only half the story, and perhaps not even the more important half. The other half of the story—Berlin's positive liberty—has played a large role in the development of free speech in America.

In his 1948 book *Free Speech and Its Relation to Self-Government*, Alexander Meklejohn pointed out that, "The First Amendment does not protect a 'freedom to speak.' It protects the freedom of those activities of thought and communication by which we govern. It is concerned not with a private right, but with a public power, a governmental responsibility."

Meiklejohn's theory can be read in the *United States Reports*. There, free speech has been justified not for some intrinsic value of speech or individual liberty, but because it is a necessary condition for making informed decisions about matters of government, decisions that all citizens in a democracy are called on to make. Speech provides information, the raw material from which citizens can make self-governing choices. Again and again, the Supreme Court has stressed the integral role of free speech to ideas and experience that citizens require for self-government.

Sanctuary is only the starting point. By itself, sanctuary cannot resolve hard constitutional choices. Whose sanctuary prevails when a speaker allegedly upsets the peace and quiet of an audience? What about libel and invasion of privacy, where both speaker and victim rely on a notion of sanctuary? What happens to sanctuary in the face of compelling countervailing considerations, like national security, which are used in balancing relative rights?

Free speech can and must be defended on several non-First Amendment grounds. It can and should be justified in terms of sanctuary (negative liberty), which Younger proposes. But he is simply and eggregiously wrong when he says, "There is no justification beyond this."

For free speech can also be justified in terms of positive liberty, which Younger ignores. It can find support in other constitutional provisions and doctrines left unmentioned by him. Freedom of speech could arguably be inferred from the structure of the Constitution and the intent of the Framers, which he too casually rejects or does not consider. It has deep roots.

A concept so fundamental and basic as free speech is part of the fabric of American life as we know it. The notion of sanctuary, even if it did not originate with Younger, is an important, but by no means the sole nor perhaps even the most important, justification for freedom of speech. Freedom of speech is the fountainhead of nearly every other form of freedom.

IV

What is the minimum number of pages that can be put between hard covers and still be called a book? We have all seen thin but nonetheless good books with less than two hundred pages. What about under one hundred pages? Fifty pages? Is there a sliding scale on which the shrinking number of pages changes a book into a booklet?

These questions come to mind when reading the eighty-three-page text of *The Irony of Free Speech*, published in 1996 by Owen M. Fiss, who teaches at Yale Law School. It is, in terms of number of pages, a very short book. But it is by no means an unimportant work. There has never been a direct relationship between number of pages and importance of a written book. After all, how long was Einstein's 1905 article on relativity?

Exemplifying this rule of experience, Fiss's compact little volume is a fine achievement. In addition to the virtues of brevity and conciseness, *The Irony of Free Speech* contains the much rarer merit of original thought on fundamental issues. Fiss undertakes that most difficult of tasks: to try to get us to think in a new way about old and familiar issues, and he does so with a clarity and precision, style and grace, that is both stimulating and impressive.

The book's stated purpose is to reexamine the conventional wisdom that the state is the "natural enemy of freedom." Fiss argues that the state "may also be a source of freedom," and he explores this "irony" in the free speech field.

To demonstrate his thesis, and to take it from the abstract to the concrete, Fiss asks us to consider three of today's most controversial free speech issues: hate speech, pornography and campaign finance. Each of these highly charged topics, according to Fiss, tests received ideas about the First Amendment. As to each category, sound and even cogent arguments can be made for—irony of ironies—state intervention on free speech grounds.

The heart of Fiss's approach, and what makes it truly exciting, is what he calls his "reconceptualizing" of the relevant problems. Reconceptualizing is a word that acts as a crucial signal to the reader. It means we are in some strenuous mental gymnastics.

Reconceptualizing any legal issue involves a number of steps. First, we have to identify the reasons (that is, the public policies) for a given rule. Then we have to see if new policy considerations or new configurations of old public policies exist. Finally, we need to see if the new evaluation leads to a different rule. This is, in essence, what law is all about.

Fiss is a master at reconceptualizing. At the outset he identifies two different theories of free speech, one "libertarian" and the other "democratic." The libertarian view is based on the notion that the First Amendment protects the individual interest in self-expression. The democratic theory of speech, by contrast, stresses social rather than individualistic values and aims to "broaden the terms of public discussion as a way of enabling common citizens to become aware of the issues before them," and to act on them.

These two basic theories tend to see the state differently. The libertarian view traditionally presumes that state involvement is antagonistic to free speech. The democratic theory views the state as having a need "to act to further the robustness of public debate, in circumstances where powers outside the state are stifling speech."

Then we get to the hard part—balancing the values in free expression against the countervalues advanced by the state to support regulation. Here we see "reconceptualization" in action. We cannot avoid the balancing, says Fiss, by taking the easy way out and saying that the activities at issue are not speech. Fiss, moreover, sees equality as a countervalue that has grown in importance over recent decades, so that free speech cases now pose a conflict between liberty and equality.

But choosing between liberty and equality presents its own problems. Fiss brushes aside the "preferred position doctrine"—the firstness of the First Amendment—as "little more than an assertion or a slogan" because "no reason is given for preferring liberty over equality." But then he says it is perhaps impossible to choose between such transcendent commitments, and the Constitution provides no guidance. Here Fiss sounds like Isaiah Berlin, the Oxford political philosopher who has often written about the "necessity and agony of choice" between "ends equally ultimate, equally sacred."

Fiss escapes this dilemma by recognizing a new countervalue: democracy itself. In other words, state intervention in the free speech area may be justified by a goal of ensuring the robustness of public debate. This creative use of policy analysis is Fiss's most significant contribution, even if it does not work in all cases.

For example, of the three categories Fiss looks at, only one—political expenditures—seems to fall squarely within Fiss's new countervalue. The *Buckley v. Valeo* and *Citizens United* line of decisions holding unconstitutional, on First Amendment grounds, mandatory limits on political contributions has come under mounting attack for essentially the reasons given by Fiss. A limit on campaign contributions would appear to enhance democracy and permit new or other voices to be heard in the political arena. Such limits would level the playing field and improve the fairness of the electoral process itself.

Unlike the *Buckley* and *Citizens United* situation, hate speech and pornography are less obvious candidates for his new analysis. Fiss argues that both hate speech and pornography have a "silencing effect" on would-be speakers and therefore skew public debate. The premise here is the "silencing effect," which Fiss claims is a "subtle psychological dynamic—one that disables or discredits a would-be speaker." Although justifications may exist for regulating hate speech or pornography, Fiss's "silencing effect" hardly seems the strongest or the most persuasive.

But the problems of particular application in no way lessen the magnitude of Fiss's achievement. This is a complicated area, and Fiss gives us a rare glimpse of how law changes and grows in such a complicated field. It is the methodology that counts. Reconceptualizing is the essence of the creative process, in law as well as elsewhere.

On finishing *The Irony of Free Speech*, one knows that he or she has read something of genuine value and has had a real intellectual experience. Fiss's ideas stay in the mind, bouncing around, dislodging other previously held notions. Even if we cannot specify the minimum number of pages to define a book, we know that *The Irony of Free Speech* achieves all that a book can hope to achieve. And maybe it does so not in spite of its having only eighty-three pages of text, but precisely because it is so terse and succinct. Powerful brevity may be the soul of persuasion.

21

RELIGIOUS LIBERTY

If the past few decades have taught us anything, it is that people do not live by reason alone. Something beyond the rational is often necessary. For billions of people, that something is religion.

Even in our supposedly enlightened modern world, religion obviously continues to be crucial, driving force. Recent history and current events have brought home religion's still powerful influence. Indeed, despite modern science and education, the past fifty years have seen a revival of religion, and this revival has not been limited to Islam. In parts of our own country, creationism still competes with evolution for acceptance.

For such people, religion meets needs not satisfied elsewhere. It is a reaction against modern life, a life marked by secularism, uncertainty, moral relativism and self-indulgence. Modern life with its easy mobility often separates people from their roots. All religions give people a sense of identity. It helps many people cope and be better people.

Given the persistent and growing hold religion has, a prudent free thinker learns tolerance. It is no use mocking religious faith, as Richard Dawkins, Sam Harris, and Christopher Hitchens have done. You are no match for it, as Tom Paine, Friedrich Nietzsche and H.L. Mencken learned. All you do is make enemies. You persuade no one; either you are a believer or not. Faith, by definition, is not open to rational argument or proof.

The revival of religion underscores the fundamental importance of religious liberty. If religion is to some extent irrational, all the more reason for us—now more than ever—to protect the rights of religious minorities. In this country, we try to do that with the religion clauses of the First Amendment, specifically the Free Exercise Clause and the

Establishment Clause. Under those clauses, government can neither abridge the "free exercise" of one's religion, nor "establish" a religion. For almost four hundred years, going back to the colonists who came here to escape religious persecution, Americans have struggled with the meaning of religious liberty and with the height, width and impermeability of the so-called wall separating church and state.

I

That struggle is the subject of *Religious Liberty in America: Political Safeguards*, a 2003 book by Louis Fisher. Fisher starts from the uncontroversial shared premise that religious liberty needs to be protected (although he does not make clear exactly how much such liberty he would favor, which is of course where problems arise). What does make the book controversial, however, is its basic argument.

Fisher's "central thesis" is that we should look to the political branches—the legislative and executive branches—as well as to the courts to protect religious freedom. He views the issue from a separation of powers perspective, which is his specialty as a staff researcher at the Library of Congress. His thesis "runs against the grain" because we have mistakenly become too accustomed to thinking of the courts, particularly the U.S. Supreme Court, as the single most appropriate guardian of religious liberty. Most of Fisher's book is devoted to disproving, one way or another, the proposition that "judges can be trusted to protect individual and minority rights."

Fisher is correct that courts in America have not always covered themselves with glory in their rulings on political and individual liberties. As he rightly says, "The Supreme Court's record in safeguarding minority and religious rights has never been attractive or reliable." Exhibit A for Fisher is the hateful 1857 *Dred Scott* decision holding that slaves were property and not citizens. Exhibit B is the Civil Rights Cases of 1883, which struck down legislation passed by Congress in 1875 giving African-Americans equal access to public accommodations. He also discusses judicial decisions enforcing the ill-conceived Sedition Act of 1798 and denying equal rights to women.

The stars seemed to be properly aligned for the timing of Fisher's book. An article in the May 26, 2003 issue of *The New Republic* echoes the same basic theme. "It is now obvious," writes Jeffrey Rosen in that magazine, that "Congress has proved a far more vigorous defender of liberty and privacy than courts." Rosen, writing about post 9/11 judicial acquiescence to government for expanded surveillance authority, goes on: "The truth is that the vision of heroic judges bravely interposing themselves against popular opinion has always been a myth."

But, even so, there have been moments when courts have risen to the occasion and made memorable decisions in favor of freedom. Everyone's most shining example of such a ruling is *Brown v. Board of Education*. But others abound, and we all have our favorites. Indeed, Fisher writes about several of them, including *Engel v. Vitale* (outlawing school prayer), *West Virginia Board of Education v. Barnette* (outlawing compulsory flag salute), and *Wisconsin v. Yoder* (allowing religious interests of the Amish to outweigh state's interest in compelling school attendance).

Although writing about the political processes, Fisher seems to miss the importance of politics to his general approach. Whether the judicial or political branches will be more sympathetic to individual liberties often depends on politics. When one branch is stingy or crabbed in its attitude, the others may not be, and vice versa. Put another way, the courts can step in, as the Supreme Court did in the 1960s, when the political process fails to act or acts inappropriately. Or, as happened not too long ago, if federal courts interpret the U. S. Constitution adversely to individual liberties, state courts may take a broader view of liberty guarantees in state constitutions. Federalism and separation of powers create several centers of power.

In light of this well-known interplay of politics and sources of law, Fisher's conclusion is anything but controversial. Who could argue with the following statement he puts forth as it if were a new revelation: "Individual rights are best protected by society as a whole, operating through the regular political process and with vigorous exchanges between federal and state courts"? No one would disagree with Fisher's concluding line: "Who protects minority rights? You do." Such platitudes served up as profundities are unilluminating.

Far more useful and stimulating is Fisher's welcome study of Supreme Court decisions restricting religious liberty that were later overturned or modified by the political process. These chapters are fascinating case studies about the interaction between courts, politics and public opinion on basic issues of human freedom. They substantiate the claim made by Rosen in *The New Republic* that "on the rare occasions when courts have challenged a deeply felt current in public opinion . . . they have been forced to retreat in the face of backlash from the political branches." The particular vantage point adopted by Fisher is persuasive, even if it only corroborates our instinct that politics and public opinion both play vital roles in lawmaking, that practical experience counts more than abstract logic.

Fisher picks good examples. Most protections for conscientious objectors, for instance, came not from the courts, but from the political branches. In another famous example, the Supreme Court reversed its position on whether a compulsory flag salute violated religious rights of Jehovah's Witnesses. Although the Court in 1940 upheld the salute, three years later, after some intense public criticism, the Court overturned the first ruling. A 1986 decision against the wearing of yarmulkes in the military was reversed a year later by Congress. Religious liberty for Native Americans, including religious use of peyote, has been secured mainly through the political process, not by judicial rulings.

Such examples show the benefits of multiple centers of power and expose the weakness of any authoritarian system of government. When power is dispersed, no decision is absolutely final. Discussion goes on and change is possible. Judges, legislators and executive officials, at many levels, all have roles to play. Fisher's book highlights such checks and balances and demonstrates how the swinging political pendulum has affected civil liberties, especially religious freedom. And, in an era of clashing civilizations and global religious resurgence, religious freedom and tolerance are high on the list of values to protect.

II

Events of the past few decades are enough to raise doubts about the future of religious freedom in this country. Religion is pushing more and more into the public space. In the 1980s, the U.S. Supreme Court upheld the constitutionality of a city's Nativity-scene display. In doing so, the Court said that the traditional "wall of separation" between church and state is no more than in inapt metaphor.

At the same time, President Reagan, supposedly with eighty percent of the public behind him, lobbied extensively for Senate approval of a constitutional amendment to allow prayers in public schools. Although the proposed amendment fell short of the necessary two-thirds vote, the significant thing is that more than half the Senate voted for it.

Since then, conservative politicians have promoted legislation (*e.g.*, anti-abortion laws, creationism in textbooks, use of public facilities for religious instruction) based on religious attitudes. These events show that two of the most crucial lessons of history and our national experience are being ignored.

The first of these neglected points is the relationship between religious tolerance and pluralism. Governmentally composed prayers caused many colonists to leave England for religious freedom in America. But, unfortunately, some of these very colonists, when they found themselves sufficiently in control of colonial governments, passed laws making their own religion the official religion of their respective colonies. This sad historical fact strongly suggests that people are more prone to favor religious tolerance when they are a minority than when they are a controlling majority.

The truth of this insight is borne out by recent events in other countries. In Poland, where the population is ninety-five percent Catholic, there have been widespread demonstrations protesting the removal of crucifixes from classrooms. In Israel, Ultra-Orthodox Jews have protested and sometimes used violence against fellow citizens who violate the Sabbath by using cars or keeping businesses open or whose dress is supposedly immodest. Neither Poland nor Israel—nor a host of other lands—has the religious diversity or the heritage of religious tolerance that America has. What is right for Poland or Israel may not be right for the United States with its unique national experience.

Tolerance, then, has a better chance for survival in a pluralistic society. Where there are many religious sects and no one sect is dominant, each one is more likely to favor tolerance. Where any one sect predominates, there is a greater possibility for intolerance. America has been and still is a pluralistic society in terms of religion. For inexplicable reasons, this point has received little attention in the recent past.

The second crucial, but for the most part undiscussed, point is the true nature of what is at stake in these recent controversies over religious freedom. From media accounts, one would think the issue was no more than simply prayers in school, a municipal creche, anti-abortion laws, or competing scientific theories about the beginning of the universe. If that were the whole issue, there would probably be no debate, and certainly much more subdued feelings. But those are not the real issue; they are the first faint hint of potential trouble, the blip on the constitutional radar screen that triggers the First Amendment's distant early warning system.

The real concern is that such things as school prayers, a city creche, anti-abortion laws and creationism will inevitably create a climate that could lead to fearsome consequences. As the Supreme Court wrote in the 1962 case banning school prayer, "governmentally established religions and religious persecutions go hand in hand."

In and of themselves, school prayers and municipal creches are perhaps even relatively innocuous. The Republic would survive them. But they represent a step in the wrong direction by encouraging divisiveness. They inevitably stress distinctions between religious beliefs. Ultimately, it is a question of line-drawing, and it is better to draw the line so as to take no chances. Religious intolerance, a product of religious divisiveness, must be stopped in its incipiency.

Religious tolerance in America is a fragile thing. Freedom of conscience has always occupied a special place in American thinking. Of course, as the Supreme Court has said, "the history of man is inseparable from the history of religion," and religion has helped countless millions lead their lives. But the world has seen too many holy wars and religious persecutions not to make us wary of any effort, no matter how slight, innocent or well intentioned, to reduce or infringe on religious freedom.

The danger of religious intolerance is not merely a curiosity from the far distant past. The most cursory glance at the current world picture shows continuing religious conflicts, even in otherwise civilized places. Northern Ireland (Protestant against Catholic), the Mideast (*e.g.*, Jew against Muslim, Sunni against Shiite) and India (Hindi against Muslim) come quickly to mind. Every day we see sectarian conflicts with their appalling toll in casualties. And the memories of those still living recoil at the thought that more could have been done for victims of religious persecution in Europe seventy years ago.

Perhaps the recent assaults on religious freedom should be chalked up to politics. Perhaps something deeper is at work. At any rate, recent events are not calculated to create a climate of tolerance. If we are lucky, such events will be an aberration.

At the very least, recent events teach us that each generation must be tested. The old battles are not won forever. They must be fought anew lest our precious freedoms gradually slip away through inattention or lack of vigilance. "The greatest dangers to liberty," wrote Justice Louis Brandeis in 1928, "lurk in insidious encroachment by men of zeal, well-meaning but without understanding."

22

DEFINING PRIVACY—A TASK STILL UNDONE

In our complex modern world filled with data banks, credit information, tax returns, sophisticated and intrusive electronic equipment, the notion of privacy is attractive, if not essential. A massive surveillance states makes us all dearly want a zone where what we do or say is not public property. In a famous passage, Justice Brandeis once referred to the right of privacy as "the right to be let alone—the most comprehensive of rights and the right most valued by civilized man."

But thus to describe privacy fails to enlighten in a meaningful way. No one seriously doubts the importance of privacy as a value. Yet what is it? It is a shorthand, catch-all phrase that we tend to use loosely in common speech. Loose language breeds fuzzy thinking.

The need for privacy, we all know only too well, is a highly vexing problem of modern life. One of the most controversial and polarizing social and political issues in contemporary America—abortion— is often discussed in terms of the right of privacy. So are other, only slightly less volatile, issues. Despite all that has been written about the right of privacy, however, little has gone to the heart of the problems of diminished privacy in today's world and to the basic reasons for recognizing such a right.

The real and agonizingly difficult question is when, if ever, privacy should yield to accommodate other, perhaps equally important or conceivably even more precious values. We need to find guides in the past and present to help us cope with the future.

Part of this task is accomplished by *The Right to Privacy*, published in 1997, by Ellen Alderman and Caroline Kennedy. Caroline Kennedy the co-author of a book on the right to privacy? It is a little like Zsa Zsa Gabor co-authoring a book on the pleasures of being single, or

Woody Allen co-authoring a book on parenting, or Anthony Weiner co-authoring a book on how to sext.

And yet the combination works, at least here. *The Right to Privacy* is a serious and worthwhile treatment of a fundamental problem. These co-authors, lawyers both, have written a fitting sequel to their 1991 best seller *In Our Defense: The Bill of Rights in Action*. In their second book, Alderman and Kennedy explore the right of privacy in a number of different contexts: law enforcement, family life and procreation, the media, public disclosure of intimacy, the workplace, and cyberspace. It is an illuminating and useful canvass, as far as it goes.

But it could have gone much further. For all the virtues of their book (and there are many), for all the cases and contexts in which they examine the right to privacy (and they are wide-ranging), Alderman and Kennedy fail to grapple with the most fundamental, essential and overarching controversies surrounding the right to privacy.

Those controversies concern more than particular contexts in which privacy is balanced against some other countervailing value. Left unaddressed in the Alderman-Kennedy book is a larger, more far-reaching thesis, one that exposes the proper approach. That approach goes behind the particular controversies to the constitutional, philosophical and political tensions enveloping an implied right.

This larger, unstated thesis starts with the frank recognition that privacy is a grab-bag term for a host of problems, many of them quite different from one another. As Alderman and Kennedy say at the outset, "Privacy covers many things." The "things" that "privacy" covers are quite disparate, ranging from solitude for thought and contemplation, to self-actualization, to keeping government and the media at bay. Privacy is a common, not a technical, term, and the many different topics it encompasses should make us wary about generalizations.

Second, privacy is an evolving concept. Like the meaning of "equal protection of the laws" and "cruel and unusual punishment," privacy takes on different definitions in different times and places, and under different historical, societal and technological circumstances. Our notions of privacy change, as do the threats to it. "There is less privacy than there used to be," Alderman and Kennedy rightly observe.

Add to this the bedrock problem of the lack of standards surrounding the right of privacy. Inasmuch as the Constitution does not explicitly mention the right to privacy, courts and legislatures (both federal and state) must give content to the term.

Privacy thus becomes a focal point—even a battleground—for two strong traditions in American constitutional law. One tradition emphasizes—as the primary protector of freedom—law as opposed to discretion, written laws opposed to unwritten law, precise rather than vague laws and judicial restraint rather than judicial activism.

This tradition worries about judges exercising arbitrary power, roaming at large in the constitutional field, and drawing on merely personal and private motives. It is exemplified by Justice Hugo Black, who in 1969 wrote, "If the judges, in deciding whether laws are unconstitutional, are to be left only to the admonitions of their own consciences, why was it that the Founders gave us a written Constitution at all?"

An equally long and honorable tradition seeks the same goal— protection of liberty—by another, very different approach. This second tradition is based on the premise that courts must have power and discretion to protect freedoms not covered by written law and to protect minority rights from majority power. In the eyes of this second tradition, no written constitution is ever capable of enumerating all of the rights of the people. Courts must, this tradition argues, find some sort of safety valve in the Constitution to cover such unenumerated rights.

The right to privacy is one of those constitutional safety valves. As a matter of text and nothing else, several passages in the Constitution and its amendments might support inferences—so-called penumbras—to protect unenumerated rights like the right to privacy. This was the creative thrust of the Supreme Court's 1965 famous (or infamous, depending on your point of view) *Griswold* case.

That odd case involved a vestigial state law prohibiting married couples from using or receiving information about contraceptives. Finding no explicit or specific constitutional right of privacy, a majority of the Court in *Griswold* reasoned, in an opinion written by Justice William Douglas, that "specific guarantees in the Bill of Rights have penumbras, formed by emanations from those guarantees that help give them life and substance." The anticontraceptive law in *Griswold*, ruled the Court, violated a "penumbral right" of privacy, radiating from several specific constitutional provisions creating a "zone of privacy.

Griswold meant that, even without an explicit or specific right of privacy mentioned in the Constitution, there are certain areas of life beyond the reach of government intrusion. Whether based on *Griswold*'s controversial "penumbra theory" or the liberty protected by the Fifth and Fourteenth Amendments, the idea of privacy is to ward off interference, to preserve an area of life independent of social control. It embodies the desire not to be impinged upon, to be left to oneself, to prevent the encroachment of public authority.

In 1977, fully twelve years after *Griswold* was decided, the Supreme Court said that, "The concept of constitutional right of privacy still remains largely undefined."

The one certain conclusion to be drawn here is that we deal not with absolutes, but with a balancing of interests. The real and unavoidable task is to reconcile the tension between privacy and the value in competition with it. Alderman and Kennedy are right when they say, "We need to take privacy apart and analyze the competing legal principles and societal interests." It is a task still to be done.

PART THREE

PERSONALITIES

Civil liberties mean nothing without people—judges, lawyers, clients, commentators—to give them content and bring them to life. A high-sounding right on paper is only that—a piece of paper. But that observation is true about much in the law. Only flesh and blood people take the law out of the library, off the shelves and make it live. Like any other field, law has some interesting personalities. Here are a few that have caught my eye.

23

HUGO BLACK, FELIX FRANKFURTER AND CIVIL LIBERTIES

"No two members of the modern Supreme Court have been more important in developing the contemporary constitutional debate than Hugo Black and Felix Frankfurter." This thought forms the premise of a superb book published in 1989 called *The Antagonists: Hugo Black, Felix Frankfurter and Civil Liberties in Modern America* by James F. Simon, a professor at New York Law School. *The Antagonists* excels in every way: it is original in concept, unique in approach, brilliant in execution. Not since *Gideon's Trumpet* by Anthony Lewis has a book about the Supreme Court succeeded so well.

Simon's volume ranks with the best writing on the Court. It is special in its use of the adversary relationship between two leading justices as its theme. Simon is also unusual in the balanced judgment he displays throughout. Since *The Antagonists* was published almost twenty-five years ago, Simon has shown the same balanced judgment in the more recent series of books he has written the relationships between a number of chief justices and presidents (Marshall and Jefferson, Taney and Lincoln, and Hughes and FDR).

The success of *The Antagonists* flows in large part from its luminous style. The book is an easy read, clear, and extraordinarily accessible, ensuring wide popular appeal. By writing in a conversational, familiar tone rather than hiding behind the thick, obfuscatory veil of some academic scholarship, the author sacrifices nothing in terms of insight, while at the same time greatly broadening his audience without condescension. To write so accessibly often takes far more care, skill, and understanding than to lapse lazily into jargon and commonplace habits of arcane professional thought.

Simon's popular writing style is no accident. At Yale Law School, he studied under the late Fred Rodell, a maverick law professor who specialized in teaching how to write about law for the general reader. Rodell hated footnotes and all other badges of pseudo-scholarship, and his teaching profoundly affected Simon—for the better.

One of the author's most winning stylistic devices enlivens the start of each chapter where he includes a fascinating and evocative vignette related to the chapter's theme. For a chapter on Justice Black's background, it is a word portrait of a Populist candidate campaigning for governor of Alabama. For another, it is a conversation during oral argument on the Supreme Court bench between Justice Frankfurter and Justice Frank Murphy complaining about Justice Douglas's political ambitions. Yet another depicts Justice Robert Jackson's surprisingly bad cross-examination of Nazi air marshal Hermann Goering at the Nuremburg Trials.

These gripping vignettes set the stage for the author to explore in sparkling prose the nature of Supreme Court justices, how they are selected, and how they perform. The "central purpose" of the book, according to the author, is "to trace Black's and Frankfurter's backgrounds, explain their very different responses to fundamental constitutional questions and gauge the consequences of their work for their nation." A "second focus" is "personal" and appears in "off-the Court portraits of Black and Frankfurter in an effort to understand them as individuals and as they interacted with each other."

Simon portrays Justices Frankfurter and Black as vying for leadership of the Court. Frankfurter, with his extraordinary academic credentials, expected to emerge in control. The turning point for Frankfurter was the flag salute cases.

In *Gobitis*, the first flag salute case, Frankfurter had written an opinion in 1940 for an eight-justice majority (which included Justice Black) holding, for reasons for patriotism and judicial restraint, that it was constitutional to require schoolchildren, over their religious objections, to salute the flag.

Three years later, in the *Barnette* case, Frankfurter's influence and majority had so eroded that *Gobitis* was overruled in one of the Court's most eloquent tributes to freedom of conscience and the transcendant nature of civil liberties. "With the *Barnette* decision," writes Simon,

"Frankfurter's leadership of the liberal wing of the Court . . . was obliterated."

Although Black's influence grew as a result of *Barnette*, he too fell to his judicial nadir during World War II. For it was none other than Black who wrote the Court's opinion upholding the government's conduct in the Japanese-American exclusion cases. According to Simon—and most of us—*Korematsu* was "the worst judicial opinion that Hugo Black wrote in his thirty-four years on the Court . . . Black's suggestion that the policy was justified by military necessity was ludicrous."

Unlike Earl Warren, who later regretted his role as California governor favoring the wartime relocation policy, Black "never revealed the slightest tremor of remorse." All of this suggests that the stress and anxiety of war makes for strange and often repressive judicial rulings. Fear is no friend of civil liberties.

The author has the extreme good sense to avoid falling into the trap of classifying the Justices by political labels. As the author intelligently notes, Black's and Frankfurter's interpretations of the Bill of Rights could be "confusing to those who automatically place Black in the liberal camp and labeled Frankfurter the Court conservative."

On Fourth Amendment search and seizure questions, for instance, Frankfurter was consistently more liberal than Black. In *Everson*, a famous First Amendment religion case, it was Black, who over Justice Frankfurter's dissent, wrote the majority opinion upholding public funding of busing for private religious schools. And during the Cold War, with the exception of the *Dennis* case, both Justices "compiled an impressive record" of protecting civil liberties.

In the *Rosenberg* atom spy case, the two Justices were the only ones who voted in each instance to hear argument. (This does not even include Black's votes, after Frankfurter left the Court, against civil rights protests and against finding a constitutional right of privacy.)

Yet we persist in thinking of Justice Black as the more liberal of the two. No doubt this feeling is attributable to his grand, absolutist reading of the First Amendment—the famous "no law means no law" approach—as opposed to Frankfurter's balancing approach. Adding to Black's liberal reputation was his longstanding debate with Frankfurter over whether the Due Process Clause of the Fourteenth Amendment incorporated the Bill of Rights and made them applicable to the states.

In support of his constitutional positions, Black was able to mount simple and compelling arguments, cast in plain and moving English, that often sounded like rousing stump speeches for individual rights in a democracy. More importantly, perhaps, Simon observes that "Felix Frankfurter was left behind" by the Warren Court's egalitarian revolution and protection for individual rights and liberties.

The author's final assessment of the two antagonists is unusually fair and balanced, perhaps too much so. Simon says the open challenges to each other often pushed them to their best and most impassioned advocacy. He also points out how much they "shared basic goals for the nation" and agreed on such issues as individual rights, even if they disagreed on how to protect them. As Simon writes: "Justice Frankfurter's judicial contribution was vitally important to the development of the jurisprudence of individual rights on the modern Supreme Court. The expansion of civil liberties and, particularly, First Amendment rights was firmly established in our constitutional literature because of Hugo Black. But the limits of judicial authority were better understood and more fully appreciated because of the opinions of Felix Frankfurter. In the end, both Justices served as the nation's constitutional guardians, bound together by the recognition that they should have an absolute faith in America's democratic institutions and the individual freedoms those institutions protect."

The evenhandedness of Simon's judgment is belied by unpleasant descriptions elsewhere in his own book. The author recognizes how Frankfurter was "overbearing," an inveterate flatterer, an "intrepid meddler," and "hypocritical" when he complained of his colleagues' political concerns. Frankfurter's diaries are filled with nasty comments about people he pretended to befriend. And he instigated some of the worst feuds among members of the Court: Frankfurter infuriated Douglas and Warren, who would not speak to him for long stretches. Black, in contrast, remained unflappable amid controversy.

This is not a book only about the past. It reverberates with current issues, constantly moving the reader's reactions from past to present. From the start, with the prologue's description of Frankfurter's Senate confirmation hearing, the book strikes a familiar chord in the reader's mind. In the wake of the 1987 Robert Bork confirmation hearings, we read with fascination how in 1939 Frankfurter "was the first nominee in the one hundred fifty-year history of the U.S. Supreme Court to be subjected to a full inquiry by a Senate committee." We learn how Frankfurter thought the "proposed public examination was in bad taste" and "potentially damaging to the best interests of the Court."

Memories of Bork's more recent experience crowd in on us as we find out more about Frankfurter's performance before the committee. Although he initially declined to appear, Frankfurter changed his mind after two days of "poisonous swill concocted for the committee by assorted oddballs, witch-hunters and anti-Semites who testified that Justice Frankfurter's confirmation would threaten the Republic." When he finally testified, he announced that he would not "discuss anything he considered inappropriate." He told the senators, "I should think it improper for a nominee no less than for a member of the Court to express his personal views on controversial political issues affecting the Court." Since his views were contained in his many published writings, he said "he had no intention of supplementing his past record with 'present declarations.'"

Contemporary reaction to Frankfurter's credentials remind us again of Bork. According to *The Nation*, "Frankfurter's whole life has been a preparation for the Supreme Court, and his appointment has an aesthetically satisfying inevitability. No other appointee in our history has gone to the Court so fully prepared for its great tasks." In 1987, *The Wall Street Journal* used almost the same words to describe Bork.

Simon's new book underscores how hard it is to predict a justice's performance. Frankfurter, the liberal crusader before his appointment, became on the Court a conservative proponent of judicial restraint. And Black the former member of the Ku Klux Klan, earned as a justice a reputation as a champion of civil liberties. As retired Justice Lewis Powell said, after he wrote an opinion at odds with his pre-Court views, "It is different when you are a justice. You wear a different hat, have a different responsibility."

Other now-then comparisons abound. The chapter on Frankfurter's background opens with a description of a 1919 meeting between the future justice and Arabia's Prince Feisal at the Paris Peace Conference following World War I. Justice Brandeis had asked Frankfurter to let Arab representatives know that American Zionists were "committed to Arab rights" and "peaceful coexistence" in Palestine. Frankfurter's dispute in the 1920s with Harvard over the so-called Jewish quota makes us think about the current Asian quota used by many American college admissions officers.

These echos of past and present highlight the recurring nature of legal issues. To prevent slippage, each generation must fight some battles anew. Progress is not always obvious.

Summing up, Simon judiciously concludes that, "The Court and the nation were stronger because Black and Frankfurter served *together*." And so too, we are wiser and have a better appreciation of the synergy created by these two jurists because Simon wrote this sympathetic, sensitive, excellent, and wonderfully clear book.

24

ERIC NEISSER AND THE SPIRIT OF CIVIL LIBERTIES

Forget that the Bicentennial of the Bill of Rights has, in a technical sense, long passed. Do not worry if you let 1991 slip by without reading a book on the Bill of Rights. What matters is that the spirit animating the Bill of Rights thrives and flourishes in our time, and affects our controversies, regardless of the precise year for a calendar celebration. And now, at least, we have a book that is up to the task of celebrating the Bill of Rights the way it ought to be celebrated.

Recapturing the Spirit by the late Eric Neisser of Rutgers Law School is not a dry history of the drafting of the first ten amendments to the Constitution, but a stimulating, exciting and provocative collection of essays about current civil liberties controversies. History plays a role in Neisser's writings, to be sure, but only insofar as the past helps us deal with the present, not as an end in itself. Neisser "remind[s] the reader of our Constitutional roots," and the result is a tremendous success.

"The principles of the Bill of Rights, which is now two hundred years old, are immutable," the author writes in his opening sentence. "But," he continues with his credo, "they must be rediscovered by each generation and applied to the realities of each age." Neisser devotes the rest of the book to applying the Bill of Rights to the realities of *our* age.

If we literally heeded those who advocate adherence to the Framers' original intent, we would not apply the Bill of Rights at all to wiretaps, respirators and television, because the Framers obviously did not think about such problems. Such an approach, however, would render the Bill of Rights a dead letter—a quaint eighteenth-century monograph. But the Framers were not just drafting a campaign platform; they were writing for the indefinite future. We live in that future, so we must work with the document, and the principles, that they left us.

Commenting on the Founders' future as our own, Neisser divides his book into several sections. After an overview of constitutional rights today, he focuses on free expression, privacy, civil rights and discrimination, poverty and the right to choice, the criminal process, freedom of religion, and a grab-bag on war, schools, youth and love. Such a broad canvas allows scope for the author's constitutional views. But to list the subjects covered by his masterful pen fails to convey the impact of his persuasive and powerful writing.

One of the most gracious of Neisser's essays is the tribute to Justice Brennan on his retirement in 1990. "Some have the title," Neisser begins. "Some hold the pursestrings. Others lead by force of personality, example or plain hard work. William J. Brennan Jr., though never the Chief Justice in title, essentially led the Supreme Court for most of his thirty years there." According to Neisser, the "Brennan Court" gave "life to abstract principles" and "brought the Constitution home to everyone." In a sentence with meaning to a whole generation, he writes: "Many of us who chose the law profession in the 1960s did so because of Justice Brennan's assurance that the law, and in particular constitutional law, can be a positive force for social change."

These writings, many of which were published first in his "Civil Liberties Today" column in the *New Jersey Law Journal*, are, by every measure, first-rate.

Neisser is a consummate essayist. He writes with grace, verve and conviction, managing to compress within a few pages impressive analyses of difficult constitutional issues. His essays are models of legal writing at its best. For example, one essay begins: "There are two problems with privacy: we are not sure exactly what we mean by it, and it is not mentioned by the Bill of Rights." Blessed with a keen awareness of both logic and language, he dispenses his insightful commentary without complicating sentence structure or off-putting legal argot.

A law professor Neisser may have been, but he did not write like an academic trying to wow or impress readers with hard-to-understand theories. His conversational and idiomatic American prose, like the judicial opinions of Supreme Court Justices Hugo Black and Robert Jackson, is a delight to read. And the readability of the prose greatly enhances the clarity of what he has to say. Indeed, the one quality these essays epitomize more than any other is clear thinking and clear writing.

Neisser, who died much too young in 1999 at the age of fifty-two, has a special vantage point and superb credentials for writing this book. He was a teacher of constitutional law and litigation at Rutgers Law School. At the time of his death, he had just become the dean of Franklin Pierce Law Center in New Hampshire. Before teaching, he was for two years Legal Director of the American Civil Liberties Union of New Jersey. Having litigated, even up to the Supreme Court, the types of civil liberties cases he writes about, he knows at first hand what the issues are and how they are played out, not always happily.

This was Neisser's first and only book, death having sadly deprived us of others. A proud product of New York City public schools, he graduated near the top of his class from the Bronx High School of Science in the mid-1960s. He raced through the University of Chicago in three years, having been allowed to skip the freshman year based on placement exams. His next stop was Yale Law School, where he excelled and became note and comment editor of the *Yale Law Journal*.

Neisser could have worked anywhere on graduating from law school. He could easily have gone to a large firm and begun the climb to lucrative partnership. Instead, he consistently chose a course closer to his heart, even if not his wallet. After law school, he clerked for Judge Frank Coffin of the First Circuit, one of the most respected and intelligent appellate judges in the federal system. No doubt the later, more potent combination of Yale Law School and Judge Coffin, with their stress on public service, overcame the Chicago School market theories he imbibed at the fount as an undergraduate.

Following his clerkship, he went on to teach, and to think and to write about law. He wrote his share of academic law review pieces, and worked at reforming the federal courts on the West Coast. But throughout his career, the one abiding theme was his concern for civil liberties. So it is that, while relevant, neither his job history nor his extraordinary academic talent is what uniquely qualifies him for the task of having written this book. Neisser's special qualification was his professional attitude, his way of viewing the law.

Neisser admits, "One need not agree with all, or indeed with any, of my positions." But his hope for the book is not to make converts. His objective is broader. He wants to "help people re-think the work of James Madison and his colleagues and determine its meaning for today."

25

HITCHENS vs. HOLMES

Christopher Hitchens, the journalist and author who died in 2011, is known for his vibrant expression of strong and contrary opinions on a wide range of topics, including that towering giant of American law, Oliver Wendell Holmes.

Most of us in the law revere Holmes, and with good reason. We first meet him in our course on constitutional law and never forget him. Civil War hero, philosopher, jurist, Holmes lived a full and active life that inspires us. We still read his crisp, penetrating, memorable judicial opinions with pleasure and admiration. His lively personality, his deep reading, his intellectual tolerance, and his astonishing way with words make Holmes a brilliant legal beacon and, to many of us, one of the greatest judges in American history.

Hitchens disagrees. In a 1994 book review, Hitchens refers to the "power-worshiping jurisprudence of that old coward and fraud Oliver Wendell Holmes." And in 2006, Hitchens describes the "clear and present danger" test as "the fatuous verdict of the greatly overpraised Justice Oliver Wendell Holmes." Hitchens does not mince words, nor did he elaborate or explain.

So much for Oliver Wendell Holmes! There goes another glittering reputation. Or does it?

We who get paid to argue for a living are allowed, maybe even obliged, to examine what Hitchens says about Holmes. The adversary system we are fond of permits a brief on Holmes's behalf, so that we can all make up our minds properly, after hearing both sides.

Although Hitchens does not explain what he means by a "power-worshipping jurisprudence," we know what he is driving at. As a judge, Holmes believed in democracy. That belief meant, for Holmes, that the power of the people, as expressed through majority vote of their elected representatives, should generally determine what the law should be. That is why Holmes rarely used judicial review to void laws except when the majority violated certain cherished individual rights.

To Hitchens, such deference to democratic majorities means Holmes worshipped the power of people, the tyranny of the majority. Hitchens forgets that the alternative is judges imposing their own subjective values on society. The really tough question has always been *when* unelected judges in a democracy should override the wishes of the people's elected representatives. Hitchens supplies no answer. Of course the fundamental debate over judicial review and constitutional interpretation continues to this day.

Hitchens next calls Holmes an "old coward." Old, yes (Holmes retired from the Court when he was almost ninety-one), but a coward? Hitchens cannot mean coward in the sense of lacking physical courage. Holmes dropped out of college (Harvard) to enlist in the Union Army and was wounded three times before the Civil War was over. Those searing wartime experiences may have influenced Holmes's later attitude toward freedom of speech during war.

Hitchens must be alleging that Holmes was guilty of some form of intellectual cowardice. But Holmes never took a position publicly out of fear, when he privately believed something else. His dissent in a high profile antitrust case brought down the wrath of Teddy Roosevelt, the president who appointed him.

Likewise, how was Holmes a fraud? Hitchens does not say. Presumably Hitchens means that Holmes had a reputation as a "liberal" but often made "conservative" rulings. But it is all a matter of context and balance. Compared to almost all of his fellow Supreme Court justices, Holmes did indeed seem liberal. Whom does Hitchens prefer to Holmes? Rufus Peckham? Edward Sanford? Come on.

In calling it a "fatuous verdict," Hitchens seems to be saying that Holmes' famous "clear and present danger" formula for resolving free speech cases was silly. Hitchens implies that Holmes pretended to rely on his supposedly inane (that is what "fatuous" means) test only to rule frequently against free speech claims. But those unfortunate rulings came before Holmes saw the light in 1919 in the *Abrams* case.

Holmes's deep and tolerant attitude toward freedom of expression still shines through brightly in those wonderful, stirring, almost poetic dissents of his in *Abrams* ("free trade in ideas"), *Gitlow* ("Every idea is an incitement . . . . Eloquence may set fire to reason"), and *Schwimmer* ("freedom for the thought that we hate"), cases familiar to all first-year law students and lovers of freedom of the mind.

It is simply impossible to review those Holmes free speech opinions and call them "fatuous." They are anything but. One may disagree with them, one may even try to improve on them, but they are great judicial opinions, rhetorical masterpieces, among the finest defenses of freedom of thought ever written.

We come finally to what is probably the core of Hitchens' critique of Holmes—that Holmes has been "greatly overpraised." If there is one dominant theme running through Hitchens's entire body of work, it is his pose as a contrarian and iconoclast. For Hitchens, it was a way of separating himself from the rest of the herd of commentators. If most of the world thinks one thing, Hitchens the contrarian takes the opposite point of view and asserts it, often with a slash-and-burn, take-no-prisoners style of argument. Hitchens seemed to relish playing the role of contrarian, of taking a combative approach to what everyone else believes. One can easily imagine what a legal brief written by Hitchens would have looked like: a scorched earth personal attack on his adversary.

So it was with Hitchens on Holmes. Most people praise Holmes; therefore Hitchens, true to form, harshly criticizes him. To what end?

Hitchens's iconoclastic attitude toward Holmes is ironic. For Holmes in his time was himself considered a great iconoclast. He led a revolution against the purely deductive approach to judicial decisionmaking that had dominated nineteenth-century legal thinking. The clarion call of Holmes's legal revolution famously stated that "experience" and "the felt necessities of the time"—policy considerations—count more in the "life of the law" than logic. Holmes the iconoclast has now become the target of an iconoclast like Hitchens.

A clue to evaluating Hitchens's criticism of Holmes can be found in the writing of the American author Hitchens most resembles, H.L. Mencken. Like Hitchens, Mencken too was an iconoclast, perhaps the iconoclast par excellence. Like Hitchens, Mencken too deployed a muscular, memorable prose style that left the objects of his withering critiques—people, books, ideas—torn to pieces.

Once having read it, who can forget Mencken's devastating description of William Jennings Bryan making a fool of himself at the Scopes evolution trial? Like Hitchens, Mencken too wrote much on a vast range of topics. Mencken, was, in short, Hitchens's literary godfather and role model. Hitchens is a modern Mencken.

Mencken also showed Hitchens how to view Holmes. In a May 1930 issue of the *American Mercury* magazine, Mencken reviewed a collection of Holmes's dissenting opinions and pointed the way for Hitchens. According to Mencken, "To call Holmes a Liberal is to make the word meaningless." Zeroing in on Holmes's opinions in Espionage Act cases, the Sage of Baltimore went on to to say that, "They may be good law, but it is impossible to see how they promote liberty."

It is hard to distinguish between Mencken's and Hitchens's dour perspectives on Holmes. They are almost identical. Hitchens's 1994 critique of Holmes appeared in a review of a biography of Mencken. In that review, Hitchens described Mencken's 1930 article and wholeheartedly agreed with it.

Hitchens was a great friend of the First Amendment. He exercised to the fullest his right of free speech and argued for others to have the same right. His life, his ideas about freedom of expression, his argumentative style, and his controversial view of Justice Holmes are all worth our attention. Even when we disagree with him, and we do often—including about Holmes—Hitchens makes us think, and that enlarges our own mental universe and makes us feel more alive.

Old Holmes would approve, even as he winced.

26

BILL BUCKLEY THE WITNESS

The death of William F. Buckley, Jr. in 2008 produced an immediate outpouring of commentary, mostly focused on his well-known conservative politics and his unusually extensive vocabulary. Newspapers and magazines ran long obituaries eulogizing his many contributions to the political, intellectual and literary life of contemporary America. Buckley was a prolific writer, the founder of *National Review*, and the host of "Firing Line" on television, among other things. A number of people also published moving first-person accounts of how Buckley influenced them personally (particularly when they were young and unknown), helped their careers and nourished them with long-lasting friendship.

To these tributes I want to add a trial lawyer's reminiscence. In 1987 Buckley testified for me as an expert witness at a jury trial. It was a brief, little-known, but truly unforgettable performance. And he did it without asking for a fee.

The case itself was unusual and still remains controversial. The subject of a true crime book sued the author of the book for allegedly misleading him about what the book would say. The plaintiff was Jeffery MacDonald, a Green Beret physician who had been tried and found guilty in 1979 and sentenced to life imprisonment for brutally murdering his pregnant twenty-six-year-old wife and their two young daughters. The defendant, my client, was Joe McGinniss, author of a popular book about the case called *Fatal Vision*. In the book McGinniss concluded, to MacDonald's great dismay, that MacDonald was in fact guilty. People have been loudly debating MacDonald's guilt or innocence ever since.

One issue in this grudge civil suit was whether a writer is ever justified in allowing a subject to believe what he wants to believe about how a book will portray him.

Enter Bill Buckley, expert witness.

Buckley, who had known McGinniss and admired his work, agreed to testify for us as an expert on the relationship of authors to publishers and authors to their subjects. He refused any compensation and flew to Los Angeles where the trial was being held, at his own expense. Arriving at eleven p.m. (two a.m. New York time) the night before he was to testify, the then-sixty-one-year-old Buckley, tired though he must have been, stayed up preparing another two hours, until five a.m. his East Coast time. His stamina and enthusiasm, coupled with is famous ability to be a quick study, were impressive as well as encouraging.

Next morning, I stood up in court and announced, not completely knowing what to expect, "Your Honor, the defendant calls William F. Buckley Jr." Buckley took the stand and, after some qualifying background questions, was accepted without objection as an expert witness.

Buckley's testimony focused on the need for a non-fiction author to have full discretion to arrive at his or her own conclusions about a subject. "One as an author is supposed to write what one thinks based on the objective evidence as one evaluates it," Buckley testified. "There would be no sense in which I would feel obliged to tell [the subject] what my conclusions were as I progressed with that endeavor." And "under no circumstances" would Buckley feel any obligation to show the subject a copy of the manuscript before publication.

As to whether an author should allow a subject to continue to believe whatever the subject may want to believe about how the writing is turning out, Buckley replied: "Writing is in part an art, and if you're doing a biography of [then-California Senator] Alan Cranston and you feel you are capturing a portrait of him by listening to him, by encouraging him to talk about subjects, say, that he wouldn't talk about to his constituents, by all means you encourage that because you are an investigative artist, you want to capture that person, and under the circumstances the last thing you would do is interrupt any tendency to spontaneity by arresting a flow of conversation by any suggestion that you found something that he was saying contradictory or incriminating."

Alan Cranston? Where did he come from? I asked myself. What was Buckley doing referring to the Senator from California? This was not part of our preparation. And this was on my direct examination! What would cross-examination be like?

Senator Cranston became, without any prior warning to me, a favorite (if unexpected) metaphor for Buckley's direct testimony that morning. In response to my questions about the scope of an author's discretion to encourage self-deception in a subject, Buckley explained: "That's an artistic question. If Senator Cranston, let's say while I was writing a biography about him, began to make references that sounded to me as though he had another wife living in Florida, I would from time to time return to that subject to encourage him to give me more details, but I wouldn't alert him to the fact that I was suddenly discovering that he was a bigamist, but I would certainly want to know if I was going to write a comprehensive authoritative biography. So I would follow the leads."

Now I began to really wonder what Buckley was up to and where it might lead. Was he suggesting—and would the press at the trial conclude—that Senator Cranston did have another wife? Looking back more than twenty-six years, I think Buckley was just having fun performing.

"What is your opinion," I asked, "of the effect on authors and writers if they didn't have the discretion that you've been talking about today?"

"It would destroy the profession," Buckley replied. "I don't think people would read or have any appetite to read books that were merely mechanical reflections of formulas that had been arrived at before the books were written . . . . So all that's interesting about freedom of speech, I think, would simply evaporate."

On that good note, I soon wound up my direct examination and sat down.

The highlight of Buckley's testimony, however, at least in terms of audience reaction, came on cross-examination. MacDonald's lawyer asked Buckley if it was the "custom and practice in the literary field" for authors to "lie" to subjects "in order to get more information out of them." Buckley asked for a definition of "lying," because "it is not that easy." He then gave the following example: "If the Gestapo arrives and says, 'Was Judge Rea [the presiding judge] here? Where did he go? and I said 'Well, he went that way.' Am I lying? Thomas Aquinas would say I was lying, a lot of other people would say I wasn't lying, I was simply defending an innocent life."

Buckley paused for a moment, looked thoughtfully at Judge Rea, and then, in that inimitable signature voice and with raised eyebrows, added archly: "I hope it's innocent." At that point the entire courtroom erupted in laughter, absolutely amazed and charmed by Buckley's quickness of mind and his ability to improvise on the witness stand.

Buckley was soon done with his testimony. I never saw him again, but we corresponded occasionally. His star turn as an expert witness impressed me. He had no dog in the MacDonald/McGinniss fight. Conservative politics were not at stake.

Others may speak of what Buckley did at *National Review* and elsewhere; I will always remember him as a stand-up guy who declined any fee to testify on behalf of a friend and freedom of expression.

27

SIMON RIFKIND—A SACHEM OF THE LAW

My first job out of law school was with the prestigious Manhattan law firm of Paul Weiss Rifkind Wharton & Garrison. The firm's senior partner at the time was a seventy-three-year-old former federal judge named Simon Rifkind. I stayed for only a year and a half before I was lured away by a small firm looking to start a litigation practice. But for part of my time at Paul Weiss my office was right next to Judge Rifkind's, and I got to know him a bit. We were on a first-name basis; he called me "Danny," and I called him "Judge."

In some societies—the Chinese, most famously—a person of old age is automatically revered and respected. Such cultures value age for the hard-bought experience, store of wisdom, and accumulated judgment it usually represents. By contrast, no one has ever accused American society, either now or in the past, of worshiping old age. Rather, even as more and more of us live longer and longer, so much so that the Social Security system fears bankruptcy in the decades ahead, America still prizes youth and energy above all. Sometimes this attitude is error.

The crucial lesson of this error brightly shines through four volumes of Judge Rifkind's collected writings. Rifkind continued to come to his office at Paul Weiss each day until he was ninety-five to advise clients and colleagues. He showed just how terribly wrong is the American tradition of ignoring the wisdom of age. On the contrary, we need to study and learn from what such wise old sachems of the law have to say.

Rifkind had a long and distinguished career. Born in Russia in 1901, Rifkind came to America when he was nine years old. After Columbia Law School, Rifkind became an assistant to New York Senator Robert F. Wagner and later his law partner. As Wagner's assistant, Rifkind helped shape the New Deal, particularly the Wagner Act concerning labor relations. With Wagner's backing, Rifkind became a federal trial judge at the age of forty, and he remained on the bench for ten years. He took six months off in 1945 to become adviser to General Eisenhower on Jewish affairs in Europe. In 1950 he resigned from the bench and joined the Paul Weiss firm where he remained for the rest of his long life as he won great praise for his lawyering ability.

While Rifkind's career may be well known, his miscellaneous writings perhaps are not, and they do warrant attention. For five decades now, ever since Marshall McLuhan first said it, we have been told again and again that the electronic age will replace reading and writing. Nonsense. To be sure, we lawyers practice what is essentially a plastic art, but if our fleeting thoughts are caught in print on a page, they may, like prehistoric organisms trapped in amber, last forever. The written word is a form of immortality.

Three of the volumes of Rifkind's writings, which comprise a matched set, look as if they were bound to last forever, or at least as long as Rifkind's own long life span. Privately published in 1986 and 1989 by his law partners, they have never been discussed in print other than in a dismissive and sarcastic column in the *New York Times* that overlooked their significance. The three volumes are handsome indeed, large in size, set in a big easy-to-read type, and printed on 1,315 heavy vellum pages. These three books are called *One Man's Word* and are an impressive display of two arts: the art of printing and the art of lawyering.

How nicely these three beautiful volumes are bound and printed, pleasing as that may be aesthetically, is nowhere near as important as what they contain substantively. Rifkind's collected works consist of all manner of writings: speeches, addresses, judicial opinions, appellate arguments, jury openings, and closings, letters, eulogies and tributes, and office memoranda on grand themes. Although his subjects vary widely, the most vital professional theme treated again and again by Rifkind focuses on what it means to be a lawyer, and that is a theme of burning and abiding interest to us all.

For Rifkind, being a lawyer was a vigorous experience, and he is unusually able to pass on his deep feeling for this great experience to contemporaries, to younger lawyers, and to generations of lawyers yet unborn. These full volumes are not meant to be read from cover to cover in one sitting; rather, their pleasure, wisdom and instruction can and should be spread over years. They are perfect for occasional weekend reading as a form of professional uplift. Reading what Rifkind says makes you feel good about practicing law, and it makes you try harder.

Rifkind's writings on the legal profession have several notable characteristics. They are marked by enthusiasm and strength, clarity of thought and expression, personal and professional integrity, and, overarching all, a noble vision of the lawyer's role in society. He sprinkles his comments with apt literary and biblical references.

Rifkind's topics themselves tell a large part of his tale. One piece is entitled, "A Lawyer's Credo"; another is a soaring "Statement of Firm Principles." "The Spirited Lawyer Representing Political Defendants" will put backbone in any advocate who ever had or may have an unpopular client. In "The Lawyer's Role and Responsibility in Modern Society," Rifkind gives us a controversial view of a fundamental subject. He also writes on private practice, oral advocacy, pro bono activities, and whether the law is a profession or a trade.

The key to Rifkind's many comments on the legal profession is his sense of values. Rifkind's values are traditional, and that explains much of his outlook. "The old ideals are neither dead nor abandoned," he writes in a philippic against the trend to make law more of a business than a profession. "It is still possible to revive [the old ideals] and have them prevail as the creed of lawyers, faithfully observed."

Consider, for example, Rifkind's view of a lawyer's ethical duty to defend an unpopular client, a duty always much discussed. William Kunstler, who represented his share of such clients, said, "I only defend those whose goals I share." Rifkind takes "the contrary view—the more unpopular the defendant, the more hateful he appears, the better and stronger must I have a reason for not accepting his assignment."

Rifkind clinches the point memorably: "If Lucifer himself comes to retain me to prevent his eviction from the Garden of Eden, I would take his case unless the Archangel Gabriel had already retained my partner to get the order of eviction." I love that line.

It is impossible to read these selections and not draw inspiration from them. They leaven with a lofty outlook the quotidian activities of practicing law. They ennoble our task. In some ways, Rifkind's writings do for the legal profession what Cardozo's writings did for the judicial process: they hold the banner high for the rest of us marching behind. In short, this is powerfully good stuff.

It is highly practical stuff as well. A 1988 address to Paul Weiss lawyers, for example, "articulates practical bits of wisdom which have proved helpful in the day-to-day practice of our profession." It sets forth some forty rules that bear reading and rereading by those of us in private practice.

Rifkind also has a keen awareness, born of his own long experience, of what it takes to be a trial lawyer, of the sacrifices and joys. One passage well sums up our lives: "If you entertain a goal of a nine to five workday and daily dining with your family, of taking your holidays when you schedule them, of well-spaced opportunities for leisure and reflection, you will be confronted by repeated disappointments. But if you hunger for high adventure, if you can stand the tedium when rabbits rather than lions appear in your rifle scope, if you can absorb the ecstasy of triumph as well as the dejection of defeat, then trial advocacy is in your horoscope."

No one, of course, will agree with all of Rifkind's views—perhaps even Rifkind had over time changed some of his opinions. Rifkind's unyielding defense of Judge Irving Kaufman's handling of the Rosenberg spy case, for instance, has always seemed a bit rigid and emotional. Similarly, one gets the feeling from Rifkind's writings that he was not entirely comfortable with many of the social and cultural changes that took place in our country since 1960. A long-haired hippie Simon Rifkind was not. But these are small quibbles with a vast output of an energetic life in the law, and a person is allowed to get a little crotchety as he or she gets older. Age has its privileges.

Crochets pervade the fourth, unrelated volume of Rifkind's writings, which consists of excerpts from his diaries in old age. Called *At 90, on the 90s: The Journal of Simon H. Rifkind*, this slim (one hundred and eight pages) book shows Rifkind's views during this ninetieth year on a number of controversial public issues. In a simple style, with short declarative sentences, Rifkind here gives, in random entries often without transitions, his brief musings and reactions to issues of the day and developing trends. He comments on the Supreme Court, selection and confirmation of judicial nominees, freedom of speech, as well as non-legal topics such as the Gulf War, the future of Israel, and Jewish inter-marriages.

Rifkind here is pessimistic and unhappy. Regarding judicial nominees, he thinks, "The prospect is dismal." That same month, he adds: "The current forces are all negative." "All this depresses me," he writes in his diary on September 11, 1991. "Can anyone cheer me up?" The same date ten years later certainly would not have cheered Rifkind up.

In the end however, it is Rifkind in these four books who cheers *us* up. Whether he is happy or sad, inspiring or critical, Rifkind tells us what is on his mind, even if it occasionally makes us uncomfortable. He cheers us with the vibrancy of his writings and the positive attitude he has toward our profession. In his diary, he notes that, "Some of the greatest steps in the progress of our society have been achieved by private litigation." He cheers us with his indefatigable energy, his life-affirming gusto, and most compellingly of all, his example.

Old age, as Rifkind, demonstrates, can still be a time for productive work. Like Justices Oliver Wendell Holmes and Hugo Black and John Paul Stevens, like Judges Learned Hand and Harold Medina, Rifkind too was magnificent in old age. All of them echo the aged but restless hero in Tennyson's poem "Ulysses": "How dull it is to pause, to make an end,/To rust unburnished, not to shine in use,/As though to breathe were life!" As Holmes said, "To live is to function, that is all there is in living."

Rifkind was an esteemed elder of our tribe of lawyers, and his books pass on what he knew to the younger warriors of the law. "Only by an apprenticeship under a good master," Rifkind wrote in a 1986 piece in the *New York Law Journal* called "The Teaching Law Firm," "can a young law school graduate achieve the skills necessary for the craft of lawyering." These books prove again that he is such a master, and that he can send a spark to those who come after.

I was very lucky with my apprenticeship.

28

ARTHUR LIMAN, LAWYER OF VIRTUE

Arthur Liman was one of Rifkind's law partners. A renowned litigator, Liman was a superb example of that rare and endangered species: a virtuous lawyer. When he died in 1997 at the age of sixty-four and at the peak of his powers, he left a gaping hole in the fabric of the New York bar.

A lawyer of virtue who can find? For her (or his) price as far above rubies. This paraphrase of Proverbs 31.10 is prompted by the posthumous publication of Arthur Liman's memoirs, and has nothing to do with his hourly rate.

His autobiography, written during the months of his final illness, unintentionally explains by the example of his professional life why he is now so revered and so missed. His memoirs recount the shaping of a lawyer of virtue.

Unlike most lawyer autobiographies, this book is not simply "Liman's Greatest Cases" or "How Liman Always Outsmarted the Other Lawyer or Made a Monkey Out of the Hostile Witness." On the contrary, this is a sensitive, introspective, highly intelligent, literate man's sincere and probing description of his lifelong love affair with the law, the important influences on his professional development and his views of the changes of the practice of law since his graduation from law school in 1957.

Of course he talks about his famous clients and cases—and there were many—but not to enhance his own reputation. Rather, he blames himself for errors and graciously gives credit to others. Without flinching, Liman took a lot of unfair public criticism during the Iran-Contra investigation and when his client Michael Millken was sentenced to ten years after a plea bargain (later reduced to twenty-two months).

In this (unfortunately his only) book, Liman dissects his own psyche, trying to understand himself and to make sense of his extraordinarily active and varied lawyer's life. Liman uses his memoirs to explore his motives and choices in life.

If Liman had spent his entire professional life as a lawyer in a prestigious law firm working on private matters, it would have been enough. In that event, his life and his autobiography would still have been exciting and fascinating. The memoirs of a good trial lawyer are like that, and Liman was nothing if not a good trial lawyer.

But what takes Liman's autobiography to another level, what makes his memoirs special and inspiring, are his several splendid intermittent stints of public service for little and sometimes no money. From the start, Liman knew that "somehow, I was going to combine private practice with public service."

Liman's public service took many forms. For a while as a young lawyer, he was a federal prosecutor under one of his mentors, the legendary Robert Morgenthau, here in Manhattan. (Liman's other mentor was Rifkind.) Liman headed the investigation into the 1971 Attica prison riot. He was chief counsel to the Senate committee looking into Iran-Contra. Liman was active in leading the Legal Aid Society and other organizations that provide legal services to the poor. He represented governmental entities. He was a bar association leader. The list is awesome.

Liman's memoirs touch today's headlines. Although Liman died before any of us ever heard of Monica Lewinsky, his autobiography talks about independent counsels, legislative investigations and, yes, even impeachment. It is not so much that Liman was prescient, but that he was discussing some of his own "firsthand experience with impeachable conduct." One was with the Iran-Contra legislative inquiry and the other was as prosecutor in the proceeding that disbarred Richard Nixon from practicing law in New York.

As to Nixon, Liman writes with an eerie, rasping echo for the future: "It was disheartening to hear the President of the United States plotting false testimony just like some member of the Mob." As to Reagan and Iran-Contra, Liman says: "We had no comparable evidence" and "we could never prove whether President Reagan was actually told of the diversion." As to the grounds for impeachment, Liman says that it should involve "severe misconduct" but "an act need not be criminal to warrant impeachment," adding, "A serious dereliction of duty could suffice."

Liman even has a section entitled "Presidential Accountability and Criminal Liability." In it he criticizes the trend of independent counsel investigations starting with Iran-Contra. "This all seems more relevant today than it did then," writes Liman, "given the activities of Kenneth Starr." Remember that Liman wrote those words in 1997. Even then, Liman thought Starr was not using an independent counsel inquiry properly.

The greatest long-term consequence of recent goings-on in Washington may not be to the presidency but to Liman's bedrock belief in the concept of voluntary public service, what was once called civic virtue. The Monica mess culminated more than a decade of events that could discourage good people—especially lawyers—from ever wanting to be in the public eye.

Liman defied the trend. Ever since Robert Bork's confirmation hearings in 1987, lawyers and non-lawyers have become acutely aware of the new and biting sacrifices that have to be made for the chance to work in the public interest. John Tower, Clarence Thomas, Douglas Ginsburg, Zoe Baird and Kimba Wood are just a few of the people who might in retrospect wish their names had never been mentioned for higher public office. And this does not even count the several cabinet officers who have been indicted.

Sadly, it is almost as if public service is the surest way these days to ruin your reputation. It used to be that a temporary cut in a pay was all that you gave up if you took a public sector job. Now, in Washington's highly partisan and bitter atmosphere, for the privilege of earning less money, you also run the serious risk of having your private life invaded and publicized, your family and friends hurt and embarrassed, and your life's work mercilessly attacked on political grounds.

Is public service worth it? No doubt, Liman would say yes, but these are new and daunting considerations to be carefully weighed in the scale, and they skew some of our most cherished ideas about the role of lawyers in our society. Are sensible lawyers as eager today as they used to be to be appointed to high visibility government jobs? The tone of our public life depends on good and talented people stepping forward, as Liman did again and again.

Arthur Liman was an admirable lawyer-Cincinnatus. He went back and forth between his private plow at Paul Weiss and his many public accomplishments. We really need more lawyers like him, wonderfully competent, modest, thoughtful, quietly heroic, uninterested in personal power or glory, intrepid in representing their clients and the public interest, and unafraid of the dangers of public life.

"The heroes of the legal profession," writes Liman knowingly, "are not the lawyers who achieve celebrity status by self-promotion or mugging for the cameras." No, the true heroes of the legal profession are the lawyers of virtue, like Liman. His autobiography should inspire others to follow his example, as Clarence Darrow inspired Liman.

29

BEN FRANKLIN AND CLAUDE-ANNE LOPEZ

Benjamin Franklin was not a lawyer, but he helped frame our Constitution in addition to all the many other contributions he made. Few figures in American history have won the stature that he has. If George Washington was the Father of Our Country, Franklin— seventy years old in 1776—was the nation's wise, experienced, prudent and genial grandfather, with a kindly face and twinkling eye that Norman Rockwell could have drawn.

More than two hundred twenty years after his death, we revere him, and rightly so, as America's first and perhaps greatest polymath. Statesman, scholar, patriot, writer, scientist, printer, philosopher, diplomat—whatever he touched turned out superbly well.

Self-taught and self-made, Franklin accomplished his many successes and lived his rags-to-riches, Horatio Alger life story in a way that has inspired generations. We still read his *Autobiography* and *Poor Richard's Almanack*. From a distance of more than two centuries, we view Franklin as one of those gifted and lucky heroes who founded our nation. Many biographies have told us countless facts about Franklin's long and active public life.

But Franklin's well-known public life is only part of his story, albeit an important part, but by no means the only part. As with all great historical figures, and Franklin is no exception, private, hidden facts fill in and round out the portrait, adding texture, shading and nuance to our understanding of the human being. *My Life with Benjamin Franklin* by Claude-Anne Lopez does exactly that for Franklin, with great success and admirable, elegantly simple style.

In *My Life with Benjamin Franklin*, published in 2000, Lopez reveals "little-known episodes" of Franklin's life "as well as unexplored nooks and crannies" of his personality. Lopez, as one of the nation's leading authorities on Franklin, brings to her task not only the skill and depth of a scholarly historian but also the writer's eye for telling anecdote and the immigrant's enthusiasm for her adopted country's ideals. For many years as editor of *The Papers of Benjamin Franklin*, Lopez has in the past published books from a similar perspective on Franklin's relationships with his family and with the women of Paris. The most well known of these is her *Mon Cher Papa*.

Lopez carved out a niche for herself. Faced with an daunting avalanche of writing on Franklin, she dreamed of making his personal life her "turf." But she felt that her approach might not be academic enough. However, her "out-of-fashion attachment to the text, the fact, the vignette" has a secure place in historical and biographical literature. As Lopez explains, "I love stories. Those I love the best are woven from scraps of information found here and there and brought together, like a quilt, into a pattern." Such stories make up her book.

Her research credo is one with which a lawyer can identify. Lopez says her "hope never dies that the next letter, oyster-like, will contain a pearl, something hidden up to now and suddenly glittering with promise." Change "letter" to "case" and her thought also embraces an advocate researching a point of law.

Lopez's delightful and unusual introduction to this book is by turns clever and candid, professional and personal. She addresses her introduction directly to Franklin himself. "Franklin," she starts, "you have been my passport to America." Lopez then explains how during the Second World War she emigrated as a young woman from Belgium to the United States, married a Yale history professor, had children, but still felt stifled and unfulfilled. All that changed for the better when she was offered a job in the 1950s with the *Franklin Papers*. There and then she found her life's work.

My Life consists of eighteen fascinating and nicely written essays drawn from Lopez's happy and fruitful research in the *Franklin Papers* at Yale. The essays range widely. One is a convincing refutation of an anti-Semitic forgery attributed to Franklin and currently circulating on the Internet. Three mini-detective stories show Franklin on the fringes of the world of espionage. Some pieces describe Franklin's efforts to outfit the Continental Army and to choose the first dinner set for the Foreign Service. One essay tells the misadventures of a French utopian scheme he sponsored. A memorable high point of the book is an imaginary dinner party during which, on the first anniversary of his death, six illustrious Frenchmen discuss Franklin's influence on their country.

By the end, the reader feels like sending the author a letter (which we did), thanking her for a pleasant and enlightening reading experience. What we enjoyed most—and what, besides Franklin, unifies the collection—was the way the essays reflect the author's special cast of mind and attitude toward life, in short, her personality. The essays in this book are not only about Benjamin Franklin, not really. Like any piece of writing, they are also about the author, and when the author is Claude-Anne Lopez, that is good too.

A number of Lopez's essays, for example, are animated by a subtle but distinctive feminism. This is not surprising in view of her personal experience. In her introduction, Lopez quietly laments the sex discrimination she felt as a young faculty wife after World War II. In those days, she recalls, the wife of a professor "was supposed to provide elegant entertainment for her husband's colleagues, to help her husband prepare the index of his latest work—or to do it herself if she was exceptionally gifted—and above all to keep clear of any personal goal." She was resigned to a noncareer of typing other people's dissertations until she was asked to work on the *Franklin Papers*.

As with her other writing, in this book too she focuses on Franklin "from a French woman's point of view." But the women she draws, young and mature, are all women of intellect, spirit and accomplishment. When Lopez writes about Franklin's dealings with lively teenage girls interested in philosophy or literature, we feel she is making both a personal and a universal point. This is Lopez striking a blow, in her own quiet and disarming way, for the rights of women.

The author is a careful and pleasing writer. She demonstrates that good historical scholarship does not have to be wrapped in dense, abstruse, difficult or boring prose laden with academic jargon. Her writing has the wonderful virtues of being readable, accessible and vitally interesting.

She keeps the reader uppermost in mind. Each essay has a personal introduction that gives her reason for writing it and knits the collection with smooth transition. Lopez constructs all her sentences well, but some of them really sing. One, referring to publishers who initially rejected her personal approach to Franklin, goes: "The publishing finger is not always on the public pulse." Using short words, it combines good rhythm, cadence, balance and alliteration. Another, dealing with Internet falsehood, points out that, "These days the only legs a lie needs are virtual ones." A third gem refers to "the warmth of the embers without the devastation of the flame." What excellent use of the English language from an author whose mother tongue is French!

Such good balance and memorable metaphors usually do not spring full blown from the pen or computer keyboard on the first try. They require much effort and rewriting. We know this from personal experience.

Like the close and astute observer she is, Lopez sees both beneath and beyond the superficial. She looks for the hidden significance of events, the deeper and larger pattern of human behavior. She tells us how her curiosity is always piqued when "I sense a human drama buried among the commercial, legal, diplomatic, or purely routine topics that constitute the bulk of the Franklin papers." That "human drama" is of course what also makes practicing law endlessly fascinating. Technical proficiency is one thing, but seeing the "human drama" quite another, much more important thing.

That human drama is not always happy. It is reassuring, in an odd way, to read that Benjamin Franklin had his share of sadness. He made enemies, was estranged from his son, and spent long times away from his family. His letters late in life show "an old man whose private dreams have been shattered." The longer we live, the more we suspect that everyone falls into that category in one way or another. Shattered private dreams are part of life. But it lifted my spirits to learn from Lopez that even the immensely successful Benjamin Franklin had his share of deep disappointments.

In her introduction, Lopez disappointed us by suggesting, with foreboding, that this would be her last book. She was seventy-six years old. "My very first book was published by Yale," she writes, "and this one closes the cycle." How sad! Say it isn't so. We object!

But Lopez did not have time to change her mind. Unfortunately, she was not blessed with many more years of good health in which to continue to write at least one more volume filled with her valuable insights and stamped with her unique and sensitive personality. Such gifted historians are almost as important as the Franklins they write about. Claude-Anne Lopez died in 2012, at the age of eighty-eight.

PART FOUR
OBITER DICTA

To lawyers, obiter dicta are those statements in a judicial opinion not strictly necessary for the legal rule announced in the case. Dicta are not an essential part of the court's reasoning or holding. But such dicta are often the most interesting, most memorable parts of court opinions. By their very irrelevance they offer glimpses of the judge's personality and character. A judge may, for a number of reasons, good or bad, expound on irrelevant facts, hypothetical variations of the facts, or a theory of law that was not applied. Dicta sometimes get cited or quoted more often than holdings.

Dicta have no authority, though they may offer insight into how the author thinks. So too here. Webster defines obiter dicta as incidental remarks, and that aptly describes the pieces in this section. They form a miscellany.

30

THE SUCCESS OF THE WORD: THE LITERARY CRITIC AS CONSTITUTIONAL THEORIST

The study of literature may be good preparation for the study of law. One of our most eminent legal scholars, the late Grant Gilmore, took his Ph.D in French literature, writing a dissertation on Mallarmé, before ever setting foot in a law school. Perhaps this is not surprising. After all, literature, like law, deals with human nature and experience. At its best, the study of law furnishes us with insight into human nature and the human experience. Like law, literature is built on texts that must be read, studied, and interpreted. As a result of their training, sensitivity, and cast of mind, students of literature might make excellent students of law.

Despite the obvious similarities of the intellectual tasks involved, blending law and literature into a distinct discipline is only a relatively recent development. In 1973, James Boyd White, in his seminal book *The Legal Imagination*, drew heavily on readings from literature "to establish a way of looking at the law from the outside, a way of comparing it with some other forms of literary and intellectual activity, a way of defining the legal imagination by comparing it with others." Since the publication of White's pathbreaking book over four decades ago, literary studies and critical techniques have increasingly become an explicit part of legal debate. Even the recondite word "hermeneutics," a term used by literary critics for the study of interpretation, has started to find its way into the pages of legal periodicals. Within the last few years, such journals have sponsored a textual interpretation. Law and Literature, as a separate study, has come out of the closet.

One of the more interesting books in this genre is *The Failure of the Word: The Protagonist as Lawyer in Modern Fiction* by Richard Weisberg, a professor at the Benjamin N. Cardozo School of Law in Manhattan. *The Failure of the Word*, published in 1984, is a good example of the combined disciplines of law and literature. Weisberg's book realizes the potential of the new field of study. Weisberg's stated aim is to expose some of modern literature's malaise in the "futile wordiness" of lawyerly protagonists, and he succeeds in achieving this goal. On its own terms, *The Failure of the Word* is a subtle and provocative volume bound to spur much creative thinking about the role of lawyers in modern fiction. But Weisberg's book is much more.

In addition to its manifest content, *The Failure of the Word* has a vital, and no less important, latent content. The subtlety, fertility, and richness of the book invite us to view it not as mere literary criticism, but as a separate text that is itself open to interpretation. In referring to Herman Melville's *Billy Budd, Sailor*, Weisberg himself says that his "analysis need only be considered one of the many responses to an incredibly evocative story." By the same token, Weisberg's own book is "incredibly evocative" and suggests more than one possible response.

The latent content of *The Failure of the Word* is a theme larger than literary criticism. Like the literary lawyers he analyzes, Weisberg communicates, at least in part, by indirection, using the ability to "mask" true purposes behind "politic outward displays." Although ostensibly about literature, Weisberg's book is really about law. *The Failure of the Word* can be understood, in its broadest sense, as an original and penetrating essay on constitutional law and legal interpretation. Only by reading Weisberg's work in this way can it be fully appreciated and put into the context of Weisberg's own intellectual development.

In view of Weisberg's achievement, one learns with interest that he had something in common with Grant Gilmore. Like Gilmore, Weisberg studied French and Comparative Literature before studying law. Like Gilmore, Weisberg earned his doctorate with a thesis on Mallarmé. Something in the poetry of Mallarmé must stimulate and inspire future law professors. In reading Weisberg's book, we should perhaps keep Mallarmé in mind as a frame of reference.

MANIFEST MEANING

The manifest content of *The Failure of the Word* consists of literary analysis. Weisberg uses eight examples of modern literature as a window on various cultural phenomena. Analyzing well-known works of Dostoevsky, Flaubert, Camus, and Melville, Weisberg gives insight into what they wrote. Through this analysis, Weisberg reaches certain unique conclusions about literature, law, and culture generally.

Weisberg's stated theme is original. One of the hallmarks of originality is the ability to see connections between apparently unrelated phenomena. Where others have seen nothing, Weisberg discerns genuine links between several apparently unrelated pieces of modern fiction. It is no small achievement to perceive vital connecting patterns in works as diverse in time, setting, and subject matter as Dostoevsky's *Brothers Karamazov, Notes from Underground,* and *Crime and Punishment*; Flaubert's *Salammbô* and *Sentimental Education*; Camus's *The Fall* and *The Stranger*; and Melville's *Billy Budd*. Weisberg's achievement is enhanced by the far-reaching implications he is able to draw out of those connecting patterns.

Weisberg sets out to show nothing less than the relationship between modern cultural malaise and the lawyer-like protagonists in nineteenth and twentieth-century literature. According to Weisberg, the use of lawyer-like protagonists in modern literature is the key to understanding basic aspects of modern culture. In such characters are combined two fundamental cultural themes: the twin themes of *ressentiment* and legalism. These themes, in turn, combine to produce the "legalistic *ressentiment*" so central to modern fiction.

At the heart of Weisberg's literary analysis lies the concept of *ressentiment*. That concept, which Weisberg ascribes to Nietsche, means perpetual rancor. *Ressentiment* involves disguised rage taking the form of public "revenge" against imagined "insults." Ressentient individuals have a lingering sense of injury without a firm sense of values. They generally feel a discrepancy between what they consider their own worth to be and the actual worth and position accorded them by others.

Ressentiment is, for Weisberg, "modern Western culture's own deepest malaise." To understand *ressentiment* and ressentient injustice is to understand law and language today, says Weisberg. *Ressentiment* is a "negative force in society and history," and plays a major role in the novels that he interprets. In each literary work examined by Weisberg, *ressentiment* mars the protagonist. And in each such work of fiction, the protagonist is a lawyer or lawyer-like character.

These fictional lawyer-types, flawed by *ressentiment*, are the bridge of Weisberg's other major theme: legalism. These literary-legal figures have several other distinctive traits. Weisberg describes the lawyer-like protagonists as well educated, hard working, insightful individuals, blessed with subtle and careful minds, endowed with superior powers of perception, distinctively articulate at their best. Weisberg sees these fictional lawyer-types, at their worst, as avoiding and distorting reality and life, as maladjusted, repressed, and violent individuals who adhere to resentful values. They are inactive, promoters of injustice, indirect with hidden motives equivocating, dissembling, and above all too wordy. This verbosity is a primary trait, making the fictional lawyers prolix verbalizers who use words to avoid reality and action. Such people, do not act; they react, with words. "These protagonists prefer the safety of wordiness to the risks of spontaneous human interaction."

Juxtaposed against the predominantly negative traits of lawyer figures are the primarily attractive qualities of the "just individual." Such an individual, while nonverbal and less articulate, is more popular, basically well adjusted, and fulfilled. He has a keen intelligence and couples action with reason. Unlike his verbose legal counterpart, the just individual responds quickly and effectively to evil, though nonverbally. He is associated with happiness, power, beauty, goodness, and other positive forms of life. He spontaneously partakes of all the fullness of reality.

Tension between these two sets of character traits generates the energy of Weisberg's thesis. According to that thesis, the bitter and resentful verbosity, the sheer wordiness, of fictional lawyers has produced what Weisberg sees as the prevailing failure if modern Western culture. Speech is an inadequate replacement for legitimate action. Yet we have been plagued by the "futile wordiness of legalistic protagonists." Hence the genesis of Weisberg's title, *The Failure of the Word*, and his subtitle, *The Protagonist as Lawyer in Modern Fiction*.

But Weisberg's thrust is not pessimistic. Like a physician, he examines the symptoms of modern cultural malaise and diagnoses the causes of legalistic *ressentiment*. Having made his diagnosis, Weisberg offers a prognosis of guarded optimism: "*reseentiment* can yet be altered." Negative forces "yield eventually to the ebullient creativity of self-willed people with a firm sense of communal ethics. Literary art, ever the reflection of a culture's sense of itself, may again join a positive system of law to generate admirable language.

LATENT CONTENT

As Freud used the term, *manifest* dream-content is "what the dream actually tells us." By applying Freudian terms to the interpretation of a text, we may be able to find in *The Failure of the Word* something besides its manifest content. In Freudian psychoanalysis, *latent* dream-thoughts, by contrast, are the concealed material. In Weisberg's book, latent, partially hidden themes co-exist with the manifest content.

On the surface, the manifest content of Weisberg's book is a matter of literary analysis, albeit literature involving lawyers and law. On a deeper level, and perhaps not even consciously perceived by the author himself, the latent content of Weisberg's book is an essay on constitutional law and legal interpretation. Seen on this level, Weisberg uses literature as a symbol of law, so that his comments about literature should properly be read as comments about law. It is possible, of course, that Weisberg never intended literature to be a substitute for law in his book. However, as Weisberg would be among the first to recognize, an author's intent is not necessarily binding on a reader's response. A text, such as *The Failure of the Word*, is open to more than one interpretation.

Interpreted as an essay about law, and not about literature, *The Failure of the Word* has much to tell us that is important to contemporary legal discourse. It evaluates the dichotomy between speech and action, a basic distinction in constitutional law, from a new perspective. From Weisberg's discussion of the speech-action dichotomy, we can generalize to the larger theme of judicial activism versus judicial restraint. Weisberg's book yields further insight into judicial review and constitutional interpretation and subjectivity in law, and the habit of lawyers to speak by indirection. The jurisprudential quest for original intent provides a controversial yet enlightening way to illustrate these aspects of Weisberg's theory.

The Speech-Action Dichotomy

Running through Weisberg's book is a crucial theme that has a clear parallel in constitutional law. Weisberg sees an important distinction between speech and action in the works of literature he examines. Weisberg's distinction between speech and action in modern literature resembles a similar distinction used by the Supreme Court in First Amendment cases. Ultimately Weisberg rejects the distinction as empty and pernicious. In rejecting the distinction between speech and action in literature, Weisberg reaches the same conclusion as do some of our most eminent constitutional scholars.

A major link between the eight literary works studied by Weisberg is their distinction between speech and action. In each of the works, "inactive, wordy characters" try to rule others who are both active and nonverbal. Such characters lead mere half lives, as they verbalize and narrate rather than live. In *Salammbô*, for instance, Flaubert pits a castrated priest, a lawyer-like protagonist and a "wordy adversary," against his opposite, a "virile rival." Similarly, in both *The Stranger* and *Billy Budd,* the nonverbal innocent heroes must suffer formal legal trials at the hands of lawyerly adversaries who manipulate justice through their verbal skills. As Weisberg explains, the protagonists in these works embody the speech-action dichotomy.

In practice, the Supreme Court has frequently cited the distinction between speech and action in deciding First Amendment cases. Under the stated rationale of these cases, where the conduct in question is "pure speech," it is entitled to full First Amendment protection. If the conduct is "speech plus" (for example, labor picketing for illegal purposes), it is entitled to lesser protection. If the Court views the subject as conduct, and not as speech (such as a demonstration on the premises of a county jail), the First Amendment does not apply. In all these cases, the crucial question is deciding which category, speech or action, is appropriate.

That question has never been an easy one for constitutional scholars to answer. The cases are hard to reconcile, and the Supreme Court has never spelled out a basis for its distinction. When the Supreme Court differentiates between speech and conduct, it is more often than not announcing its conclusion, rather than setting forth an analytic process, as the dissenting justices frequently point out. Professor Laurence Tribe writes that "[t]he distinction between 'expression' and 'action' or 'speech' and 'conduct' is essentially unhelpful because it asks a question which is answerable only if one has already decided, on independent grounds, whether the act is protected by the First Amendment."

Based on this kind of analysis, more and more constitutional theorists have recently begun to reject the speech-action dichotomy in constitutional law. They believe that dichotomy is "empty" and "has no real content." All communication involves conduct, and such conduct, such as "symbolic speech," is expressive. "Expression message and medium are thus inextricably tied together in all communicative behavior." This development in constitutional law is analogous to Weisberg's own thinking in his book.

In the last analysis, Weisberg also rejects the speech-action dichotomy. At the end of his book, Weisberg makes clear that he thinks speech and action should be inseparable. To illustrate his point, Weisberg quotes from Melville's *Billy Budd*: "the poet but embodies in verse those exaltations of sentiment that a nature like Nelson, the opportunity being given, vitalizes into acts." This passage is crucial to understanding Weisberg's point. With the passage from *Billy Budd*, says Weisberg, "[w]e have truly entered the holy of holies. The mystery of this paragraph remains with us." What "mystery"? Why is it "the holy of holies."

The excerpt from Melville fascinates Weisberg because it collapses the distinction drawn by Dostoevsky, Flaubert, and Camus—not to mention the Supreme Court—between speech and action. "Ethical action and writing, we learn here," says Weisberg, "have not always been dissociated phenomena; Nelson symbolized the symmetry of art and heroism." According to Weisberg, Melville seems to be calling "for a renewal of the old alliance of artistry with just action," and the "classical unity of literature and action," when "heroic action and narrative act were inextricably linked." "One arm acted, the other wrote," adds Weisberg. "The match of outer form with inner man achieved artistic harmony in such figures."

Breaking the link, that is, distinguishing between speech and action, had led to serious problems. Weisberg sees the distinction as symptomatic of everything wrong with modern literature, as a reflection of *ressentiment* in our culture. "Only ressentient modern-day verbalizers," writes Weisberg, "see alienation from heroic activity as the sine qua non for the verbally expressive life." One could produce a fascinating analysis of certain Supreme Court justices as "ressentient modern day verbalizers."

In some ways, by breaking down the distinction between speech and action, Weisberg is only recognizing the obvious. But, as Justice Holmes once advised, "[w]e need education in the obvious." Perhaps Weisberg had Winston Churchill in mind when writing: "in other ages political leaders combined strong-willed ethics with verbal force." President Kennedy, for example, said that Churchill "mobilized the English language and sent it into battle." The core of Weisberg's critical view of the speech-action dichotomy is: "use of words in the service of positive values remains . . . a magnificent possibility."

Judicial Activism vs. Judicial Restraint

Weisberg's affirmative view of the link between speech and action, the "magnificent possibility" of using "words in the service of positive values," suggests a certain view of the role of courts in a democratic society. In America, courts have extraordinary power. In performing their duty to interpret laws, courts in this country can take either an active or passive view of their role. As Alexander Bickel wrote, judicial review is a "counter-majoritarian force in our system" because it allows unelected judges to thwart the will of the people's elected representatives. The unusual aspects of judicial review have made it a perennial subject of legal debate.

The debate continues. Today, as in the past, participants in the debate over the proper role of courts use the terms judicial activism and judicial restraint. Despite their imprecision and frequent inappropriateness, these terms convey the primary thrust of the two opposing viewpoints. As the daily newspapers attest, politicians and journalists assume most Americans understand the difference between judicial activism and judicial restraint. When President Nixon spoke of favoring "strict constructionists" as judges, and when presidents seek judicial nominees who supposedly will not impose their own personal values if put on the bench, the American people understand the meaning behind these phrases.

It is hard to read Weisberg's book without interpreting it, at least in part, as a psychological critique of judicial restraint. Weisberg favors action over inaction. He associates inaction, "fatal hesitancy," with verbosity. Rather than act, legal protagonists in fiction, like Hamlet ("the first great literary lawyer"), talk at length.

The result of such wordy inaction is, for Weisberg, continued wrongdoing. "Injustice has endured," Weisberg says, "and even expanded through the verbal predilection of the protagonist as lawyer." "Passivity," he continues, "has often allowed and sometimes encouraged, the dominance of injustice on earth." Weisberg criticizes those who always find reasons not to act. "The noble strength of his sensitivity," Weisberg writes about a legal protagonist, "wars with the ignoble effects of his wordy investigations."

Weisberg's activist tone sharply contrasts with some of the precepts of judicial self-restraint. One cannot imagine Weisberg saying, as Justice Brandeis said, that "[t]he most important thing we do is not doing." Nor would Weisberg be likely to find totally congenial the self-restraining principles announced by Brandeis in *Ashwander v. Tennessee Valley Authority*. As a matter of temperament, if nothing else, Weisberg would probably disapprove of the way Justice Franfurter was "forever disposing of issues by assigning their disposition to some other sphere of competence." The "passive virtues," exemplified by Frankfurter, and written about by Bickel, would hold no attraction for Weisberg.

The conclusion that Weisberg views the self-denying ordinances of judicial restraint with great skepticism is inescapable. Undoubtedly, Weisberg sees such principles as excuses for not acting. Lack of justiciability, mootness, ripeness, and the political question doctrine would strike Weisberg as reasons sought out by judges to justify a psychological reluctance to act. Of great relevance is Weisberg's description of the inactive, verbalizing legal protagonist: "he creates so many doubts for himself . . . that he does not ever make a move toward reacting to a deeply felt insult. Primary causes (the justice of the charge against the oppressor, no matter what the odds of success) are replaced by endless second-guessing (Should I act? Will there be a better time to act? Was my enemy really wrong? Don't I admire him deep down? Will I look ridiculous? etc.)."

The leading modern examplar of judicial self-restraint, Felix Frankfurter, would surely strike Weisberg as having many of the qualities found in the fictional lawyers in modern literature. Frankfurter was a brilliant and learned lawyer, superbly educated, capable of great insight, blessed with a complex, subtle, and extraordinarily articulate intellect. At the same time, Frakfurter was verbose, passive, hypertechnical, long-winded, persnickety, and more concerned with process than with substance. His advocacy of judicial restraint was maddening to those who admired his libertarian crusades before he joined the Supreme Court. In a trenchant and controversial psychobiography, *The Enigma of Felix Frankfurter*, H.N. Hirsch goes so far as to describe Frankfurter as "a textbook case of a neurotic personality," what Weisberg would identify as a "disjoined inner state."

In the view of Hirsch and others, Frankfurter's life is filled with what is the grist of Weisberg's mill. Throughout his life, Frankfurter hid his true motives, using flattery and other means to manipulate people. On the Court he was capable of great insight and felicitous expression. Yet he repeatedly avoided substantive issues, and perpetuated what others considered to be social wrongs by relying on the "passive virtues," that is, by "creat[ing] . . . many doubts for himself" and by "endless second-guessing." Fed up with Frankfurter's wordiness, Justice Frank Murphy dismissed Frankfurter's scholarly opinions as "elegant bunk."

In many ways, Frankfurter personifies the ressentient legal figure. Like the classical ressentient type, Frankfurter, according to Hirsch, lacked a firm sense of personal values due to a fundamental ambiguity in his choice of an identity. Frankfurter, writes Hirsch, was "someone whose self-image is overblown and yet, at the same time, essential to his sense of well being." Frankfurter's early years on the Court represented his first confrontation with a sustained challenge to his exaggerated self-image in a field that he considered his own.

The turning point for Frankfurter came in the flag salute cases. After the second flag salute case, in which the Court overruled his earlier majority opinion, the remainder of Frankfurter's tenure was, in a sense, devoted to refighting a recurring battle. Frankfurter's stance cast him in opposition to the rest of the Court; his leadership has been rejected. From Frankfurter's psychological viewpoint, he felt perpetual rancor, as if he were under siege and had no choice but to remain where he was and fight it out. He reacted to his opponents with vindictive hostility. Such opposition pushed Frankfurter according to Hirsch, "into jurisprudential corners from which he never extricated himself." Frankfurter became so intent on beating his adversaries on seeking revenge for the insult to his pride, that he became obsessed by an austere doctrine of judicial self-restraint.

Frankfurter's career vividly illustrates Weisberg's views. With Frankfurter, as with other ressentient individuals, "vengeance takes the form of a Hamlet-like torrent of words directed against an irrelevant object;" in Frankfurter's case, many long opinions rationalizing his inaction. Surely Frankfurter's critics would say he "saturates the page with vindictive verbosity," that he "retreats into language" with "wordy cowardice." What Weisberg says about one of Camus's characters applies with equal force to Frankfurter: he was afflicted with the "massive evil which intellectuals endure when they allow formal structures to replace their native sense of justice." Wordiness leads "to passivity in the face of clear injustice or, worse still, to the creation of injustice itself."

Many of Frankfurter's critics say that he lost an "opportunity for truly creative jurisprudence" because his judicial self-restraint got in the way. Such criticism calls to mind Weisberg's comment that, "highly formalized language mediates between [ressentient legalists] and the exigencies of life, protecting but also gradually distancing them from the sources of positive and creative action." Just the juxtaposition of the comments underscores the power of Weisberg's analysis and its tremendous utility. It would be a great surprise if Weisberg turned out to be a Frankfurter fan. Much closer to Weisberg's world view is the remark of Justice Douglas, who once wrote: "[i]t makes a mockery of judges who insist that if they were not imprisoned by the law they could do justice."

Legal Interpretation

Judicial activism and judicial restraint are aspects of legal interpretation. Just as Weisberg's book gives insight into the activist-restraint conundrum, it also illustrates various facets of endemic problems in legal interpretation. Weisberg's analysis of fictional works displays his views on basic interpretive problems. Those views, when drawn out, are interesting in their own right, and suggest new devices for discussing old problems.

1. Law and Values. If Weisberg's book is a symbolic essay about law, its implications are broad and relate to the most current debates in constitutional law. Weisberg bemoans literature without values. According to Weisberg, the "absence of deep-rooted values" causes severe problems for literary characters. Clamence, one of Camus's existentialist heroes, has learned nothing because he failed to "conceive the positive, ethical value system which must replace the rotten present code." On the very last page of his text, Weisberg welcomes the "seeds of a revivified genre" that includes "reintegration of language and values." Our generation, he says, should be especially "wary of language systems bereft of ethical referents."

Weisberg's discussion of values in literature sounds much like a similar discussion in law. Indeed, Weisberg may actually be discussing law obliquely. At one point, for example, he directly states that "European religion, law, scholarship, and literature . . . may have rationalized their own values out of existence."

The role of values is crucial to the controversy over the legitimacy of judicial review in a democracy. That controversy has focused on what values, if any, courts should implement in interpreting the Constitution. Several scholars think courts should use such values, whether they be conventional morality, fundamental rights, the judges' own values, neutral principles, natural law, consensus, or tradition. In *Democracy and Distrust*, John Ely took a different approach. Ely proposed reinforcing participation and representation in a democracy. Ely argued that all the value-filled approaches were defective and noninterpretive in the sense that they were not found either explicitly or implicitly in the Constitution.

In time, however, Ely had to bear the brunt of his own criticism. His "process-oriented" strategy struck an astute observer as itself "covertly value-laden." Paul Brest argued that electoral participation, so stressed by Ely, was as much a value as any of the values that Ely had exposed. In the end, Brest called Ely's effort a "detour" and concluded that no system of judicial review can be value-free.

Against the background of the debate over values in judicial review, Weisberg's book takes on more meaning. Presumably Weisberg would eschew a value-neutral form of judicial review, "bereft of ethical referents." Presumably Weisberg would strongly favor a form of judicial review based on "deep-rooted values," that "conceive the positive, ethical value system." Precisely what values Weisberg would enforce through judicial review is more difficult to tell. The "salutary traits" referred to by Weisberg—vitality, sincerity, passionate involvement with others, ethical leadership, refusal to let clear wrongdoing survive—differ from the sort of values usually associated with constitutional law.

2. Objectivity and Subjectivity. Weisberg draws a central distinction between objective and subjective interpretation. The thrust of his analysis in this regard is that law is riddled with subjectivity. He does not necessarily use "subjective" in a pejorative sense. In describing incidents in Dostoevsky's novels, he points out the artistry and imagination involved in legal investigation of the facts, which lead to a "personalized vision of reality." Such "artistic legality" and "idiosyncratic vision" can be brilliant accomplishments, even if subjective. But, Weisberg says, they explode the myth of legal "objectivity."

Exploding the myth of objectivity in law, as well as elsewhere, has been a recurring and controversial modern theme. During the late nineteenth century, for instance, the dominant view in America was that judges were oracles of the law, that they "found" the law as it had always existed, and mechanically applied such law to the facts in particular cases. In theory, such Legal Formalism, based as it was on deductive logic, made law seem objective by reducing the subjective element in limiting the scope of a judge's discretion and creativity. This formalistic view lulled people into thinking that they were living under a "government not of men but of laws."

With the publication of Holmes's *Common Law*, in 1881, Legal Formalism started to come under attack. Judicial decisions, which had hitherto been cloaked in the guise of logic, began to be seen as choices between competing public policies. Inspired by Holmes and later by Cardozo, the Legal Realists showed that judged do in fact make and change law. The Realists advocated the use of sociological facts and empirical research to justify the social policies, or sets of values or goals, on which judicial decisions rested. Recognizing the subjectivity of judicial decision-making, the Legal Realists called for bringing the relevant factors out into the open.

Even the Legal Realists, however, failed to resolve the tension between objective and subjective legal interpretation. Such tension figures prominently in all discussions of the judicial function. Should a judge impose his or her own vague preferences as law? No one publicly supports such arrant subjectivism. But if the legal text to be interpreted is vague or ambiguous, where is the judge to find guidance, especially when the drafter's intent is unclear or when times have changed. Such tension creates the crucial problems of legal interpretation.

Weisberg's book reveals him to be a modern Legal Realist. Like the Legal Realists of the past, Weisberg recognizes the subjectivity inherent in the legal process. Captain Vere in *Billy Budd* is "the apparent voice of disinterest, reason and formality." But Vere is disingenuous in describing the choice he says the law compels him to make. Weisberg sees "the articulate figure's [*i.e.*, the lawyer's] fundamental subjectivity" as part of a process where "law disguises with seeming rationality an arbitrary value system."

Legalistic characters in fiction "disguise a ferociously negative subjective tendency with a coolly rational outer form." Vere, like other lawyer-types, "deliberately distorts the operative law" to arrive at a conclusion "harmonious with his deepest *private* urges." *Billy Budd,* Weisberg says, is an "inquiry into the uses of external forms to justify intense subjective urges." Thus, "we begin to see how quickly an intelligent individual can muster "cool, outer forms" to serve "formless, subjective ends."

Weisberg's literary investigations may suggest a tentative and partial solution to the riddle of subjectivity and objectivity in law. First, he says, we "need to examine the premises upon which articulations are based." At least then we can know the actual dynamics of decision. Having examined those premises, we can consciously seek the "possibility for creative craftsmanship divorced from underlying subjective motivations." How this "possibility" is achieved is not exactly clear, but, at a minimum, it is a step in the right direction.

3. Hidden Motives: A Current Example. Weisberg's comments about objectivity and subjectivity have great immediacy. To Weisberg's mind, literary lawyers tend to speak covertly and by indirection, often with "organic mendacity." As Weisberg writes, the "seemingly cool outward forms of legal procedures often mask the bitter subjective aims of those who employ them—aims which are, in Melville's words, 'never declared' and which can only discovered through careful analysis.'" Further along these lines, "one who calls loudest for a purely formal analysis of a phenomenon may be one who most subtly conceals some private animus."

Although Weisberg is purportedly writing about fictional lawyers, what he says has striking relevance to a running debate among real lawyers and judges. At least since 1985, conservatives have favored a jurisprudence of the original intent of the Framers in order to resurrect the original meaning of constitutional provisions. Such a jurisprudence shows uneasiness about the vagaries of constitutional interpretation. The uncertainty and subjectivity of judicial policy-making can be cured only by resort to more objective principles. Lack of standards and guidelines creates unpredictability. Hence, to some people, the need for a jurisprudence of original intention.

However, we have to be careful, especially in constitutional law, to search for certainty and objectivity in original intent beyond the language actually used in the Constitution. Original intent may appear to be objective, when in fact, such supposed objectivity is mere illusion and a mask for equally subjective policy-making.

It is unclear whether originalists have proposed a new constitutional approach or are merely expressing substantive disagreement with certain Supreme Court decisions they dislike. Given the vast difficulties of determining original intent, the supposed objective nature of original intent may be a delusion. If such objectivity is illusory, may not jurisprudence of original intent be a disguise for equally subjective policy choices by Supreme Court justices?

Originalism has provoked great debate, much of which has revolved about possible hidden motives. In a rare public statement, Justice Brennan said, "[w]hile proponents of this facile historicism justify it as a depoliticization of the judiciary, . . . the political underpinnings of such a choice should not escape notice." Although originalism "feigns self-effacing deference to the specific judgments of those who forged our original social compact," Brennan added, "in truth it is little more than arrogance cloaked as humility." Likewise, it may be that what really interests originalists is not judicial philosophy but particular political results.

Regardless of which side one finds oneself on in this debate, the debate itself demonstrates the utility of Weisberg's analysis. Indeed, insofar as it turns on originalists' candor, the debate is being carried out on Weisberg's terms. The debate fits nicely into Weisberg's analysis. That analysis puts the originalist proposal into a larger perspective.

SYMBOLISM

To understand fully *The Failure of the Word*, we must keep three things in mind. First, we must remember that Weisberg is a lawyer. Second, we must recall that lawyers, according to Weisberg himself, speak by indirection. Finally, we must recollect that Weisberg has written on Mallarmé. Mallarmé is the key that unlocks the deep secrets of *The Failure of the Word*.

Mallarmé was a poet of the Symbolist school in France in the late nineteenth century. One of the primary aims of the Symbolists was to intimate things rather than to state them plainly. Language must make use of symbols. Direct statements or description gave way to a succession of words and of images, which suggest the idea. Some poets, wrote Mallarmé: "take the thing just as it is and put it before us—and consequently they are deficient in mystery: they deprive the mind of the delicious joy of believing that it is creating. To name an object is to do away with the three-quarters of the enjoyment of the poem which is derived from the satisfaction of guessing little by little: to suggest it, to evoke it—that is what claims the imagination." Mallarmé chose symbols as a sort of disguise for his ideas.

Weisberg writes in the Symbolist tradition, and like Mallarmé, the subject of his thesis, Weisberg suggests by way of symbols. In *The Failure of the Word* Weisberg uses literature as a symbol for the law, and fictional lawyers as symbols for real lawyers. By writing about literature and literary lawyers, Weisberg suggests ideas to the reader so that he or she can create the connections that are not explicitly spelled out. In this sense, *The Failure of the Word*, is itself a work of art.

As a result of Mallarmé's influence, Weisberg's book is richly textured and can be read on levels. On its face, it is a first-rate book of literary criticism and analysis, filled with original insight. This is the manifest content of *The Failure of the Word*.

But the true success of Weisberg's book is gauged by its latent content. Underneath the literary analysis lies a subtle and suggestive essay on law. The full value and complete achievement of *The Failure of the Word* emerges only when it is viewed on both levels. On the deeper level, the book evokes ideas, concepts, and insights that add further meaning to the understanding of law.

Weisberg offers us a new way of looking at law: with the sensitive and discriminating eye of the thinking artist. Throughout history artists have given us useful and penetrating insight. If they would train their sights on law, we might all gain further understanding. Weisberg's technique is fruitful, his concept of "ressentient legalism" is creative and useful. Weisberg's book may be a step on the road to a new jurisprudence.

Weisberg is a law professor with a fertile and provocative imagination. With *The Failure of the Word*, his first book, he showed himself to be in the forefront of the creative blending of law and literature. His performance belies the title of his book. His writing proves, not the failure, but the success of the word.

31

ADAM AND EVE HIRE A LAWYER

Imagine Adam and Eve, after being banished from the Garden of Eden, consulting a lawyer operating under twenty-first century American legal precedent. The meeting might go something like this:

"Let's see what we have here," the lawyer says, opening their file. As he turns the pages, he asks "Any prior record?"

"No," they both answer.

"Well, at least that's something. Why don't we take it from the top? Tell me what happened in your own words. Try not to leave out anything."

"God created us," Adam says, "and put us in the Garden of Eden. He told us we could eat anything except the fruit of the Tree of Knowledge of Good and Evil."

"One day," Eve goes on, "the Serpent persuaded me to eat from the Tree of Knowledge of Good and Evil. And I convinced Adam to eat from it too." Adam glares at Eve; tears well up in Eve's eyes, as her cheeks redden with embarrassment.

Seeing her discomfort, the lawyer gives her a tissue from a box he keeps on his desk for just such occasions and gently says, "That's all right. Relax. Don't hold anything back. Everything you tell me is absolutely confidential and protected by the attorney-client privilege. Now, are you saying that before you ate the forbidden fruit you didn't know the difference between good and evil?"

"I think so," Adam says, and Eve nods in agreement. "God once told us that if we ate from that darn tree we would become like Him, 'knowing good and evil.'" A hint of a knowing smile, almost a smirk, slowly crosses the lawyer's lips.

"We may have something here, a good point for appeal. It is an axiom of criminal law that no punishment can be given to anyone who does not know the difference between right and wrong, good and evil."

The lawyer makes a note and says, "Please go on with your story."

"God soon came looking for me," Adam says. "He confronted me and I confessed."

"Did He read you your rights? Did He give you the *Miranda* warnings?"

"No."

"Continue."

"God then punished us by banishing us forever from Eden so we could not become immortal by also eating from the Tree of Life. He went further and condemned us to a mortal life of hardship. That's about it. We left Eden, now we're here. We don't know what to do."

"Are you telling me God imposed a death penalty on you and all your descendants?"

"I guess so," answers Adam, not fully understanding the meaning of the word death.

"Interesting," said the lawyer. "I've never heard of capital punishment before. It sounds cruel and unusual."

"Wait a minute, Adam," Eve interrupts. "You forgot to tell him that my punishment is a little different from yours."

"What do you mean?" asks the puzzled attorney.

"I was sentenced to the pains of childbirth and to be subservient to man. And I don't like that one bit. Why is biology my destiny?"

"A good point, madam. It sounds like discrimination based on nothing but sex. But there's something else that bothers me. You say that the punishment not only affects you but also your descendants?"

"Yes."

"That doesn't sound right. Why should all of future humanity be punished for your sin? Eve, let me ask you this: whose idea was it to eat the forbidden fruit, yours, or the Serpent's?"

"The Serpent's; he put the idea in my head. I wasn't predisposed to do it."

"As God's creation, the Serpent was God's agent, albeit an undercover one—and you both were innocent victims of entrapment! We might also argue that the forbidden fruit stands for knowledge and wisdom, the acquisition of which no government may prohibit. Was the forbidden fruit 'classified information'? Who classified it and why? Is national security involved? Did you give information to WikiLeaks? You have First Amendment rights, you know. Or if the forbidden fruit symbolizes sexual maturity, and the loss of innocence that comes with it, then the basic right of matrimonial and sexual privacy comes into play."

The lawyer, enjoying himself now, was picking up a head of steam.

"In the Garden of Eden, there was a pure theocracy; God was the State. His commands, coming as they did from the highest possible religious authority, may violate the separation between church and state."

Adam and Even look at each other with hope, even if they do not really understand what the lawyer is saying.

"Your case is shot through with serious procedural violations. Your confessions should be totally inadmissible. There was no grand jury indictment. There was no trial. You were denied assistance of counsel. Reliance on your confessions violated your privilege against self-incrimination. The trier of fact was not impartial; He was accuser, judge and jury all rolled into one. The so-called proceedings made a mockery of your right to a jury trial. There was no jury, much less a jury of twelve of your peers. You had no peers."

Already the lawyer is interested. He hasn't had a case like this in years, not since Satan was expelled from Heaven. Now that was a good case, the lawyer thought to himself. A difficult client but a good case.

"I'll take your case," the attorney announces, "but on one condition."

"What's that?"

"I'll need you either to sign a conflict waiver, or Eve, you will have to get a separate lawyer."

"Why?" asks Eve.

"Because you and Adam may be in different legal positions. Adam might want to argue he is less culpable, that you Eve were the one who broke the law and you seduced Adam to eat the apple, and he merely acted out of love."

"Okay," answered both clients in unison, "we'll sign a conflict waiver."

"Now let's talk about an uncomfortable subject, my fee."

"Fee?!?" Adam and Eve exclaim together.

"If a retainer is a problem, then I'll take half the profits from the book and the movie and all other subsidiary and electronic rights. This could have legs, could be a bestseller. Who knows?"

32

POLITICS AND LITIGATION

Election campaigns have something of importance to teach lawyers. Now that we are in the era of permanent campaigns, the possible lessons practically stare us in the face. But the lessons for lawyers may be unclear or ambiguous, or both, and different lawyers, with different temperaments, may take away different lessons.

An election campaign is, like litigation, an adversary process. The two (or more) candidates resemble the opposing lawyers. Each depends on the art of persuasion to accomplish his or her goal. One set tries to persuade voters, the other tries to persuade judges and jurors.

Part of this process of persuasion involves each side trying to make itself or its message look more compelling, more correct, more appealing, than the other side and its message. This effort often employs some sort of criticism of the other side. In one context, such criticism may take the form of attack ads or scandal rumors; in the other, accusations of misinterpreting precedent, distorting evidence, or even litigation misconduct.

In both situations, the big question, requiring a prompt answer, is how, if at all, to respond. Should political candidates or lawyers answer every argument and criticism? Much—the outcome of an election or a lawsuit—may depend on the response, or lack of one. Yet not everyone agrees on what to do.

One approach in politics is aggressive and energetic. During the 1992 presidential election, for instance, Bill Clinton's campaign famously set up a 24/7 war room run by James Carville and George Stephanopolous to respond immediately to any and all attacks or criticisms of their candidate. No charges, no matter how trivial, were allowed to go unanswered. Many political analysts attribute Clinton's success in 1992 at least in part to this strategy of quick defense and counterattack.

Failure to use just such a strategy is often blamed for John Kerry's loss in 2004. For weeks Kerry's staff ignored the Swift boat attacks on his military service in Vietnam, assuming no one would take them seriously. How, they thought, could the public be fooled by such unsupported charges made, ironically, on behalf of someone who never saw combat, against someone actually wounded and decorated? The Kerry campaign staffers thought wrong. Too late, they responded, but the response was less than overwhelming and failed.

On the other hand, the Democratic presidential candidate in 2008 used self-restraint successfully during the primary campaigns. Barack Obama made a widely publicized point of refusing to engage in the "old politics" of attacking his opponent personally or defending himself against every attack. Obama said he would stick to the issues, not personalities.

This attitude became a signature, a distinctive characteristic, of his campaign, frustrating those who opposed him but making him appear "above" the undignified pettiness and nastiness of shot-for-shot attacks and defenses. But questions lingered and still linger over whether such a nice-guy, statesmanlike stance will work in other elections.

What should a practicing lawyer make of this recent political history? How does a litigating lawyer translate these political lessons into his or her daily professional life? And is there even one clear lesson? Or are the lessons from politics complicated? Do they point in more than one direction, without sure guidance to lawyers?

Suppose an adversary in a lawsuit makes several arguments, some important, some not. Is it absolutely necessary to disprove all of those points? Is it even good practice? It would seem better to concentrate on the main themes and not waste precious time and space on minor or irrelevant points. But we are taught to be thorough and we worry that the unanswered argument, however trivial, might somehow prevail.

A litigation scenario closer to the political context occurs when one attorney attacks his or her adversary personally. Suppose a lawyer was once sued for malpractice or was criticized in a court opinion. Should an adversary hoping for spillover prejudice mention such past events in an unrelated lawsuit? And if they are raised, how much space, if any, in this age of page-limited briefs, should the lawyer being attacked devote to explaining that the malpractice suit was dismissed or settled for nuisance value or is otherwise irrelevant? Or that the judge who made the criticism was simply wrong?

Similar points of personal privilege arise all the time. Lawyers representing clients in litigation often accuse their adversaries of conflicts of interest, spoliation of evidence, misrepresenting the law and distorting the facts, lying about oral agreements between counsel and bringing up endless irrelevancies. Some of these categories— misrepresenting, distorting, lying—resemble the charges made in political campaigns. In his 2004 book *The Winning Brief*, Bryan Garner says that "you know you must counter it, but how do you do so without getting in the muck?"

The temptation for the lawyer to respond, to dispel misinformation, is huge and often irresistible. The lawyer wants to set the record straight and defend himself or herself. Absent a response, moreover, the judge could well get the wrong impression. The lawyer, like the politician, wants to win and has a professional bent to refute every allegation.

But perhaps the temptation to respond should be resisted. What about the Obama approach? Should not a lawyer following Obama's successful example, focus on the real issues and not be distracted by or drawn into personal attacks or other irrelevancies? A 2008 book by Justice Antonin Scalia and Bryan Garner, *Making Your Case*, advises, "Don't show indignation at the shoddy treatment your client has received or at the feeble or misleading arguments raised by opposing counsel." (This advice might raise an eyebrow or two among readers familiar with Justice Scalia's own sometimes fiery judicial opinions.)

Does responding to an attack, moreover, appear defensive and reinforce the thrust of the attack itself? Shouldn't we trust judges to see through arrant nonsense and rule wisely on the merits? Does not professionalism dictate a certain lofty standard of style in these matters to avoid making and responding to personal attacks? Surely the job of judges would be simpler and easier if they did not have to wade through all the irrelevancies and ad hominem passages in legal papers. According to *Writing to Win* by Steven Stark, "You do not have to answer each allegation and charge raised by the other side."

There may be no one simple right answer, either in politics or in litigation. Experience in both fields is ambiguous and ambivalent.

Sometimes the war room approach wins, sometimes the opposite substantive, dignified approach succeeds. Which one will prevail in a particular context is not always easy to predict with certainty. Either course of action has its risks.

Lawyers may think that they are acting to counter misinformation by pointing out it is not true. But by repeating an adversary's argument, if only to refute it, they may inadvertently make it stronger.

This dilemma and paradox has always plagued libel plaintiffs who, by suing, risk giving more publicity and currency to the defamatory comments that may not have been so widely circulated. In any effort to rebut the other side, lawyers may want to keep this in mind.

33

ENGLISH REVOLUTION REDUX

Books sometimes surprise us, and that is one of the many joys of reading. We choose a volume because we like the author or are interested in the subject, but then, as we are reading, the unexpected suddenly happens. The pages we are perusing come alive all at once and take on new meaning. They connect with current events or other things we have been reading and illuminate other subjects in stimulating and previously unseen ways.

The Tyrannicide Brief, published in England in 2005 by Geoffrey Robertson, a prominent barrister known for his defense of human rights, vividly tells the story of the relatively unknown lawyer, John Cooke, who in 1649 prosecuted King Charles I for treason during the English Civil War. The main thrust of *The Tyrannicide Brief* is to explain how Cook conducted the first trial of a head of state for waging war on his own people, which foreshadowed the prosecutions in our day of Pinochet, Milosevic and Saddam Hussein.

But as I read about the causes of the English Civil War over three hundred and fifty years ago, I could not help thinking about current events. Today's hot-button controversies—executive privilege, torture, extraordinary rendition, indefinite detention without counsel or habeas corpus, secret military trials with abbreviated procedural rights, even the power to wage war—all relate back to seventeenth-century English history.

The core issue in the English Civil War was the struggle for power between King Charles I and Parliament. Today the single most important and controversial structural issue in American government is the struggle for power between the president and Congress.

I was struck by the similarities. In each case, separated by centuries, the executive and the legislature compete for dominance.

I would read a page about seventeenth century English history, and it often seemed as if I could have been reading the front page from tomorrow's *New York Times*. The cliché about history repeating itself leaped to mind.

The similarities between then and now have not been lost on everyone. Some of those who defended President George W. Bush's actions actually claimed—incredible as it sounds—to find support in the seventeenth-century powers of the English king. One such defender was and is John Yoo, who as a lawyer in the Justice Department's influential Office of Legal Counsel played a key role in some of those decisions. Yoo's memoranda provided legal cover for several of the most obnoxious of our policies during the war on terror.

Yoo wrote that English political history should inform our Constitution's war powers and grant "monarchical" power to the president. In a 2002 article, Yoo claimed that the president had the "plenary powers of the king" except when explicitly abrogated by the Constitution. Similarly, argued Yoo, the seventeenth-century English king's royal "prerogative" power to "suspend" or "dispense" with Parliamentary laws is authority for an American president to ignore statutes passed by Congress—such as prohibitions on torture and warrantless eavesdropping on Americans—whenever he or she claims that "national security" or "military necessity" is at issue.

Yoo is right to compare today's events to seventeenth-century English history, but demonstrably wrong in his conclusions and the verdict of history on Charles I. Yoo ignores the end results. It is truly bizarre for Yoo to have cited Charles I's actions as reliable precedent.

Charles I favored what some now call a unitary executive. He relentlessly tried to gather all power into his own hands. He dissolved Parliament in 1628. He used what was referred to as his "negative voice" (what we might call a veto or signing statement) to nullify what Parliament did. He removed judges whose decisions displeased him. The notorious Court of Star Chamber used the power to arrest, to torture and to sentence to indefinite imprisonment ("at his Majesty's pleasure") for political offenses such as seditious libel.

In the 1600s, for instance, the English king had the right to declare war, but Parliament alone could decide whether and how to raise any tax to fight that war. But Charles I, violating this rule, chose to raise taxes himself, and an obsequious court in 1638 generated much discontent when it upheld the king: "The King may dispense with any laws in case of necessity . . . . Rex is Lex . . . . The King can do no wrong." Another judge on the same court said the King had unlimited discretion to act for what, in his unchallengeable subjective view, was the public good: His good faith had to be assumed on the question of whether the kingdom was in danger.

But the outcome of England's Civil War repudiated those royal claims. The court of history ruled against Charles I's notion that the king is above the law. Charles's fundamental error, according to barrister Robertson, was to pit his "single judgment" against the law made by the people of England through their elective representatives. Charles's prosecutor thought tyranny occurred when rulers showed "their fixed intention to govern without Parliament or an independent judiciary or any other democratic check on their power."

Rather than support an imperial presidency, the history of seventeenth-century England militates compellingly against it. On regaining power after the Restoration in 1660, some highly placed monarchists wanted to keep republican diehards in prison indefinitely. But since the Magna Carta allowed anyone in England to use habeas corpus to challenge his or her imprisonment, someone in authority came up with a pernicious idea that echoes today. The king would keep his political "enemy combatants" in custody forever not in England but the off-shore islands of Jersey and the Isle of Man. This attempted end run was so unpopular that the official who came up with it had to leave office, and Parliament in 1679 passed the Habeas Corpus Act, which made the "great writ" apply extraterritorially. In 2004 the U.S. Supreme Court cited this history in *Rasul v. Bush*, a case dealing with detainees at Guantanamo.

Perhaps we should not be surprised that the causes of the English Civil War still play themselves out in current American history. Much of American legal and political experience has its roots in the ferment of seventeenth-century English history. Englishmen settled the American colonies during the seventeenth century and as colonists took with them the prevailing ideas of the day and then built on those ideas, adapting them to American soil. Those intellectual, legal and political ideas of the American colonists—which created certain lasting concepts of liberty that would have an important role in the American Revolution and after—included ending the divine right of kings.

And perhaps we also should not be surprised if any nation has continual governance struggles. That is what separation of powers and checks and balances are all about. They are "essential to the preservation of liberty," as Madison wrote in *Federalist* No. 51.

A review of current events in light of the English Civil War calls to mind a famous speech by Patrick Henry, a self-taught Virginia lawyer, in the run-up to the American Revolution. Speaking in 1765, patriot Henry, complaining about the unpopular Stamp Act, referred to the events of seventeenth-century English history and declared, "George the Third may profit from their example."

Our George the Second and his successors should also have profited from their example.

34

BILL CLINTON AND THE DRAFT

Ever since 1975, with the advent of the all volunteer Army, the military draft has ceased to be a factor in the lives of young Americans. It was not always that way, as millions of men in their mid-sixties and early seventies may recall. When my law school classmate Bill Clinton ran for president in 1992, his failure to respond to the draft during Vietnam became an issue. But it was a false issue.

I

We should not punish politicians for their virtues, yet we almost did that to Clinton over his Vietnam draft status. The real issue was neither whether the Arkansas governor was a draft dodger, nor whether he was disingenuous to his draft board and ROTC in 1969. Nor was there a genuine question about the depth or sincerity of Clinton's opposition as a student to the Vietnam War.

The main point cuts deeper, straight to the never-completely-healed wound of our emotionally scarring national experience during the Vietnam era. How to respond to the Vietnam draft was the greatest personal moral crisis in the lives of men of a certain age. Vietnam is the skeleton in America's political closet, and talk about draft evasion during that era resurrects a national "character issue." To discuss how Clinton responded to the draft in 1969 is to reopen the wound of an unfinished and bitter debate about the true meaning of patriotism, courage and democracy at a unique moment of American history—a moment that defined those who came to political consciousness during it.

Vietnam was not World War II. Opposition to the Vietnam War was as honorable as serving in it. If we disqualify candidates who avoided the draft during Vietnam, we unnecessarily and drastically limit the pool of available talent.

No one of Clinton's generation who has lived through the same times and faced the same hard choices and real dangers will have— and no one else should have—any serious criticism of his behavior regarding the draft.

For those of us who were draft bait during the Vietnam era, Clinton's now famous letter to the ROTC colonel resonates loudly and meaningfully. With heartfelt and impressive prose from a pen far more mature, thoughtful and fluent than an ordinary twenty-three-year-old, the letter recaptures a difficult time in our lives, when the nation was riven over the war. Breathes there a man then subject to the draft who did not nod knowingly and with understanding and empathy as he read Clinton's passionate description of his personal crisis of conscience?

Unfortunately, at one point Clinton seemed to back away from his earlier, forthright position on the draft and the Vietnam War, as if he was ashamed of it. That was a mistake. He tried to portray himself as patriotically and bravely putting himself in harm's way by making himself available for the draft. But that portrayal is dubious. All it did was unnecessarily create new questions about his credibility.

Rather than put a new spin on his personal history, Clinton should have proudly reasserted the honorable position he took back in 1969. All Clinton had to do was remind people how it really was to be a graduate student in 1969 without a draft deferment, and explain what patriotism and courage meant then.

It is not hard to recall a law student's feelings about the draft in 1969. Like Clinton, I graduated from college in 1968, after graduate-school deferments had been eliminated, and I started my first year of law school that September. Overhanging that whole first year was the somber, ever-present threat of the draft, which dominated the thoughts and conversations of law students far more than course work.

Each night during supper, the television in the law school dining room broadcast the evening news. Color film clips showed the latest jungle battles and body counts. Some of us, preoccupied with our personal fates, would become quiet and have trouble eating. Others would talk about their draft strategies, ranging from joining Reserve or National Guard units to exploring conscientious-objector status and trying teaching as a deferment.

Certain events were more depressing than others: receiving your reclassification from 2-S (student deferment) to 1-A (draft eligible) was one. That night it was impossible to study. Abstraction turned to reality when you got your notice to report for a physical examination. My exam was at Whitehall Street in lower Manhattan, a strange experience recalled with gallows humor each time I hear Arlo Guthrie sing "Alice's Restaurant." Once you passed your physical, you knew the inevitable was going to happen—unless you did something to avoid it.

In this peculiar setting, "patriotism" and "courage" were not simplistic, one-dimensional terms. People of intelligence, integrity and good will wondered aloud who was more patriotic, who loved his country more: the young man who, like millions before him, answered his country's call to don a uniform; or the one who, believing that an ill-conceived, unwise, unnecessary, unpopular, undeclared foreign war of uncertain purpose violated our nation's credo, refused to be part of the military. Opinion was split over whether it was braver to be in the military at the risk of physical harm or to avoid the military at whatever personal cost. Neither side in that national debate had a monopoly on patriotism or courage.

In retrospect, especially as we fight back tears while walking slowly by the haunting Vietnam Veterans Memorial in Washington, we feel the horrible waste and futility of our tragically misguided Vietnam policy. On the other hand, as Clinton recognized in his letter, we should ask why any of us should not have shared the burdens and risks that others—others less well-educated or less affluent or less articulate—were shouldering. How much of our reactions to the draft were colored by moral antipathy to the war and how much by mere selfishness?

More than anything else in our history, Vietnam tested the limits of that beguiling but dangerous phrase "my country right or wrong."

Clinton and I took different paths. I was drafted into the Army in October 1969, during my second year of law school, in the last draft call before the lottery system and went into the Army as a private. But I was lucky: I wasn't sent to Vietnam and I didn't get maimed or killed.

By not being drafted, Clinton missed an important aspect of the democratic experience; serving for a time as a citizen-soldier with other Americans drawn from all walks of life. I was the only Caucasian drafted from New York City that day, and I learned at least as much from my Army experience as I did from law school about equality under the law.

Missing that experience, however, in no way disqualified Clinton from the presidency. Military service would be useful but is no prerequisite for a good chief executive. I can think of many soldiers I knew who make me shudder at the thought of their being in high elective office.

When my tour was over in 1971, I returned to law school anxious to start my second year again. Among my new classmates were, in addition to Clinton, several who had delayed or interrupted law school because of the war. Yet, no doubt because of the draft lottery and the phased withdrawal of troops, there was now less talk about the war, and what talk there was seemed less strident. Those who had served nursed no sense of injustice against those who did not. Nor should they now more than four decades later.

It would have been absurd if Bill Clinton draft status during the Vietnam era had in any way been held against him.

II

Thinking about Clinton and the draft made me introspective and wonder about myself and the draft. Why, I now ask myself forty-five years later, did I not try somehow to avoid military service as most similarly situated law students at ivy league schools did? Over the years I have thought about this question a lot. My friends and classmates thought I was nuts. There were not many ivy league law student draftees in the Army during the Vietnam War.

After long self-analysis, I have the following layered response, which may not be reliable, as most of our important choices in life are non-rational and difficult to fathom. I may fall prey to the subjectivity and kaleidoscopic permutations that memory can work on reality. In any event, I have finally come to the conclusion that I must somehow have *wanted*, subconsciously, to be drafted, but not necessarily for patriotic reasons alone. Other factors were at work, and if you did not duck, you got hit.

The first layer of my reasons is, in a sense, the most obvious and the most superficial. Patriotism and love of country are instilled in us early on, and they played a role, although I did not at the time have strong beliefs one way or the other about the merits of the Vietnam War. I was too busy with my studies. I was more concerned with and more interested in contracts, torts and civil procedure than in the politics of the falling domino theory in southeast Asia. I was not a conscientious objector.

Maybe I had seen too many John Wayne war movies and watched too many episodes of "Victory at Sea." Perhaps I had read too many of Winston Churchill's stirring wartime speeches. I know that during basic training I imagined myself at Valley Forge with George Washington and the Continentals, with the Union troops at Gettysburg, and with the GIs landing at Normandy on D-Day. I felt like I was one with them. The day I was inducted I experienced a real emotional *frisson* as I swore, just like the president of the United States does at every inauguration, to "protect and defend" the Constitution, the same Constitution I had been so recently and so carefully studying in my first year of law school. But this response, strong as it is, hardly scratches the surface.

The next layer down is more interesting. I thought of the draft as part of the social contract I implicitly made with America. I remembered Plato's dialogues about the last days of Socrates, which I had read in college. After being sentenced to drink the hemlock, Socrates chooses not to escape from prison when offered the chance. He asks his friend Crito to imagine what the Laws of Athens would say if they were now to appear in his cell and discuss the matter with him. In this imaginary conversation described by Socrates, the Laws explain the concept of law as a contract between the state and the individual citizen. The Laws argue that Socrates, after benefitting all his life from the Laws of Athens, would now be breaking that contract if he ran away rather than obey a lawful decree simply because he considered it unjust.

I was like Socrates. I had received many substantial benefits from our society, in my case, a first-rate free education at New York City public schools (including the Bronx High School of Science) and college (City College of New York when tuition there was free), access to whatever books I wanted to read at fabulously well-stocked free public libraries, admission to an elite law school (Yale), and unlimited opportunity. It was as if America (and the City and State of New York) had said to me: "Son, we will give you the best we have to offer. You can go to the best schools, study with the best teachers, read whatever you want, and become whatever you want. We will give you every advantage we can. All we ask in return is, in essence, that you pay your taxes and, if we need you, that you serve for a few years in the military."

That was the implied contract, a good and more-than-fair one as far as I was concerned. Rather than a Faustian bargain, I felt I had greatly benefitted from a generous, one-sided deal with my guardian angel. I thought I was getting by far the better of the deal and that society was asking little in return from me. So when the time came for me to honor my part of the contract, how could I say no? To do so would have been churlish and ungrateful of me. Being a citizen-soldier struck me simply as one assumed aspect of citizenship, like being a Minuteman, whether you regard it as a burden and obligation or an honor and a privilege.

It also seemed to me to be hypocritical to talk in class in an ivy league institution about democracy and liberal ideas and equality before the law and then let military service in an unpopular war fall primarily on the shoulders of underprivileged young men. You cannot utter clichés and platitudes about how we are all equal and live in a classless society, and then avoid obligations just because they are onerous. You have to walk the walk, not just talk the talk. Kids in the ghetto should not be the only ones drafted. Author and former Marine Karl Marlantes captures this thought in *Matterhorn*, his novel about the Vietnam War, when he has an African-American soldier explain: "The draft is *white* people sending *black* people to fight *yellow* people to protect the country they stole from the *red* people." One of the young men drafted with me was a recent immigrant from Castro's Cuba who had just started college. Not yet even a citizen, he was drafted. Why? Why should those who had benefitted least from our society be drafted, but those who had benefitted most not be? It made no sense to me. It was grossly unfair.

If we mean what we say, we must all share in such obligations. It is unclear to me, moreover, how much draft avoidance was the product of deep and sincere moral opposition to the Vietnam War and how much sprang from a desire not to have one's life interfered with and put at risk. Fear, anxiety and self-indulgence are insufficient reasons for avoiding one's duty, especially if such true reasons are masked by high-sounding, even sincere, political opposition to an unjust war. In my mind, being drafted was part of what it meant to be an American. In retrospect, however, I suspect this second group of reasons is more after-the-fact intellectual rationalizing than anything else.

We come then to the final layer, to what I think was really going on in my head, though hardly on a rational or even conscious level. The more I think about it, the more I believe that my decision not to avoid the draft was primarily psychological and subconscious. Part of me was probably competing with my father, who was drafted into the Navy in World War II and earned two battle stars in the Pacific Theater.

Generational rivalry can be a powerful motivator. Perhaps out of my own insecurity, I wanted to prove I was as good, as patriotic, as brave as he was. I guess I wanted, craved my father's approval and love. I think he understood, for, unlike the rest of my family, he never discussed my decision with me, let alone tried to talk me out of it. The only time I ever recall him hugging me was when I left our family's Bronx apartment at five in the morning to report for induction, as he said softly: "Don't do anything stupid."

Perhaps I saw military service as a rite of passage, a test of manhood, a chance to prove myself, a way to show that the blood was not running thin. In my first year of law school, before I was drafted, I had read Oliver Wendell Holmes's inspiring Memorial Day speeches about his Civil War service, and they affected me greatly. In one of them, called "The Soldier's Faith," Holmes criticized the attitude of those "who think that love of country is an old wive's tale." I was young (twenty-one), physically fit and reasonably athletic, and had gone straight through school—high school, college, law school—without a break. Maybe I saw the Army as a form of what we now call the gap year or as an opportunity—albeit risky—for a very different kind of experience or adventure far away from home.

Another very personal impulse was at work there too, one not easy to discuss publicly. I am Jewish, and very often Jewish men, especially young men, are unfairly portrayed as thin, sickly, unathletic talmudic scholars, separate and apart from the rest of society. I am not that way, did not want to be thought of that way, and did not want to think of myself that way. That stereotypical portrait encourages anti-Semitism. I was of course familiar with and admired the heroic Israeli War of Independence in 1948, the courageous fighters in the 1943 Warsaw Ghetto uprising, and the impressive Israeli battle victories in 1967. That was the kind of strong, robust, physically capable Jew I wanted to be, as American as anyone else, willing to defend, at bodily risk and with one's life if need be, what was important, if only an ideal. My Army tour of duty would be my version, my pale imitation, of the early waves of Jewish settlers in Palestine who adopted the achetype of the New Jew—plow in one hand and rifle in the other.

So being drafted was an easy decision for me, though full of different strands of thought and feeling on different levels, only some of which were conscious. I understand and appreciate that others, like Clinton, came to different conclusions for their own reasons. The thought of avoiding the draft never entered my head. I have never regretted my decision for a minute, am immensely proud of those two years of military service, and I think a lot of my contemporaries missed out on a valuable and unique life experience. The volunteer Army has, unfortunately, culturally separated the vast majority of Americans from any first-hand contact with anything military.

Outspoken cultural critic Camille Paglia pointed to the current diminished status of military service as a symptom of "how a civilization commits suicide." In an interview with the *Wall Street Journal* at the end of 2013, Paglia explained that, "The entire elite class now, in finance, in politics and so on, none of them have military service—hardly anyone, there are a few." She went on, "But there is no prestige attached to it anymore. That is a recipe for disaster."

If it were up to me, I would reinstitute the draft (or at least some form of compulsory national service), and make it absolutely fair (no exemptions). If everyone had to serve, including women and the children of those with wealth and power, we would have fewer wars. But, with a political platform like that, I, unlike Clinton, would never get elected anything.

35

ABOLISH PRIVATE SCHOOLS?

In addition to reinstituing the draft, an equally unpopular plank in my imaginary political platform would be to abolish private schools.* Here is why.

It is always a good time to consider the status of public school education in America. I had a great New York City public school education in the 1950s and early '60s. "Today," as Andrew Delbanco writes in 2013, "when the state of teaching and learning is bemoaned, it is usually the public schools that get the blame." The sixtieth anniversary of the 1954 decision in *Brown v. Board of Education*, which outlawed racial segregation in public schools, is upon us. And more than ten years have passed since the June 2003 decision by the New York Court of Appeals that the existing system of state funding of New York City public schools violates the New York State Constitution. These events both highlight the problem and suggest the pressing need for a new, different, even drastic solution.

Hopes raised by *Brown* have not been fully realized. In terms of racial balance, public schools in many big American cities, including New York City, are largely non-white out of proportion to racial breakdown in the general population. In 2005 Jonathan Kozol, author of *The Shame of the Nation*, wrote that New York "has the infamy today of being the most segregated and unequal state for black and Hispanic students in the nation," reflecting the "conditions of near-absolute apartheid [that] now prevail in New York City schools and those of a growing number of its suburbs."

---

* The third plank of my wildly impracticable political program would be to abolish inherited wealth. Luckily, I never plan to run for political office, be the subject of a Senate confirmation hearing, or be in a position to implement my ideas.

Brown's promise went beyond mere racial integration; it was a promise of opportunity. But failing urban public schools proportionately affect minority children most in need of educational opportunity. That broader promise of *Brown* has failed not only blacks, but everyone. Kozol criticized "those people in New York and other Northern cities who pretend to honor Dr. Martin Luther King while ripping apart the dream for which he died."

Brown's partial failure is a symptom of a larger problem. As the New York case—*Campaign for Fiscal Equity v. New York*—demonstrates, public school education today is, by general agreement, a mess. According to Chief Judge Judith Kaye speaking for the majority in 2003, "New York City schoolchildren are not receiving the constitutionally mandated opportunity for a sound basic education." Three years later, in 2006, Chief Judge Kaye said the State had still "failed to fund the New York City public schools adequately." One intermediate appellate judge in that case pointed out that "a nascent educational crisis has been growing over the years, with roots decades deep, but with consequences that are taking on a new urgency." And the problem is not confined to New York City.

Today's crisis in public school education calls for a fresh solution. We need to approach the problem in a new, perhaps even radical, way. We have to think like Alexander the Great when he dealt with the Gordian Knot. To cut the Gordian Knot of public school education problems, the best solution may be the simplest, may be to—dare we say it?—abolish private schools This plan is not offered as a tongue-in-cheek "modest proposal" à la Jonathan Swift, but as a genuine answer.

Abolishing private schools would make more money available for public schools, improve the average level of education, help racial integration, and lessen discrimination against the poor. Can anyone have the slightest doubt that if there were no private schools and all children—rich and poor, white and non-white—had to go to public schools, then those public schools and their students would be infinitely better off than they are today? Everything would improve: in the argot of the educational field, "inputs" children receive—teaching, facilities and instrumentalities of learning—and their resulting "outputs," such as test results and graduation and dropout rates. The current problems of public schools would then no longer primarily affect only the children of the poor or minorities.

The New York case focused on whether the state's method of funding public education in New York City violates the Education Article of the State Constitution. The Court of Appeals held in 2003 that there was a constitutional violation. "The political process," ruled the Court, "allocates to City schools a share of State aid that does not bear a perceptible relation to the needs of City students."

The Court went on: "New York City schools have the most student need in the State and the highest local costs, yet receive some of the lowest per-student funding and have some of the worst results." The Court's analysis coincided with Kozol's analysis that "New York's whitest and most wealthy suburbs spend approximately twice as much per pupil as is spent on the black and Hispanic kids" in the South Bronx. As a remedy, the Court gave the State until June 30, 2004 to determine the actual cost of providing a sound basic education in New York City and to enact appropriate reforms. A decade later, appropriate reforms have still not happened. In November 2013, the *New York Times* published a long article under the headline "In Public Education, Edge Still Goes to the Rich."

Better or more equal public funding, however, is not nearly enough. It does not address some of the basic, most urgent problems of public school education. Those problems can only be met by banning private schools.

Abolishing private schools will make more money available. The dollars now spent on private school tuition, enrichment and extra-curricular activities could instead be spent on public schools. Public pressure on politicians to spend more money on education would be irresistible. If private schools were banned, wealthy parents would use their considerable resources for the public schools where their children attend.

As Malcolm Gladwell wrote in a *New Yorker* magazine article, "The worst thing that ever happened to incompetent public school districts was the growth of private schools; they siphoned off the kind of parents who would otherwise have agitated more strongly for reform."

By the same token, if everyone went to public school, the average level of education would rise. Inputs would get better. Teacher quality, school facilities, classrooms, class size, classroom supplies, textbooks, libraries and computers would all improve. With improved inputs, it is highly likely that outputs measured by school competition and test results would also rise.

Abolishing private schools will also fulfill the delayed promise of *Brown*. Private schools now allow white students of means to opt out of *Brown*'s corrective sweep. Private schools in New York City are overwhelmingly white, and public schools are overwhelmingly non-white. Just as southern states once used private schools to evade *Brown*'s integration decree, so too New York parents do now, if they can afford it. Without private schools, school integration will at last be a reality.

Finally, eliminating private schools will remove a huge means of discrimination against the poor. Next to inherited wealth, private schools are the most anti-democratic, anti-egalitarian and anti-meritocractic feature in our society. Educational opportunity is the key to social mobility. Private schools, which are often a conduit to prestigious colleges, charge tuition, so that poor people as a group are shut out from them. The reality familiar to almost every family with school-age children in Manhattan is that you send your children to private schools if you can afford to do so. Abolition of private schools would halt such economic discrimination.

In spite of these real advantages, any proposal to end private schools can expect strong emotional opposition. People—especially Americans—do not like change, nor do they like being told they cannot do something they have been doing for a long time. They will invoke other values that they will claim are not simply shields for racism. When the South hid behind "other values" sixty years ago to defend its apartheid system, we saw it as transparent racism. Now "other values" become a convenient excuse for Northern states.

One such objection will be that abolishing private schools would interfere with parents' basic right to choose how and in what manner to educate their children. But that particular "right" is not explicitly mentioned in the Constitution; it is judge-made and can be unmade, especially when it is seen as a mask for entrenched privilege.

It might also be argued that abolishing private schools violates the free exercise of religion by parents who wish to educate their children at religious schools. Although this objections is a thorny one, it can be dealt with in either of two ways. First, religious schools can teach religion, and public schools can teach everything else. If that approach fails, the second solution might be to make an exception for bona fide religious schools.

A more subtle objection has to do with choice. If private schools are done away with, choice in education disappears. The result is one and only one type of schooling, with perhaps uniform curricula dictated by the state. But of course public schools do not produce cookie-cutter, conformist graduates, and private schools have no monopoly on cultivating independent critical thought. In their 2013 book *The Public School Advantage,* Christopher and Sarah Lubienski argue that public schools actually outperform private schools.

These and similar objections are not imaginary. They are real and strongly felt. When I published an earlier version of this essay ten years ago, I received many irate letters. One dubbed my idea "absurd." Another, from a Long Island lawyer, was more colorful: "Sir: We have a great Constitution! It supports the publishing of pap like your article. If Thinker-Kornstein had his way, we citizens could look forward to further guidance from Comrades Putin and Weingarten. It's like the Plessy case—'Dumb but Equal.'"

Another lawyer thought I was "engaged in parody," but when he realized I was "serious, bemusement turned to anger." The thought of abolishing private schools made his "blood run cold." He went on: "It has been tried already, in Soviet Russia, Communist China, Cuba and North Korea. It never works out quite the way theory anticipates. The less fortunate are not elevated. Everyone is dragged down to the lowest level of 'equality.'" He concluded by telling me not to "crush the freedoms and rights of the rest of us. Leave free markets and free people alone."

Education of our children is too important not to at least explore new ways to improve and make it more fair, even if that means sacrificing some other, less important values, especially when those "other values" may be veils for racism. It is the Constitution's compromise with slavery all over again. If we really believe in quality education for all our children, if we take seriously the meaning and thrust of *Brown,* if we want a long last to make of *Brown* more than a mirage, it is time to start talking about abolishing private schools.

36

THE BERTRAND RUSSELL CASE REVISITED,
OR DO WE EVER LEARN?

Despite the verdict of history against McCarthyism, some American institutions still seem to fire people for political activities or views unrelated to their jobs. The facts are ominous. In 1982, the Boston Symphony Orchestra hired Vanessa Redgrave to narrate an opera oratorio at its centennial celebration, but then cancelled the performance because of opposition to Redgrave's political views about the Mideast.

At a faculty meeting in 1988, a distinguished but benighted professor of criminal law, procedure and jurisprudence opposed an Israeli teacher's coming to New York University unless the foreign scholar disagreed with the policies of his government. The NYU professor called for an investigation of the Israeli professor's politics. The Israeli was to teach trusts and estates law.

And, more recently, in 2011, Harvard's faculty of Arts and Sciences cancelled two summer courses on economics taught by a politically active scholar from India named Subramamian Swamy. Why? Because Swamy wrote an article in a Delhi newspaper after the Mumbai bombing, an article that some considered anti-Muslim and inflammatory. Students and parents petitioned Harvard—that bastion of academic freedom—to sever its links with Swamy.

Lest we forget, these controversies bring back bad memories of a bizarre New York case involving an esteemed, world-renowned thinker—Bertrand Russell—who was prevented from teaching in New York City because of opposition to his views.

The strange controversy over Bertrand Russell started in February 1940, when the New York City Board of Higher Education (BHE) unanimously approved the appointment of Russell as Professor of

Philosophy at City College (CCNY). For the length of his eighteen-month appointment, from September 1940 to January 1942, Russell was to teach only three courses a term, all of them advanced: (1) logic and its relation to science, mathematics and philosophy; (2) problems in the foundations of mathematics; and (3) the relation to the pure to applied sciences and the reciprocal influence of metaphysics and scientific theories.

A coup for free public higher education in the eye of the faculty, the Russell appointment nonetheless fell far short of pleasing everyone. Episcopal Bishop William Manning led a public protest with religious and moral overtones. The same day that the BHE voted to reconfirm Russell, Jean Kay—a Brooklyn housewife with no children attending CCNY—asked the state courts to annul the Board's action because Russell was an alien, had never proved himself on a competitive examination before getting his post, and was an advocate of sexual immorality.

The City Corporation Counsel moved to dismiss Kay's petition solely on the ground that Russell's lack of citizenship was irrelevant. He neglected to mention Kay's two other claims. The motion to dismiss came before one Justice McGeehan, who, two days later, announced his decision denying the motion. Not only did McGeehan reject the challenge to the citizenship claim, but he also upheld Kay's contention regarding a competitive examination and immorality.

Judge McGeehan's ruling, of course, was absurd. It is preserved forever in the case reports, and there it remains for all of us, including the faculties of NYU Law School and Harvard University, to study.

To settle the citizenship question, the judge invoked the statute requiring teachers in "public schools"—generally understood to mean only elementary and secondary schools—to be citizens. Ignoring the widespread practice of hiring foreign scholars as visiting professors, McGeehan said, "Other universities and colleges, both public and private, seem to be able to find American citizens to employ."

Regarding the issue of competitive examination, the judge apparently equated philosopher-mathematician Bertrand Russell to an average kindergarten teacher, who is required to take an examination. McGeehan chose not to follow recent cases specifically exempting college professors from such examinations. Nor did Russell's impressive credentials make much of a difference either. Maybe the judge thought someone else could have shown in a few blue books more competence than Russell had displayed in his dozens of books and hundreds of articles in journals and general magazines on mathematical, philosophical, scientific, political, and social subjects.

The rulings on citizenship and competitive examinations are obviously strained and overly technical, but the discussion of immorality—the heart of the suit—is what makes the case truly memorable. Setting the pitch of that discussion, the housewife's attorney at oral argument accused Russell of being a nudist and running a nudist colony and labeled Russell's works "lecherous, salacious, libidinous, lustful, venerous, erotomaniac, aphrodisiac, irrelevant, narrow-minded, untruthful and bereft of moral fiber."

After this bombastic lecture, Judge McGeehan found "most compelling" the housewife's contentions that Russell's appointment "violated the public policy of the state and nation because of [his] notorious and salacious teachings" and because "he is not a man of good moral character." By the end of his opinion, McGeehan had described Russell's appointment as "an insult to the people of the City of New York," and had concluded that in appointing him the BHE was "in effect establishing a chair of indecency."

Rather than stress Russell's moral character, the court focused on Russell's writings, which "amply sustain . . . the contention . . . that Mr. Russell has taught in his books immoral and salacious doctrines." Although McGeehan said it was "not necessary to detail . . . the filth . . . contained in the books," he could not resist the temptation to quote several passages dealing with casual marriage, premarital sex, adultery, nudity and homosexuality. Judge McGeehan saw a conflict between these writings and state laws prohibiting certain sexual crimes. On the basis of Russell's mild, almost bland criticism of the status quo, and without even ascertaining whether Russell still adhered to views between eight and fifteen years old, Judge McGeehan revoked Russell's appointment because it would tend to incite the commission of sexual crime.

McGeehan did not care if Russell was hired to teach only mathematics. Even if Russell refrained from promulgating suspect doctrines, said the judge, ". . . his appointment violates a perfectly obvious canon of pedagogy, namely, that the personality of the teacher has more to do with forming a student's opinion than many syllogisms. A person we despise and who is lacking in ability cannot argue us into imitating him. A person whom we like who is of outstanding ability, does not have to try.

"It is contended that Bertrand Russell is extraordinary. That makes him the more dangerous . . . [H]is very presence as a teacher will cause the students to look up to him, seek to know more about him, and the more he is able to charm them and impress them with personal presence, the more potent will grow his influence in all spheres of their lives, causing the students in many instances to emulate him in every respect."

As one contemporary critic sarcastically described such judicial reasoning: "The student body at City College consists of males, chaste or unchaste, some of them over eighteen, with morals poised so delicately that if Bertrand Russell expounds mathematics or philosophy, they are impelled to abduct and rape, while if he dos not appear in their midst, woman's virtue knows no peril. In the modern world such an Eden of innocence as City College is too precious to allow the serpent to intrude."

Bad as Judge McGeehan's decision was, it was unanimously affirmed without opinion by an intermediate appellate court, which would not even grant leave to appeal to the Court of Appeals, the highest state court. At that point, the City Corporation Counsel decided—perhaps for political reasons—to pursue the case no further.

It was then that the BHE called upon Emory Buckner and John Marshall Harlan for help. The Board voted to substitute Buckner and Harlan as its counsel. At that time, both men were leading trial lawyers in Buckner's Wall Street law firm. But on learning of this Bertrand Russell affair, they put aside their busy and lucrative practice and offered their services to the BHE for free.

As soon as the new lawyers became involved, they let Judge McGeehan know that the BHE had replaced its original counsel. But McGeehan, bent on assuring the result he wanted, denied the Board's request to substitute counsel.

Stunned, Buckner and Harlan immediately appealed these procedural rulings, though without success. Despite their written brief and oral argument, the Appellate Division affirmed on the theory that the Corporation Counsel, who actively opposed the substitution, was the exclusive counsel for the BHE. Nor would the Appellate Division even grant leave to appeal the affirmance.

The last attempt to reopen McGeehan's basic ruling failed when the courts denied Russell the elementary right to defend himself. The New York court thus took the paradoxical position of denying the professor, whose reputation and job hung in the balance, the right to intervene because he supposedly lacked any interest in the litigation, while at the same time permitting a taxpayer without any personal stake to challenge the morality of a professor's appointment. This is a weird view of standing.

Russell never forgot the case. Many years afterward, he still called the incident "fantastic" and a "public horror resulting from morbid imaginings of bigots." His autobiography reproduces no less than nineteen letters about the episode. Russell's obviously bitter memories show that he may never have forgiven the United States for rejecting him as unfit to teach mathematics. His strident and much-publicized anti-Americanism late in life might well reflect the deep personal hurt he received at the hands of the American legal system.

One can only hope that, in considering future appointments, the faculties of eminent universities also remember the Bertrand Russell case.

37

IN THE OPINION OF THE COURT

"I am told at times by friends that a judicial opinion has no business to be literature," wrote Judge Benjamin Cardozo in 1920. Not surprisingly, Cardozo, the most self-consciously literary of judges, thought his friends' view was wrong, saying it was based on "misconception of the true significance of literature, or, more accurately perhaps, of literary style." But the debate goes on. Today Judge Pierre Leval of U.S. Court of Appeals for the Second Circuit sides with Cardozo's friends and objects to "a movement that tells judges we should consider our opinions literature."

Of necessity, we lawyers read more judicial opinions than books—not just law books, but books on any subject. With all the judicial opinions we read, however, do we—*should we*—think of them as a form of literature? When we study a judge's opinion, do we care only about its substance—whether the holding is favorable or not to our position—or do we also think about the opinion's form, its literary style? Is it possible to separate substance and style?

These questions, which every lawyer has thought about at least a little, are the subject of a unique 1986 book, *In the Opinion of the Court*, by William Domnarski. It is the only book I know of solely devoted to the judicial opinion as literature. Even amid the growing Law and Literature movement, no other book has had this precise focus. Law review articles and book chapters have, of course, touched on the topic, but Domnarski's is the one book-length treatment. It is a book that is long overdue.

Rare not only because of its subject matter, *In the Opinion of the Court* is also rare because of its intrinsic qualities. Domnarski has written an original work of great breadth. His analyses and points of view, expressed with style and clarity, jump off the page and stay in

229

the mind. He is not afraid to be opinionated, and his views are often highly controversial. Although I often found myself disagreeing with something Domnarski said, his ability even to evoke such a reaction was one of his book's prime virtues.

Trying to write a book about the literary quality of judicial opinions is a risky business. After all, it is to comment on something about which every lawyer considers himself or herself an expert, and on which no two lawyers agree. Even so, Domnarski succeeds.

According to Domnarski, who practices law in Minneapolis, the current situation is fairly barren in terms of commentary. "Little . . . . has been written about judicial opinions as a form of literature generally," he writes. "Opinions have not been analyzed as a literary form," he continues. "Nor have they been studied for what they are at their best, a place where life and law meet in a language available to the general, educated reader."

A book like this is ideal for studying the fashions in American judicial opinions over time, and Domnarski seizes the opportunity. As for most nineteenth-century Supreme Court opinions, in Domnarski's view (and perhaps all of ours) they are "nearly unreadable to us today." Judges then were "indifferent writers" who mixed style and substance to achieve "the impenetrable effect."

But things started to change in the early twentieth century. Oliver Wendell Holmes, an "intellectual snob" according to Domnarski, is said to be a "transitional figure" in the developments of the judicial opinion. His opinions were shorter, more decisive, cited to few cases, were written with an "Olympian quality" and in a style "lively, imagistic, lucid, prone to epigram or aphorisms, and above all, brimming with self-confidence." Holmes, says the author, was "the most interesting writer ever on the Court."

Holmes's impact on opinion writing was, says Domnarski, not as great as Justice Louis Brandeis's. The inventor of the Brandeis brief, which focused more on economic facts than law, "brought the same approach to opinion writing as a Justice as he had to brief writing as an advocate." Brandeis lengthened opinions while slowing them down with footnotes. Although he "was not a particularly graceful writer," he "brought occasional flights of eloquence to his work," to wit: his memorable concurrence in *Whitney v. California*.

Then there is Cardozo, who changed opinion writing forever. He "brought legitimacy to a brand of opinion that impressed as much with style as with substance."

Unafraid to stake out controversial positions, Domnarski says that Cardozo's literary talent on the Supreme Court was followed "and surpassed" by Black, Douglas, Frankfurter and Jackson. Many of us might disagree with that assessment. During the Warren Court, Domnarski points out, opinions dealing with basic rights were shorter and aimed more directly at the average reader.

Moving along chronologically, Domnarski shows his distaste for the Burger Court, at least for the style of its opinions. They are, he says, "bloated, voiceless," "more homogenized," longer and more heavily footnoted.

Footnotes are a useful marker for the opinion-writing style of the current Court. Anyone who follows Supreme Court opinions has had to notice the dramatic decline in the use of footnotes over the last two decades. Some justices hardly use them anymore. Opinions are getting shorter and look less and less like law review articles. Something has happened; the question is what.

After this historical canvass of Supreme Court opinion styles, Domnarski goes on to formulate his own literary canon of Supreme Court opinions. This canon is Domnarski's list of the eleven "greatest and most important judicial opinions." They are: *McCulloch v. Maryland* (implied power under "Necessary and Proper Clause"), Holmes's dissent in *Abrams U.S.* (free speech), *Chambers v. Florida* (coerced confessions), *The Steel Seizure Case* (presidential power), *Brown v. Board of Education* (school desegregation), *Miranda v. Arizona* (rights of criminal suspects), *West Virginia Board of Education v. Barnette* (flag salute), *Gideon v. Wainwright* (right to counsel), *Loving v. Virginia* (anti-miscegenation law), *Skinner v. Oklahoma* (sterilization as punishment), and *Roe v. Wade* (abortion). Most of the opinions in Domnarski's canon are no surprise, but there are one or two. Never before had I seen *Roe* praised for its literary qualities. The lesson of the canon is that simple justice "calls for simple eloquence."

In an important chapter entitled "Who Writes Judicial Opinions," Domnarski seems ambivalent about a major trend over the last several decades in composing court opinions—the rise of the law clerk. In Domnarski's view, the judicial process is "undermined" by allowing fledgling law clerks rather than their non-specialist bosses to do the Court's work. Yet he also finds that judicial opinions by clerks "are all exceedingly well done." All? Come now. Domnarski yearns for the day when judges did their own work.

But Domnarski's ambivalence about law clerks really stems from the powerful role of youth in the law. Law clerks are just one aspect. Young associates at law firms draft the briefs for the cases to be decided in judicial opinions drafted by young law clerks whose handiwork is then analyzed and critiqued by even younger law students who write and edit the law reviews.

In the course of his book, Domnarski relies on quantification as a method of analysis. Again and again, he invokes numbers: of court filings, of average pages in opinions, of footnotes in opinions, of citation of opinions, of literary illusions, and of case citations in opinions. The availability of computerized information makes this all possible and easy, and adds a statistical slant to Domnarski's approach. The danger, of course, is that such measurement is illusory when trying to assess the value and importance of literary efforts that depend on non-measurable qualities of texture, style and resonance. In relying on quantification, Domnarski resembles his judicial hero Richard Posner.

Posner, a judge on the U.S. Court of Appeals for the Seventh Circuit, gets lavish praise from Domnarski. Posner, gushes the author, is the "smartest and most talented" of current judges, and "deserves special consideration because his contributions are unique in the same way that he is a unique figure in the law."

To be sure, Posner is an unusually fine and prolific writer. He understands that style and substance fuse in a judicial opinion. He recognizes that the high reputations of Holmes and Cardozo are due in part to their writing styles. It is no longer true—if it ever was—that, in Domnarski's words, "a good literary style was evidence of poor legal craftsmanship."

The final sentence in Domnarski's book reflects Cardozo's perspective as well. "We can recognize judicial opinions" concludes Domnarski, "as legal literature that can soar to the level of literature generally." I start off reading every judicial opinion with that hope.

38

THE LATEST LEGAL FICTION

The law is full of fictions. Perhaps the most famous legal fiction is the way we treat a corporation as if it were "person." An old legal fiction is the token consideration (*e.g.*, a peppercorn, one dollar) in many written contracts. Even more fictional is the notion that everyone is presumed to know the law. The list of legal fictions is long and continues to grow.

The newest legal fictions are "unpublished" opinions that are "published." In 2001, West Publishing Company started selling a new series of bound volumes of the unpublished opinions of the federal courts of appeals. West might have called this series, somewhat (oxy)moronically *The Unpublished Opinions Published*, but did not. Instead, West chose the stealth title: *Federal Appendix*.

That bland, innocuous title fooled me; at first it came in under my radar. For weeks I passed the new series of books without a second glance. The familiar buckram binding with signature red and black spaces for lettering on the spines is the same as that on West's other federal reporters. So camouflaged, it blended in with the many other books in the bookcases. The title *Federal Appendix* failed to catch my eye.

Then, one day, recently, I noticed the new books and was curious. What, I wondered, was in the *Federal Appendix*? Picking up one of the volumes published so far, I read on the first page: "Cases Argued and Determined in the United States Courts of Appeals." So far, so good; nothing unusual with that, except that they were in their own separate reporter. I skimmed the volume of opinions, which read much like any other volume of decisions from the federal courts of appeals.

But then I read, on the same first page, in smaller print: "The *Federal Appendix* contains cases that have not been selected for publication in the *Federal Reporter Third Series*. Please consult local court rules to determine when and under what circumstances these cases may be cited." "Aha," said I, in one of my increasingly frequent interior monologues, "a whole volume of unpublished opinions! It's like a form book of oral agreements. How extraordinary." Sam Goldwyn, who supposedly said an oral agreement isn't worth the paper it's written on, would have approved.

I thought it was very odd. Isn't it bizarre to publish so-called unpublished opinions? Am I the only lawyer who thinks this is weird?

The *Federal Appendix* is, of course, only the latest development in the continuing controversy over unpublished opinions. Unpublished opinions are themselves a type of legal fiction: a judicial decision that is not really a decision, an opinion that resolves the legal dispute between the parties but cannot be cited in briefs and has no precedential effect. As might be expected, such unpublished opinions have stirred the legal profession. The *Federal Appendix* undoubtedly exists precisely because of that controversy.

In August 2000, one federal court of appeals became the first to break ranks with other circuits on the issue. That case, *Anastasoff v. United States*, came from the Eighth Circuit, which held that unpublished opinions, regardless of a contrary court rule, did count as precedent. The court in *Anastasoff* held that the court rule was unconstitutional because it confers on the federal courts a power that goes beyond the "judicial." *Anastasoff* must have led West to come up with *Federal Appendix*.

Exactly what a lawyer can do with the *Federal Appendix* is unclear. Some circuits bar attorneys from even citing unpublished opinions in legal briefs. Attorneys who violate such rules are subject to disciplinary sanctions. But, one might ask, does inclusion of opinions in the *Federal Appendix* make them in some sense "published" and therefore of precedential value?

The ruling in *Anastasoff* has a short shelf-life. Four months later, in December 2000, an en banc rehearing by the Eighth Circuit resulted in the vacating of the earlier opinion, thereby voiding the original opinion's own precedential effect. As a consequence, the constitutionality of the court rule about unpublished opinions having no precedential effect "remains an open question" in the Eighth Circuit.

West was paying attention. An opportunity presented itself, and West seized it. Less than a month after the en banc decision in

Anastasoff, West began publishing the *Federal Appendix*. West knows best.

Judge Alex Kozinski may think otherwise. In September 2001, in *Hart v. Massaneri*, the always quotable Ninth Circuit judge disagreed with the original decision in *Anastasoff*. "Adding endlessly to the body of precedent," wrote Kozinski, "can lead to confusion and unnecessary conflict" and "clutter up the law books and databases [not to mention legal briefs] with redundant and thus unhelpful authority." Kozinski may have had the *Federal Appendix* in mind.

Unpublished opinions are an extremely common practice in federal courts of appeal. Those courts issue more than ten thousand unpublished opinions every year. Once they are collected in the *Federal Appendix*, the unpublished opinions, in Kozinski's words "will have to be read and analyzed by lawyers researching the issue, materially raising the costs to the client for absolutely no legitimate reason."

What a delightful if puzzling pyramid of legal fictions: unpublished opinions that are not opinions, that are published and have no precedential effect, but that clients will pay lawyers for studying. I love it.

39

JUMP IN, JUDGE CARDOZO

A news item in 2010 prompts reconsideration of one of Benjamin Cardozo's most famous opinions as a judge on the New York Court of Appeals. It is an opinion often said by scholars to epitomize excellent legal writing, good judgment, and the modern public policy approach to law. The case was *Hynes v. New York Central Railroad Co.*, decided in 1921.

The question in *Hynes* was whether a railroad was negligent when its high-tension wires fell and hit a sixteen-year-old boy, Harvey Hynes, diving off a wooden plank or springboard on the railroad's right of way on the Bronx side of the Harlem River. The lower courts had denied recovery because, they ruled, Harvey was trespassing on the railroad's land when the accident happened. According to the lower courts, the wooden plank was a fixture, a permanent improvement to the land, and inasmuch as it was horizontal rather than vertical, it was an extension of the railroad's land and therefore the railroad owed Harvey no duty.

Cardozo, writing for a majority of the Court of Appeals, disagreed. He described the results in the courts below, with his signature graceful language, as "defended with much subtlety of reasoning, with much insistence upon its inevitableness as a merely logical deduction." Rejecting those "inevitable" results, Cardozo wrote that "the rights of bathers do not depend upon these nice distinctions," and that "[r]ights and duties in systems of living law are not built upon such quicksands." Harvey Hynes was, concluded Cardozo, protected in his "enjoyment of the public waters" and the railroad had a "duty of care and vigilance in the storage of destructive forces." The lower courts were reversed, and the case was allowed to proceed.

Hynes is one of those Cardozo opinions, like *Palsgraf v. Long Island Railroad*, and *MacPherson v. Buick*, that we all study in our

236

law school course on torts. We admired them then, and admire them now. We yearn to write so well and think about the law so clearly and so imaginatively. We see in *Hynes* how Cardozo personalizes Harvey, describes an idyllic past of boys jumping in rivers, focuses us on a specific moment in time, relies on visual images, and implicitly arraigns the lower courts as the enemy. This is Cardozo in one of his best moments, and we envy his abilities.

That is why we hesitate to suggest *Hynes* may need another look in light of human experience since Harvey Hynes's accident in July 1916. To question the wise and preeminent Cardozo is to doubt one of our judicial gods; even to consider the possibility that one of Cardozo's great opinions has flaws when read today is to risk being called presumptuous or arrogant or just plain blasphemous. So we approach the task gingerly, but approach it we must after reading the newspaper a few years ago.

Fast forward ninety-four years. Many Harvey Hyneses are apparently still at it. A July 15, 2010, article in the *New York Times* brought us up to date. Entitled "A Long Jump to Manhood," the article, written by reporter Sam Dolnick, was part of a series on "Summer Rituals" and described how teenage boys continue to jump from Bronx rocks, "beyond a stretch of Metro-North tracks," into the Harlem River.

The article explained how jumping into the water from these rocky cliffs is a "rite of passage," "a tradition that mixes adolescent swagger, apocryphal love and just enough danger to keep things interesting." Generations of police officers with the Metropolitan Transportation Authority, noted the story, "chase kids all summer long" and the "cat-and-mouse games with the police go back decades."

An MTA spokesman told the *Times* reporter the obvious: that the jumping was "extremely dangerous." He specifically referred to "crossing busy railroad tracks sandwiched between two blind curves, venturing near third rails electrified with seven hundred volts of direct current." The conditions in *Hynes* were eerily similar.

Let us assume that one of today's jumping boys accidentally gets hurt. Would the MTA, on the authority of *Hynes*, be responsible? Put another way, would Cardozo's famous opinion in *Hynes* hold up a century later? Referring to Cardozo's *Hynes* opinion, Professor Richard Weisberg says: "form and substance merge and a personalized style is made to serve a strictly legal function with grace, efficiency, and effectiveness." Ah, yes, but is it still a good law? Was it ever?

One possible answer may be found in the comment of a boy interviewed by the *Times* reporter. "There is no safety net here," said a seventeen-year-old named Matt Afon. "It's your own decision. You're taking your own risk."

"You're taking your own risk." Hmmm . . . that sounds a lot like another doctrine we discovered in our first-year torts class called "assumption of risk," which is usually a defense to a claim of negligence. Does there come a point when knowing and persistent reckless conduct, despite best efforts by authorities to stop it, changes Cardozo's analysis of duty in these circumstances?

Does it matter that the boys' parents also are well aware of the danger, but do nothing to avert it? One boy's mother told the *Times* reporter that she thought about forbidding her son to jump, out of concern. But she didn't. "I felt like the kind of a hypocrite, because we were talking about things that I had done before," she said. At some point we ought to recognize that human nature is what it is, which may be another way of saying "boys will be boys."

In *Hynes*, Cardozo, rejecting the dry, deductive logic of Legal Formalism, said that "considerations of analogy, of convenience, of policy, and of justice" required the railroad to owe a duty to boys like Harvey Hynes. But Cardozo also warned in the same opinion against "pursuing general maxims to ultimate conclusions." Instead, "[t]hey must be reformulated and readapted to meet exceptional circumstances."

Should *Hynes*, in Cardozo's own words, itself be "reformulated and readapted" to meet today's circumstances"? Has the rationale of *Hynes* become a "general maxim" that we should not follow to its "ultimate conclusions"? Or would the great judge who wrote so beautifully just roll over in his grave as he contemplated the extraordinarily reckless behavior of some teenagers?

Just some random thoughts during the dog days of August, as I think about how nice it would be to jump in and go for a swim.

40

RIOT AS ALTERNATIVE DISPUTE RESOLUTION

It was my first riot. Never before had I actually been in the middle of a full-blown riot, much less one that would make front-page headlines. Sure I had gone to college in the protest sixties, but the closest I had come to physically being at ground zero of a riot was watching the 1968 Democratic National Convention on television.

Being there is half the fun, at least in hindsight. So too with the July 11, 1996 Riddick Bowe-Andrew Golota heavyweight boxing match and free-for-all at Madison Square Garden.

I was there, almost ringside, and it really was unforgettable. Consider this a dispatch from a combat zone. Luckily, my college friend Paul—fellow lawyer and fight fan—and I suffered no injuries, but things could easily have turned out differently.

What we witnessed was a good lesson about the breakdown of the rule of law. We had a peek into the abyss, and it was scary. Litigation may have its drawbacks as a way of resolving disputes, but I would not recommend riot as a new form of alternative dispute resolution.

By now everyone who was not on Mars knows what happened that night. In the seventh round, Golota led on points and was taking Bowe to school. But Golota, otherwise impressive, inexplicably could not stop himself from hitting Bowe below the belt. Finally, the referee properly disqualified Golota. I had never actually seen a boxer disqualified before.

Then came pandemonium. All of a sudden, it seemed as if everyone at the Garden was in the ring fighting. Chairs and punches were thrown. It was wild.

We watched the mayhem for about five minutes but then, as the fighting started to spread to the spectator section, we decided that, under the circumstances, maybe this was not the best time and place to test our hand-to-hand combat skills. After all, we are litigators; that means we are professionals, we only fight when we are paid to. We left, as did a number of other fans, without trouble and in an orderly way. Most people stayed.

But those five minutes in the middle of a riot are etched indelibly on my mind. It is not often that you see adults behaving as nutty as that night.

I like boxing and I hope what happened does not end boxing at the Garden. I remember the first time I saw a boxing match. It was 1956, I was nine years old, and a twenty-one-year-old Floyd Patterson was fighting veteran Archie Moore for the heavyweight title. Having gone to sleep as early as a nine-year-old should, I had to be awakened by my father for the ten o'clock fight on television. Ever since I have been hooked.

I have watched many fights over the years. Some have been on my TV, some on closed circuit, and some in person. Most of them are exciting, especially when you are actually there, the closer the better.

And there is some great writing about boxing. A.J. Liebling's book *The Sweet Science* and Joyce Carol Oates's *Boxing* leap to mind.

What happened on July 11, 1996 was the result of special circumstances. Tension had been mounting all night, way before the actual Bowe-Golota fight. Hundreds of noisy Golota fans were chanting and singing while waiving red and white Polish flags. Bowe fans, white and black, responded with chants of "USA, USA." Nationalism had taken over, just as it so sadly does at the Olympics.

Contrary to what some reports said, it was not really a racial thing. Bowe, the hometown champ, had lots of white fans in the crowd. It is just that Golota seemed to have white fans only, many of whom were speaking Polish.

In some ways, the match was like something out of a "Rocky" movie. But here Golota was playing the Rocky character. He was a ten-to-one underdog from a foreign country (although he then lived in Chicago) who was beating the odds. He was clearly in much better shape and fought much better than the sluggish, overweight Bowe. Golota was on his way to win in a huge upset.

I am still not sure *why* the riot started. After all, Bowe won, and he was lucky he did. But maybe there is something less than satisfying for a big fight to be decided by a disqualification rather than a knockout or a TKO. Without some form of knockout, there is no catharsis; and without the safety valve of catharsis, the pent-up emotions of the audience spill over into unrestrained violence.

It was crazy, all right. It drove home the point that we will always have disputes, but how we resolve them is up to us. Litigation, with all its faults, is one way.

Consider the alternative. Now we know what it looks like.

41

LIBERALISM UNDRESSED

A lifetime of reading gives us the opportunity to follow the progress of living writers. We read their early work and wonder if it is all we will ever see, or if the sparkling literary and analytical gifts on display there are merely a flash in the pan never to be repeated or improved, or, rather, a happy preview of even better books to come in the future. It is always pleasant to report on a writer and thinker whose latest work exceeds the promise of what preceded it.

Such a legal writer is Jethro Lieberman, a law professor at New York Law School. Lieberman has been around for a while and has long used his ability to write clearly about the law to put together an impressive body of work. Before becoming a law professor, he was a legal affairs writer at *Business Week* magazine. His many (fifteen or so) fine books, always written in an accessible style, move from such topics as constitutional law and history, to business law, to our society's litigiousness, to guides on legal writing. Over the years, I have read Lieberman's books for pleasure, stimulation and enlightenment.

But nothing in Lieberman's prior books, however good they were, prepared me for his 2013 literary effort. With a title like *Liberalism Undressed* and knowing Lieberman's verbal facility, I thought his new book would be just another in a long line of glib commentaries on the supposed demise of liberalism. Boy, was I wrong—and happily so!

Liberalism Undressed is Lieberman's masterwork, a brilliant, provocative, and mature product of decades of thought about some of the most fundamental issues of our time or any time. The book catapults Lieberman to the first rank of modern political and legal philosophers. His book belongs on the shelf next to the works of John Rawls, Robert Nozick, and Ronald Dworkin.

Rather than a sad eulogy over the often dissed "L" word, Lieberman here energetically resurrects, defends and justifies liberalism even as he reinterprets its basic principles. "Attacks on liberalism," says Lieberman, "have much less validity than their combined fierceness might suggest." Although liberalism means many things, the term is "useful," he says, as a "theory about the metes and bounds of state power."

In short, "What justifies the power of the state? Over what domains may the state legitimately govern against the wishes of dissenters?" Lieberman defines liberalism as the "intuition that not everything in life that matters can or should be shaped or bounded or fixed or cured by politics and law." It is a "philosophical system" that affords "the best chance of striking a livable balance between disorder and repression, from one age to another."

For Lieberman, the key is nineteenth-century English philosopher John Stuart Mill's so-called Harm Principle. Mill announced this "one very simple principle" in 1859 in his classic *On Liberty*, where he wrote that: "the only purpose for which power can be rightfully exercised over any member of a civilized community, against his will, is to prevent harm to others. His own good, either physical or mental, is not a sufficient warrant. He cannot rightfully be compelled to do or forbear because it will be better for him to do so, because it will make him happier, because, in the opinion of others, to do so would be wise, or even right."

Mill's Harm Principle is Lieberman's focus. Lieberman's book searchingly explores the "meaning and extent" of the Harm Principle. He says the Harm Principle "deserves a closer look than it usually gets" and "from it we can derive all the significant liberal commitments."

Lieberman acknowledges that the Harm Principle on its face has a negative as opposed to a positive claim for political power: the state may act to stop us from harming others, but not to force us to do good, even for ourselves. It is usually seen as an argument against paternalism and the nanny state.

Lieberman turns this conventional reading upside down. He creatively interprets Mill's text. As Lieberman points out, much depends on how you define "harm to others." "Liberally" interpreted, "harm to others" could include many forms of conduct that might otherwise be viewed, in Mill's other famous phrase, as "self-regarding."

For example, are laws requiring people to wear seatbelts, motorcyclists to wear helmets, cigarette manufacturers to put warnings on their products, stores not to sell soda above a certain size, or even Obamacare's individual mandate to buy insurance—are such health and safety laws about "self-regarding" actions or about preventing "harm to others"? Each of these laws affects societal costs as well as individual conduct and well-being.

By using such examples, Lieberman undercuts, with originality and lawyerly skill, the common, narrow reading of Mill's Harm Principle. Lieberman gives us a fresh theoretical framework for approaching and analyzing the proper role of government. He reinterprets the Harm Principle to permit government intervention to prevent harm to society. He gives a new-old philosophic justification for liberalism, and then proceeds to examine how it applies in many contexts.

He analyzes a wide range of public policy issues and, legal scholar that he is, uses famous court cases to illustrate his points. But he does so with a difference, subtly, almost subliminally. Rather than cite the familiar case name in his text, Lieberman deftly describes the facts and outcomes insofar as they help as hypotheticals demonstrating a particular principle. The engaged reader with legal training sees these passages and experiences a pleasing shock of recognition that is confirmed by a glance at the endnotes.

The endnotes themselves are special. Spread over sixty-six pages, they are an integral part of the book. They go far beyond merely supplying the source of a quotation or an idea. Like Karl Popper's endnotes to his great *Open Society*, Lieberman's endnotes constitute an essential element of his argument, filled with important observations.

Along the way, Lieberman takes us on a grand tour of political philosophy. We encounter the great political theorists of the past as well as those of the present. We recognize some familiar names: Aristotle, Bentham, Locke, Rousseau, Hayek, Adam Smith, Isaiah Berlin, and Herbert Spencer, for example. That tour, alone worth the price of the book, is especially valuable because the philosophers' views are inspected and analyzed in light of a particular problem rather than a general survey. I always like to look at a book's bibliography, and Lieberman's is a comprehensive list of works in the field. I made a note of the ones I have not yet read but would like to.

For this kind of book, an author's writing style is crucial. Philosophy (like law) is built on abstractions, and as a result philosophical (and legal) writing can frequently be dense, difficult and daunting. Lieberman avoids those common pitfalls. Co-author of the excellent *Lawyer's Guide to Writing Well*, Lieberman prudently follows his own counsel and writes lucidly and with verve. Often he will use an arresting metaphor to memorably drive home a abstruse point.

The intellectual depth and literary quality of this book is no accident. It has been gestating in Lieberman's mind for forty years. The author starting working on it in the early 1970s. He has been rethinking and rewriting, improving and polishing, off and on, ever since. It shows. Such a book probably could not have been written by a young person; life experience and mature thought and practical judgment need time to blend and ripen properly. Some things are worth waiting for. *Liberalism Undressed* is one of them.

42

VICHY LAW AND THE HOLOCAUST

Some historical events cut so deeply they leave wounds, both interior and exterior, that never completely heal. The unfinished inner healing takes the form of our continuing emotional, mental and psychological efforts to come to grips with, to understand, to remember what happened. The remaining outer tasks of unfinished business include redressing the wrong to the extent possible, and ensuring that the same—or a similar—tragedy will never happen again. One such historical event—the consequences of which we still live with—is slavery in America; another is the Holocaust.

None of us can escape the Holocaust. More than sixty-five years after it ended, it remains very much with us. Holocaust memorials and museums dot the planet, and in time more will rise. Gripping and well-made Holocaust films, upsetting through they may be, are popular and win prestigious prizes. Books about the Holocaust (even from evil idiots who deny it happened) fill bookstores and occasionally become controversial bestsellers.

It is impossible for anyone—Jew or non-Jew, survivor or not, descendant of victims or not—to read, talk or think about the Holocaust without getting emotional, without feeling at once angry and sad. That the Holocaust persists in evoking such strong emotions is a good thing.

But those emotions take a heavy toll. If we are honest, we have to admit that the Holocaust at times produces sensory overload. The facts are so awful, the images so graphically horrible, the lessons and memories so indelibly painful, that we weary of the repeated emotional strain. So unrelenting is the Holocaust's assault on our sensibilities that many of us grow numb. Some people, on the other hand, seem preoccupied by the Holocaust—almost to an unhealthy degree—and

246

never get enough of it. But, my eyes glazing over, my emotions spent, I occasionally wonder what new can be said about such a terrible and incomprehensible event. Another book about the Holocaust? Enough already, I often think; spare me, I can't take any more.

A book by Richard Weisberg proves me wrong.

To channel such frequently overwhelming emotions into a work of profound and original legal scholarship is a rare thing. But it can be done, as Weisberg's 1996 book about Vichy France demonstrates. More than that, *Vichy Law and the Holocaust in France* weaves the various strands of Weisberg's personal and professional life into a literary-legal tapestry that tells an unhappy story from a new and compelling point of view. Weisberg, with the benefit of a half-century's perspective, discovers and analyzes previously unknown legal aspects of Vichy's laws against the Jews. Weisberg makes the Holocaust in France comprehensible.

Given his particular experiences, interests and talents, Weisberg is just the right person for this intellectual task. He teaches at Cardozo Law School, a part of Yeshiva University. He was a member of the litigation team suing a Swiss bank for money deposited by Jewish customers during World War II. He has a strong affinity for French culture (including a Ph.D in French literature). He is a pioneer and leader in the Law and Literature movement, his three prior books— *The Failure of the Word*, *When Lawyers Write* and *Poethics*—having quickly become classics of their kind, and deservedly so.

With *Vichy Law and the Holocaust*, Weisberg has transcended his past work. He has gone beyond anything he has done before. His book on Vichy law, a product of many years of research and reflection brings everything together even as it offers and supports, with passages of luminous insight, a powerful thesis never before advanced. It touches the heart as well as the mind.

The thesis of Weisberg's book is both daring and enlightening. He rejects as overly simplistic the widely held notion that French anti-Semitism can "in and of itself explain the passion with which the [French] legal community authored, accepted and implemented the laws" against the Jews. One can at least understand why so many people cite anti-Semitism in France, the land that gave us the notorious Dreyfus Affair. Unlike other European countries under the Nazis, the French enthusiastically exceeded German expectations in persecuting the Jews.

But Weisberg says this explanation is wrong or at least incomplete. Instead, Weisberg primarily blames French lawyers. He propounds a two-part thesis based not on anti-Semitism but on the failure of legal interpretation. According to Weisberg, the French legal profession bears much of the responsibility for the Holocaust in France.

French lawyers wrote and gave teeth to the Vichy anti-Jewish laws, says Weisberg, by following "an ingrained approach to the reading of legal texts" that had two paradoxical aspects. The first aspect, on one hand, focused on *constitutional* interpretation and called for flexible reading that paid lip service to the noble values of the French Revolution while at the same time excluding Jews from those same protections. The second aspect, on the other, read *statutory* language narrowly so as to preclude other readings that might have led to protecting the persecuted group. Both interpretations—one flexible, the other rigid—had the common result of hurting Jews.

Drawing on the vocabulary of modern literary criticism, Weisberg labels this interpretive approach "Vichy hermeneutics." By that term, he means "the overall conception of legal discourse during Vichy," which he argues "quickly came to inform virtually the whole of legal practice and dictated more than any written set of laws" the dismal record of French persecution of Jews in World War II. The heart of the matter, according to Weisberg, is this "overriding interpretive principle."

Who was responsible for this baleful principle of interpretation? French lawyers. "All of the data," writes Weisberg, "tends to support the conclusion that legal actors could have rendered the religious statutes a virtual nullity." In this situation, "French lawyers held all the cards," but "they read the religious statutes in a niggardly and myopic manner, each stingy interpretation leading to yet another until more Jews were persecuted than even the literal language demanded."

One reads such passages with growing distress at how those spineless and misguided French lawyers missed a crucial chance to do the right thing, to strike a blow for freedom. If Daniel Goldhagen's disturbing bestseller about the Holocaust is called *Hitler's Willing Executioners*, Weisberg's book could have aptly been called *Petain's Willing Anti-Semitic Lawyers*. But lest we get a bit too self-righteous and holier-than-they as we think about the collaborationist role of lawyers in enforcing anti-Jewish laws in Vichy France, we should recall our own country's pre-Civil War experience with laws about slavery.

Weisberg rightly makes the connection to the historical precedent of "America's antebellum constitutional law." There too, constitutional due process and humaneness "managed with considerable ease to coexist with the persecution of a specific group." The dreadful *Dred Scott* case was as much a failure on the part of American lawyers as it was anything else.

Throughout the book, Weisberg explains, elaborates and supports his bold thesis. His chapter on the trial of Leon Blum—lawyer, political leader and Jew—is a stunning revelation in itself. His chapter on the professional lives of private lawyers and his thoughts on why lawyers underperformed are riveting. The entire book is sobering on several levels. By underlining the consequences of the failure of law, it enhances our awareness of the lawyer's irreplaceable role in the ranks of freedom fighters. It adds new meaning to our daily legal tasks.

Most of all, though, *Vichy Law and the Holocaust in France* inspires with a moral vision of what the legal profession might have done in the past—and could do in the future. We read about what the French lawyers did (and did not do) during the Second World War, and, thanks to Weisberg's extraordinary study, we say, with new meaning, to ourselves as lawyers, "Never again."

43

NEW YORK—LONDON: A TALE OF TWO CITIES' ANTI-SEMITISM

"Some books are to be tasted," wrote Francis Bacon in one of his most famous essays, "others to be swallowed, and some few to be chewed and digested." One of the "few" is my friend Anthony Julius's *Trials of the Diaspora: A History of Anti-Semitism in England*, which was published in 2010. It is a long, dense, provocative, complicated book about a controversial, sensitive topic, and it takes time to chew and digest, to read and mull over. Many reviewers rushed into print about it right away. Instead of responding to such a special volume like a short-order cook, however, I needed a while to collect my thoughts and clarify them, even give them time to marinate properly. Our first thoughts are not always our best thoughts.

The issues raised by Julius evoke responses that are timely even years after the book's publication. Julius's book makes each of us look inside ourselves to find our honest, personal reactions to what he describes. Julius makes us consider how where we live and what personally happens to us affect our reaction to anti-Semitism. I reacted to Julius's book differently from other commentators: I reacted as a New York Jew comparing in my mind my experiences with Julius's as a London Jew.

I

It is easy for a New York City Jew live without ever personally experiencing anti-Semitism. It is easy because being Jewish in New York is easy. Such happy forgetfulness about a most persistent and unpleasant hatred can become all enveloping if you are born in New

York, grow up in New York, go to school in New York, and work in New York. New York is a special, unique, comfortable place to be Jewish. New York is a pluralistic society with, unlike some other places, a deep ethic of pluralism that fosters a sense of citizenship and involves tolerance, cooperation and compromise.

This is so for a number of reasons. New York City's polyglot population is one important factor. The City is pluralism in action; many ethnic and religious groups live, work and visit here in harmony.

Another factor is the large number of Jews in New York. More Jews live in New York City (two million out of population of eight million) than in any other *country* in the world except Israel. And Israel—unlike New York City—is ringed by enemies and riven by religious and ethnic tensions and violence.

Moreover, because of social mobility and talent, many Jews in New York have achieved positions of influence and importance in business, the professions, the arts, politics, and philanthropy.

A fourth reason is the atmosphere and history of religious tolerance here, one of the true blessings of American liberty. That long tradition, almost from the beginning of colonial New York's existence, welcomes and encourages freedom of conscience.

As a result of this pleasant and rare confluence of liberating factors, a born and bred New York Jew often has little, if any, personal, first-hand contact with anti-Semitism, either as victim or observer. This avoidance or escape from personal anti-Semitism has certainly been my own pleasant experience for the past sixty-six years, and I do not think my experience is unique or even unusual.

Just because I do not think I have personally been an object of anti-Semitism does not mean I think it does not exist, even in New York City. I hope I am not that much an ostrich-like fool. My college history professor—Leonard Dinnerstein—wrote a long book entitled *Anti-Semitism in America*. "One who belongs to the most vilified and persecuted minority in history is not likely to be insensible" to anti-Semitism, as Justice Felix Frankfurter, referring to his Judaism, wrote in 1943, in the middle of World War II, in the most poignant cry from the heart ever to find its way into a Supreme Court opinion.

For all I know, I may have been a victim of anti-Semitism without my even having been aware of it. It may have been so subtle or genteel or hidden as to slip by me unnoticed. Prejudiced people may have had anti-Semitic thoughts or made anti-Semitic comments about me behind my back. But, again, I have not heard about such comments. I do not know if any opportunities have been closed to me because of my religion, but I know of none.

Of course my personal experience may not be the same as others. Although I have not felt the sting of religious prejudice here, other New York Jews may have. I am sure some do have some maddening tales to tell. I should not make the mistake of projecting my good fortune on to everyone else. I do not have such blinders on.

I also understand and fully appreciate that my outlook might be considered superficial or naively optimistic. After all, it could be argued, a prejudice as old and deep seated and virulent as anti-Semitism—"A Hatred That Resists Exorcism," according to a *New York Times* headline and *The Devil that Never Dies*, according to the title of a 2013 book by Daniel Goldhagen—rarely disappears completely. It is probably always there, if only slightly beneath the surface, slumbering until it is shaken awake by trogdolytes and erupts again. That has certainly been the sad, unfortunate, and dispiriting teaching of Jewish history. But, for many reasons, New York City appears to have controlled such irrational religious hatred and kept it well in check.

Yet no Jew, in New York or elsewhere, can escape history. The collective memory of the Holocaust hangs over every Jew, even those fortunate enough to live in New York. This kind of collective memory, like the memory of slavery for African-Americans, is an essential heritage. It is crucial to knowing and acting; it fosters community, identity, and continuity. It keeps us on guard. The heritage of the Holocaust tells us who we are, where we came from, and what we belong to. The Holocaust shapes our awareness whether we know it or not, and it is ultimately emotional, not intellectual, strong feeling and not dispassionate analysis. The memory of the Holocaust is not distant. It is for us, Jews in New York, a living and immediate experience. It is buried in our consciousness and focuses our view of the world. And yet I have often felt uncomfortable talking about the slaughter of the Jews in Europe. It is too large, too gruesome a subject.

Naturally, we react to persecution not only with defense mechanisms but also with a heightened pride in the traditions and characteristics of the persecuted group, particularly if we are a member of that group. Not acknowledging one's Jewishness would be a betrayal. It would, in a sense, let the bastards win and that cannot be permitted. Jewish pride may be natural, but that understandable impulse should not blind us to the reality of the here and now. The larger history of anti-Semitism does not change the good news that being Jewish in New York City is not hard. Jews in New York can and do now enjoy life and success without fear of anti-Semitic reprisals.

II

It is from this special, New York perspective and experience that I approached Julius's thoughtful book. Anthony Julius is a man of parts. A graduate of Cambridge University and a Ph.D., Julius is an eminent and highly skilled English lawyer, scholar, and writer. His many and diverse talents are impressive and of a very high order.

As a lawyer, Julius has most famously represented Princess Diana in her divorce from Prince Charles and successfully defended American writer Deborah Lipstadt against libel charges by Holocaust-denier David Irving. As a scholar and writer, he has written three other well-received books, one on T.S. Eliot's anti-Semitism, and two on modern art. He frequently contributes provocative and thoughtful essays and book reviews to newspapers and periodicals on both sides of the Atlantic. Julius is one of England's leading public intellectuals.

As the title of his 2010 book announces, he now shines a searchlight on English attitudes toward Jews, and his book brilliantly illuminates a dark and squalid history. Julius has made himself the Linnaeus of English anti-Semitism. He provides, in lucid prose, a taxonomy of it, classifying and labeling all its different forms. Revealing his personal scars, he gives examples of anti-Semitic incidents suffered in his own life, starting when he was a young boy. Some of his best and most insightful sections discuss anti-Semitism in English literature.

Like the fine lawyer he is, Julius marshals the abundant and distressing evidence of English anti-Semitism in compelling fashion. Julius lays bare and assembles so much proof that there comes a point when we feel a sensory overload and want to say, "Enough, we get it. We are convinced. You have proven your case beyond a reasonable doubt." With more than eight hundred pages and almost four thousand footnotes, *Trials of the Diaspora* is a monumental, masterful work, a testament to Julius's industry, stamina, and sustained focus on a painful topic.

But it is a good book about a bad subject. After all is said and done, one wonders about this project. One has to ask, why? What motivated Julius to undertake this herculean task? And what effect did this mission have on him?

Julius himself more than hints at some ambivalence on his own part. Toward the end of the book, Julius writes, "I have mostly engaged in the explication of nonsense—pernicious nonsense, at that. Has there been any merit in the exercise? I hope so." To study anti-Semitism is, according to Julius, "to immerse oneself in muck. Anti-Semitism is a sewer. This is my second book on the subject and I intend it to be my last." Apparently tired from his labors cleaning the Augean stable of English anti-Semitism, Julius admits toward the end of his task that, "I have derived no benefit, either in self-understanding or education, from the undertaking."

But despite such temporary fatigue, Julius ultimately seems to resolve his ambivalence in favor of what he has done, even if he regards it as a necessary burden rather than a labor of love. Confronted by anti-Semitism, says Julius, most Jews are likely to respond in either of two ways. One way is "to arrange one's defenses, and then to spend no further time on the matter." For those who choose this first way, anti-Semites do not merit study. This first response is not Julius's response.

Julius's response is different. It is to "ponder this anti-Semitism, try to understand it in all its implications, make it an object of investigation." As Julius goes on, the reader gets the distinct feeling that Julius is setting forth his personal credo, pinning his deepest beliefs to the wall for all to see. In eloquent and passionate language, Julius explains himself and declares his fundamental principles.

You will investigate anti-Semitism, he says, "because it figures in your world and you cannot live in a world in which any aspect of it remains unanalyzed." The "threat" anti-Semitism represents, writes Julius, is "potentially so overwhelming, and so profound, that unless it receives your full attention, it will immobilize you." Moreover, studying anti-Semitism "is a way of paying respect to its victims" and "a means of self-examination."

Then comes his fervent peroration, the window onto Julius's soul: "You regard anti-Semitism as an important, perhaps the most important, question in your life . . . . Your encounters with it will be high points in the psychodrama in your life . . . . Anti-Semitism will contribute to defining the person you are."

It is hard to resist and not be seduced by such a siren call. It is difficult not to be moved by Julius's powerful rhetoric, evident passion, and close reasoning. It is hard and difficult, true, but not impossible. We have to be careful not to let our strong emotions about past horrors in other places cloud our judgment and overwhelm our lives today here in New York, where conditions are different.

Except for what I learned in Julius's book, I have no idea about anti-Semitism in England. I would have thought such irrational prejudice would have little or no place in what I have always assumed was an open and enlightened society. Perhaps I am wrong.

What I do know is that the anti-Semitic conditions and circumstances in England he describes at length in his book do not correspond to the life I have lived as a Jew in New York City. The anti-Semitism he catalogs there bears no relation to my own experience here. It is hyperbole, Julius wrote in a September 2013 book review in the *Wall Street Journal*, to say, "We live in a world turning and teeming with ever-proliferating anti-Semitism." I am not marked by the same anti-Semitic wounds suffered personally by Julius.

Apparently England and Manhattan are not alike when it comes to anti-Semitism, and that may make all the difference. As a Jew, I found myself both fascinated and horrified by the many examples—some subtle, some not—of English anti-Semitism. I felt anger, but it was a vicarious anger. Living and working in New York have insulated me from anything but a second-hand experience of anti-Semitism.

I greatly admire Julius's commitment and passion for exposing our enemies. I marvel at his intellect, energy, and legal ability. I envy his analytical power, forthrightness, and rhetorical skill. I read all his books with interest, enthusiasm, and pleasure. *Trials of the Diaspora* is a classic of its kind. If and when I ever personally encounter anti-Semitism, I hope I have the courage and strength of character to take a stand Julius would be proud of.

But, unlike Julius, I do not want to become preoccupied with anti-Semitism. Unlike Julius, I have not "sought out anti-Semitism." To do so would allow anti-Semitism to dominate my life, much as sex dominates and preoccupies the life and mind of a Comstockian censor. I do not want anti-Semitism to become "the most important question" in my life. I do not want to be obsessed with victimhood. That would be handing a victory to the anti-Semites.

"[F]or sure," as Julius noted in his 2013 review, "while we must not minimize dangers [of anti-Semitism], we shouldn't overstate them either." I do not want to be so depressed or to feel so oppressed. Victimhood is tiresome and, for me, a poor fit. I do not feel like a victim, I do not want to feel like one, and I just cannot fake it. I have better things to do, more positive, more self-actualizing plans, more life-affirming goals, than devoting myself to thinking about a disgusting psychopathology like anti-Semitism. I do not want to wallow in that muck.

Whether or not I go to temple, whether or not I am observant, whether or not I am even a believer, I am fiercely proud of being a Jew and of my Jewish heritage, but I do not have to wear my religion on my sleeve. My ethnic-sounding surname does it for me. Beyond that, religion is a private matter, between me and my conscience.

I am not Shylock (one of Julius's prime examples of an anti-Semitic literary character), nursing grudges and seething for revenge from anti-Semitic slights. And New York City is neither Shylock's overtly hostile Venice nor Julius's genteelly anti-Semitic London. To get away from such nasty or polite anti-Semitism is precisely one of the reasons why our forebears left the Old World for the New. They yearned to breathe free of religious prejudice and persecution. Living and working in New York's bracing fresh air of religious freedom and tolerance have given me an outlook on the subject different from Anthony Julius's.

I have tried to read *Trials of the Diaspora* in the light of Francis Bacon's advice, in his essay "Of Studies," to read "not to contradict, and confute; nor to believe and take for granted," but "to weigh and consider." To do so required some time for reflection, and some soul searching of my own.

44

STEVE JOBS AND AYN RAND

"They're not John Galt; they're not even Steve Jobs."

Thus did New York Times columnist Paul Krugman in 2011 yoke one of Ayn Rand's fictional heroes with the late founder of Apple Inc. Krugman made the comment in an op-ed criticizing the "remarkably hysterical reaction" of some rich people to the Occupy Wall Street protests. Krugman's point was that, unlike John Galt or Steve Jobs, Wall Street's Masters of the Universe have not created anything new or of real value to justify their wealth.

Krugman's linking of Steve Jobs to Ayn Rand got me thinking. Whether or not Jobs ever read *The Fountainhead* or *Atlas Shrugged*, he was, in a sense, a real-life Ayn Rand hero. Talking about Jobs and Rand in the same breath may, in an unexpected way, offer a new, better, and more accurate explanation why her books continue to bo so hugely popular and influential.

Ayn Rand is, of course, an evergreen topic of controversy. People either love her and her perennially bestselling novels, or they hate her and her books. No one is neutral about Ayn Rand. And all the while, despite or because of the strong feelings she arouses, people keep on buying Rand's books in large numbers year after year, decade after decade.

Opinion about the true reason for Rand's popularity has always veered off in wrong directions. The new wave of commentary about Rand since the 2008 financial crisis illustrates the point. In the past several years, book-length biographies, magazine articles, newspaper op-eds, and book reviews have increasingly stressed her trademark libertarian political philosophy and conservative economic views. Many commentators have emphasized what they see as Rand's celebration of selfishness and greed, and her supposed prescience in predicting events such as an economic collapse allegedly due to government interference and collectivist ideas. These are the themes, say the commentators, that make Rand's books and ideas so popular.

They are wrong. The true reason for Rand's continuing popularity has escaped notice.

By underscoring Rand's political and economic views, all these commentators miss the real point of her persistent appeal, particularly with young people. The pundits mistakenly think that her political or economic views explain why Rand's books continue to sell ever so well and have such widespread influence more than fifty years after first being published. But the fundamental key to Rand's popularity is neither politics nor economics.

The answer is something far more basic. It is psychology. Rand's books exert an overwhelming emotional pull not because of their endorsement of free market capitalism, but because of their portrayal of autonomous, healthy, strong, emotionally secure, capable characters; because of their appeal "in the name of the best within us." That is why people are drawn to Rand's novels. Readers who are fans want to be like her fictional heroes.

The heroes in Rand's two big novels, however archly drawn, have some character traits that are distinctive, defining, memorable, and admirable. For example, they prize originality and creativity. Whether it is architect Howard Roark's daring new building designs, or physicist John Galt's breakthroughs in science, or industrialist Hank Rearden's development of a better steel, Rand's lead characters all bring into the world something new, something good, something extremely useful, something that did not exist before.

In one way or another, they are creators. They all are warmed by that celestial fire of innovation, they all have almost artistic temperaments. They think for themselves, they are independent. "The basic need of the creator is independence." (*The Fountainhead*.) In a way they exemplify the self-reliance that Emerson famously talked about in his great nineteenth-century lecture.

These character traits also describe Steve Jobs. His name is a synonym for originality and innovation. Don't live "with the results of other people's thinking," he advised seniors graduating from Stanford in 2005. "Don't let the noise of others' opinions drown out your own inner voice." Echoing Emerson, Jobs said, "And most important, have the courage to follow your heart and intuition."

Steve Jobs the creator is aptly described by Ayn Rand's architect Roark. "Throughout the centuries there were men who took first steps down new roads armed with nothing but their own vision. Their goals differed, but they all had this in common: that the step was first, the road new, the vision unborrowed."

Rand's heroes yearn too for achievement and accomplishment. They have a great passion for their work, whatever it is. Their work— how good it is—is how they define themselves. Work for them is not labor; it is what they do for love and joy, what they would do for free. Work for them is not confined to the hours between nine to five. It gives too much joy to be so limited. Dagny Taggart, a railroad executive heroine in *Atlas Shrugged*, spreads out railroad maps on the floor of her room and just studies them for the fun, for the thrill, for the sheer pleasure of it.

That is a good description of Steve Jobs' attitude toward his work. "You've got to find what you love," Jobs said in that 2005 commencement address. "[T]he only way to do great work is to love what you do."

One might be hard pressed to tell whether Jobs or Rand said, "The degree of a man's independence, initiative and personal love for his work determines his talent as a worker an his worth as a man." (It was Rand's hero Howard Roark in *The Fountainhead*.) Likewise, "The creator lives for his work." (Same source.)

Randian heroes are also very good at what they do, which makes them self-confident. They are extraordinarily able, they are extremely competent. They excel in whatever they put their hand to. Young Francisco D'Anconia, heir to a copper empire, plays baseball for the first time, steps up to the plate and hits a pitch over the outfielders' heads.

Most of all, Rand's fictional heroes set high standards for themselves. They have self-esteem. They want to do the best they can, they want to be the best they can be. How can such a goal not inspire?

Quite apart from their political and economic views, Rand's heroes love life. They do not perceive the world as hostile, overwhelming, or threatening. For them life is not just a good thing, but a great thing. It is not a vale of tears, but one glorious opportunity. Who can forget

Rand's soaring description of how Hank Rearden and Dagny Taggart feel as they take the first train ride over tracks made of the new, miraculous Rearden Steel?

These positive personality traits are understandably attractive. They especially appeal to human beings first coming to individual consciousness and forming a self-image. Rand's heroes are, in a sense, Byronic heroes, individuals in conflict with society, a conflict many teenagers feel intensely. That—not politics or economics—is why so many young people in high school and college are drawn to Rand's novels.

The Randian heroes are vivid fictional illustrations of a healthy psychology similar to that put forward in the 1950s by Abraham Maslow. Rather than focus on psychopathology, on suffering neurotics, on what is wrong, Maslow's pioneering work—especially his brilliant book *Motivation and Personality*—concentrated on psychologically healthy, self-actualizing people. So does Rand in her own way describe the highest capacities of healthy and strong people.

These piercing psychological aspects of Rand's work go far deeper than politics or economics. They penetrate to the subconscious and have tremendous power, including staying power. Ever since I first read her books some fifty years ago, I have never forgotten them, their examples of achievement, or their life lessons. Rand's descriptions of her heroes are so attractive that a reader, regardless of his or her political/economic views, keeps them as role models.

By the same token, we admire Steve Jobs for what he did with his life, not for his politics or economic views. We don't even know what they were. Jobs' status as an icon has nothing to do with his politics, whether he was conservative or liberal.

Similarly, Rand's inspiring descriptions provide a much more likely explanation for the continuing huge popularity of her books and also show why one can love Ayn Rand's books without being a right-wing extremist. But so pervasive is the common view that many people I know regard Ayn Rand fans as suffering from arrested mental development or stunted literary tastes. As a result, I often find myself avoiding any discussion of Ayn Rand. Such people just don't understand. But the next time I hear or read a comment about Rand's popularity being due to her political and economic views, I will do as her Atlas did (and as I imagine Steve Jobs would do): I will shrug.

ACKNOWLEDGMENTS

Some of the essays included here first appeared, in different form, in the *Baltimore Sun*, the *Chicago Tribune*, the *Yale Advocate*, the *New York Law Journal*, *Judicial Notice*, the *New York County Lawyer*, and the *Cardozo Arts & Entertainment Law Journal*.

I also want to thank my assistants Elina Slavina and Cielo Renta for cheerfully typing the many drafts of the manuscript.